VIETNAM
The Roots of Conflict

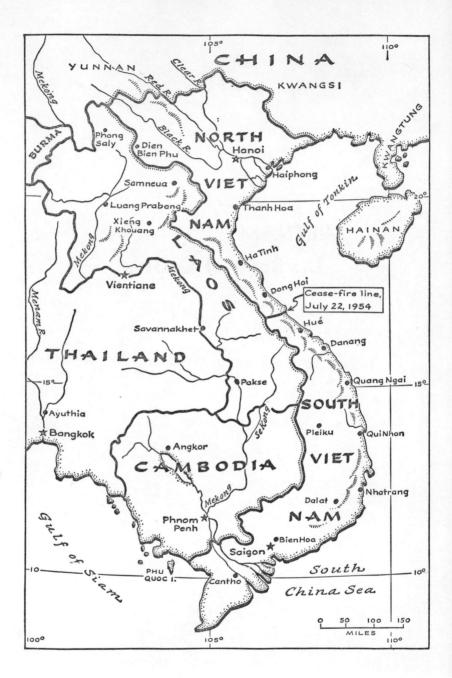

VIETNAM
The Roots of Conflict

Chester A. Bain

A SPECTRUM BOOK

PRENTICE-HALL, INC.
Englewood Cliffs, New Jersey

Library of Congress Catalog Card Number 67-18701.

Printed in the United States of America.

Current printing (last number): 10 9 8 7 6 5 4 3 2 1

Preface

The gestation of this short book dates back many years. While writing an outline history of the Far East in 1950-51, I became aware of the large gaps in our knowledge of Southeast Asia. When I left college teaching to serve for eighteen months on the Indochina desk of the Office of Naval Intelligence at the Pentagon, I was struck anew by the lack of English language materials on the Indochinese countries, and determined to examine those countries in depth. Subsequently, as part of my doctoral studies, I wrote a short draft history of Vietnam, Laos, and Cambodia prior to the French conquest, and my doctoral dissertation was *The History of Vietnam From the French Occupation to 1939*. During part of this same time, I worked with research teams for Human Relations Area Files, preparing a series of country handbooks on Vietnam, Laos, Cambodia, and British Borneo. My close interest in Vietnam continued while I was teaching at Illinois State University (1956-59) and led to my first visit to that country in the summer of 1958 during a private study tour of Eastern Asia. This tour encouraged me to become a foreign service officer with the United States Information Agency in 1959. After service with USIA in Iran and Korea, two other countries that have experienced communist aggression, I was transferred to Vietnam, where I was able to follow critical developments from the viewpoint of one personally concerned. On my return to Washington, I was assigned to research duties on Vietnam at USIA and wrote a series of papers on the Viet Cong and internal developments in Vietnam.

Believing sincerely that there was a need for more basic background material for general readers and students, I determined to write a history of Vietnam as my personal contribution to a better understanding of the Vietnamese people and their tragic conflict. The writing of the history was completely my own idea and the interpretations are solely my own. The manuscript was prepared entirely outside of gov-

[v]

ernment working hours. Fortunately, I had the able assistance of my wife who was with me in Vietnam until families were evacuated. She has served as my research assistant, editor, sounding board, and typist. The completed manuscript was read by interested government officials, but no changes in interpretation were requested or suggested. The book represents the personal view of a long-time student of Vietnamese affairs, who happens now to be a foreign service officer after many years of college teaching and private research, and should not be construed as a statement of government policy.

As in the case of Douglas Pike, author of *Viet Cong* (Cambridge, Massachusetts, 1966), which was published as I was completing this manuscript, I have been influenced in my interpretations by the reading of large numbers of translated Viet Cong documents and Communist propaganda related to Vietnam. I have also examined the problems of liberation wars and Communist tactics worldwide and have attempted to evaluate the Vietnam conflict within this context as well as within the framework of Vietnam's historical development. In a very real sense, my book is a labor of love. I have visited the Vietnamese people in their homes, offices, schools, pagodas, churches, market places, parks, and paddy fields and have never met with anything but friendliness and kindness. I have become personally involved in Vietnam and in Asia generally and care deeply what happens to their people. My present employment with the U. S. government results from that personal involvement rather than the reverse. It is my earnest hope that this little book will contribute some light on and understanding of the true plight of the Vietnamese and the other Asians who are struggling to maintain their independence and freedom against the unscrupulous and bloody terrorism of the Communists who seek to expand their conquests throughout Asia.

C. A. B.

Contents

[vii]

1: Vietnam, a Divided Land

Political Setting

The Vietnam conflict is far more complicated than a simple clash between the competing ideologies of communism and Western liberal democracy. The forces at play in Vietnam are global in scope, involving virtually every kind of trouble than can plague developing lands. They encompass all the problems of countries recently emerged from colonial rule combined with those of peoples undergoing transition from traditional to modern societies under the impact of Western technological civilization. Both North and South Vietnam are hindered by traditional attitudes and customs and shortages of skills and capital needed for modernization. Both are troubled by factionalism among their elites, the members of which avoid responsibility, a trait inherited from the traditional society and magnified by colonial rule.

In the South, apart from the Viet Cong, dozens of cliques and factions jockey for popular favor, offering solutions to problems as varied as their numbers. Few have broad support or show any capacity for the type of compromise necessary in a working democracy. This political scene is further complicated by regional rivalries and by competition between factious religious groups and subgroups. While the Constituent Assembly elected in September, 1966, has brought new young blood into the political scene and the Assembly has shown more independence and capacity than any of its predecessors, it is too early to evaluate what this means for the future.

In spite of the appearance of unity and discipline, which the Vietnamese Communist (Lao Dong) party strives to present to the world, the Communists of both the North and the South are also divided. As Vietnamese they desire in varying degrees to retain a national identity within the Communist world, yet they are torn by the pulling and hauling of the Sino-Soviet dispute in which both sides seek their allegiance. Related to this dispute are differences over tactics—whether it is better to stage a tactical retreat before superior force, or to continue the struggle at all costs on the principle that the might of the people will prevail over technical superiority. Careful reading of statements in radio broadcasts and publications intended for internal consumption shows the Communists in both North and South Vietnam are plagued, too, by such problems of the government in the South as corruption, inefficiency, and lack of zeal. Captured Communist documents complain of Communist officials who lack concern for the people's interests, who graft on tax moneys, who fear to sleep in contested villages, and who are reluctant to go into battle. The South, then, has no monopoly on problems, but it does have some 400 foreign reporters to publicize them. The North admits no journalists whom they do not believe will publish sympathetic accounts.

The two Vietnams of today are new nations created on very ancient foundations. Three thousand years ago the ancient Viet tribes (called Yüeh by the Chinese) inhabited a large area in China south of the Yangtze River. Over the centuries, most of these tribes were conquered and absorbed by the southward expanding Chinese. The Vietnamese, i.e. "Southern Viets," were pushed into the Red River delta but were also conquered and ruled for one thousand years as part of China. During this long period, the Vietnamese became thoroughly Sinicized, adopting Chinese clothing, customs, and government. Yet, they managed to retain their language and ethnic identity and finally threw off Chinese rule while China was weakened by internal strife during the tenth century A.D. For 900 years thereafter, while continuing to absorb Chinese culture, the Vietnamese maintained their independence both by paying regular tribute to their great neighbor and by repelling a series of Chinese invasions.

The Vietnamese are justly proud that they of all the Viet tribes regained and kept their independence. They are also proud that while serving as a buffer against Chinese expansion into Southeast Asia, they became an imperial power in their own right. During their nine centuries of independence, the Viets expanded southward from the Red River delta, conquering and absorbing the Indianized kingdom of Champa, colonizing the lower Mekong delta, which they took from Cambodia, and finally, at their maximum power, annexing much of Laos and becoming suzerain, jointly with Thailand, over the rest of Laos and Cambodia. Only the conquest of Vietnam by France in the second half of the nineteenth century halted this expansion.

The French conquest was a great humiliation for a people who had repelled some fifteen invasions from China. Deeply resenting foreign control, the Vietnamese produced a long series of nationalist leaders and movements that struggled for *doc lap*—independence. The first nationalist groups tried to fight with traditional methods, but with the failure of these, subsequent leaders turned to Western techniques. Among the nationalists, a clash developed between those who followed the individualistic paths of Western liberalism and those who followed communism. In the end, the Communists led by Ho Chi Minh gained ascendency over the nationalist movement by means of a superior organization, the use of deception, and the murder of opposition nationalist leaders. Although Ho Chi Minh won great prestige by setting up a Vietnamese government before the French returned to Vietnam after World War II, he made many enemies by betraying non-Communist nationalists who had supported him. Because of this and a widespread opposition to the Viet Minh's Communist tactics and goals, Vietnam came to have a second government. While this government was originally inspired and supported by the French in their efforts to defeat the Communists, it became a strongly nationalistic entity in its own right and the only hope for those millions of Vietnamese who had no desire to live under communism.

Vietnam regained full independence at the time of the Geneva Agreements of 1954, which ended France's eight-year struggle to reassert colonial control. By these agreements, which lacked clarity on important points, Vietnam was provisionally divided along the seventeenth parallel. The North fell to the Communist-controlled government of the "Democratic Republic of Vietnam" (DRV), which had been organized in August 1945 by the Viet Minh, a Communist front movement led by Ho Chi Minh. The Viet Minh's initial victory was brief, however. Nationalist elements strongly contested its authority, and the ensuing conflict enabled the French to quickly re-establish their rule in the south. By the end of 1946, French forces had driven the DRV government from Hanoi into the mountain jungles. When they returned victoriously to Hanoi in 1954, the Viet Minh still called their government a "democratic republic" and claimed to invite non-Communist participation. But they frankly admitted their Communist orientation and eliminated most non-Communist leaders in a bloody purge.

The area south of the seventeenth parallel was assigned to the government of the "State of Vietnam," which had been formed under French sponsorship in 1949 by anti-Communist Vietnamese nationalists around the figure of the former emperor, Bao Dai. After the Geneva

Agreements, however, Bao Dai was displaced through a plebiscite by his nationalist premier, Ngo Dinh Diem, and the "State of Vietnam" became the "Republic of Vietnam" with a president and an elected legislature. The governments of the North and the South each claimed to be the only legal government of all Vietnam. The North was recognized by the communist-bloc nations, and the South by the principal non-communist ones.

According to the Geneva Agreements, the country was to be reunited in 1956 by national elections to be held, in an undefined way, under the supervision of an International Control Commission (icc), which was also to police execution of the truce terms. However, the icc, composed of representatives of Canada, India, and Poland, proved itself unable to correct treaty violations by either side, and the reunification elections were never held. After signing the agreements calling for the partition and subsequent elections over the strong protests of the Bao Dai government, France withdrew from Vietnam and disavowed further responsibility. The South Vietnamese government, together with the United States, did not approve the accords. Both promised, however, not to use force to upset them. Both insisted that elections should be held under United Nations supervision. In 1955-56, the DRV propagandized its willingness to conduct elections "on the principle of universal, equal, direct and secret balloting," but the Diem government protested that conditions for truly peaceful elections and freedom of choice did not exist. Diem pointed out that the North had greatly increased its military forces in violation of the Geneva Agreements, had used armed force to block refugees from joining the more than 900,000 who fled to the South under the truce terms, had moved thousands of youths by force to the North, and had launched a reign of terror against traditional leadership elements.

In the South, activities of communist agents left by the departing Viet Minh also threatened to obstruct freedom of choice. Their operations are well described in a report by Senator Mike Mansfield following a visit to Vietnam and Laos in 1955:

While the last official Vietminh units have been withdrawn in accordance with the Geneva accord, clandestine elements remain south of the 17th parallel. Agents and propagandists are active in infiltration and subversion. Secret Vietminh village councils have been set up in many areas and function at night in opposition to the regular administration. Small armed bands even operate openly in the mountainous regions. In the event of a breakdown in the present truce, the Vietminh have in these units a fifth column ready to go into immediate action.[1]

The report expressed the fear that hostilities would be renewed in the future and added with some foresight that these might take several forms. There might be either "an uprising only of the Vietminh underground in south Viet Nam" to avoid international involvement, or "an invasion of Vietminh forces from the north, with or without the overt support of the Chinese Communists." In any event, the report predicted that "a resumption of hostilities by the Communists in that part of the world is bound to be a serious threat to world peace and would produce the gravest international repercussions."[2]

In the years after partition, the governments of both the North and the South consolidated their positions. Ngo Dinh Diem and his family organized a strong, centralized administration, which saved the South from the collapse that had been generally expected. During the same period, the North was thrown into chaos by the blood purge of traditional leaders, which got out of hand and threatened to destroy the Communist party itself. While North Vietnam suffered from food shortages and peasant uprisings in 1956, Diem held elections in the South for a constituent assembly, which drew up a constitution for a presidential-type democracy. Although it is possible that Diem's dictatorial personality would not have permitted this constitution to work democratically in any event, the Communists gave it no chance.

As the Mansfield report predicted, the Communists launched an uprising in South Vietnam on a slowly accelerating scale so as to avoid immediate international complications. During 1954-56, they attempted to maintain a holding action to prevent Diem's government from taking complete control of the former Viet Minh areas. When it was clear no reunification elections would be held in 1956, this activity was stepped up with mounting propaganda, terrorism, and sabotage. On an accelerating scale, the DRV infiltrated back into the South trained political propagandists and guerrillas—southern Viet Minh who had gone to the North in 1954-55. With them came a growing volume of war materials by sea and land to supplement caches left behind at the end of the Indo-

---

[1] U. S. Senate Committee on Foreign Relations, *Viet Nam, Cambodia and Laos: Report by Senator Mike Mansfield* (Washington, D. C., Government Printing Office, October 6, 1955), p. 8.
[2] *Ibid.*, p. 12.

china War. In 1960-62, the Communists upgraded their struggle to a "war of liberation" and set up the National Liberation Front and the People's Revolutionary Party (PRP) as their political arm in the South. These actions were clearly directed by decisions in Hanoi.[3] By 1965, the reservoir of southerners in the North was exhausted, and whole battalions and later divisions of North Vietnamese army troops moved south to join forces with the Viet Cong, as the southern Communists came to be called.

As the Communist menace increased, Diem and his family tightened their control, making their government more repressive and restrictive rather than working to broaden their base of support as their American advisers advocated. Sparked by militant Buddhist demonstrations, opposition elements in the army overthrew Diem in late 1963. Since then a series of military and civilian governments has struggled to bring stability to the country and an end to the Viet Cong insurgency. The United States had aided the French and the government of the State of Vietnam in their struggle against the Communists and continued assistance to the South following partition. In addition to large scale aid for economic and social rehabilitation and development, the U. S. sent military advisers and equipment. Military assistance was increased to match the Communist escalation, and by the end of 1966 nearly 400,000 Americans, together with forces of South Vietnam and other allied nations, were engaged in combat against Communist forces.

The Communists have been inconsistent and often ambiguous in stating the goals of their insurrection. Different goals are stated to different audiences, at home and abroad. However, a few strands may be traced from the time of partition. The Viet Cong and the DRV have consistently charged the government of South Vietnam with oppression and have advocated its replacement by what they term a national democratic government. They have also directed a continuous campaign against "imperialism" or foreign intervention, with the U. S. replacing the French as the target after 1954. The Viet Cong have maintained that their insurgency is an indigenous Southern movement representing genuine political, social, and economic discontent among the peoples of the South. The insurgents were predominately of Southern origin until 1964, when the supply of trained Southern Viet Minh who had gone North at partition was exhausted. Nguyen Huu Tho, the National Liberation Front head, is a Southerner. In the North, Le Duan, the

[3] See Chapter Six for details and documentation.

Lao Dong party first secretary, who is believed to have provided much guidance for the insurrection, is also a Southerner. Actually, many of the DRV leaders originated in the center of the country in areas now in South Vietnam. This fact somewhat complicates the definition of the insurgency's base. The DRV desired that the uprising should as far as possible be locally led and supported, for Communist doctrine looks upon overt wars of aggression as evil, an activity of only "imperialist" states, which they consider the avowed enemies of communism. Communist states must aid and support indigenous wars of liberation, but they cannot by their standards admit to direct invasion, even when it may be open and obvious. The North Koreans, for example, claimed they were not invading South Korea in 1950, but were defending themselves against attacks from the South, and Communist China claimed to have sent only volunteers into Korea.

In South Vietnam, even before Diem's government could have been legitimately termed oppressive, the Communists were calling for its overthrow in favor of a "liberal, democratic and neutral government" to be eventually reunited with the North. At the same time, however, Communist agitators were working to stir up the poorer peasants to hate their more prosperous neighbors, using such slogans as "kill the land robbers," and were undermining or destroying every constructive program of the Diem government. Gradually, there emerged the full contours of the front technique, which the Viet Minh had used in winning control of the North.

The united front is a device by which Communists use the aspirations of other parties and groups, including the middle class, to achieve Communist revolutionary ends. The goal is the forcible overthrow of the existing political, social, and economic order and the establishment of a "classless" Communist system under the direction of a disciplined Communist elite, the Party. The united front technique, conceived by Lenin and developed by Stalin, Mao Tse-tung, and Ho Chi Minh, involves a two-stage revolution. First, by duping the bourgeoisie and other influential elements, the Communists secure their aid in leading a bourgeois-democratic revolution to overthrow a "colonialist" or "feudalist" regime. After creating a facade of democratic government to appease their bourgeois allies, the Communists then stage their own revolution to establish a Communist dictatorship. Such use of others is totally justified and moral for the Party zealot who considers expedient any method or action which leads to the establishment of a Communist state.

The technique of deception was clearly explained in an editorial in the September 1966 issue of the North Vietnamese theoretical Party journal, *Hoc Tap*:

The policy of founding the Indochinese democratic union between 1936 and 1939, the Viet Minh Front between 1941 and 1951, and the Lien Viet Front; the decision of signing the 6 March [1945] accord; the present NFLSV [National Liberation Front] policy of upholding the mottoes of independence, democracy, peace, and neutrality, and so forth—all these are typical examples of the clever application of the following instructions of Lenin: "It is possible to defeat a stronger enemy only through displaying great effort and under the necessary conditions of taking advantage—very minutely, very attentively, and very cleverly—of any rift, even the smallest one among the enemy; taking advantage of any contradiction, even the smallest one, among the interests of the bourgeoisie of the various countries and among the interests of various bourgeois groups and factions in each country; as well as taking advantage of any possibility, even the smallest one, of winning over an ally who is numerically strong—although this ally is temporarily uncertain . . . unstable and unreliable." Anyone who does not understand this truth understands neither Marxism nor scientific modern socialism in general. . . .[4]

Such statements as the foregoing are obviously intended for internal Communist consumption. In accordance with their strategy of deception, the Communists publish or broadcast completely different information for different audiences. For Party members and their close followers, they may be quite frank in stating their goals. Yet, for the outside world, broadcasts in foreign languages, such as English language programs beamed toward American troops, will ignore or tone down the Communist nature of the regime in North Vietnam. Such articles as those published in *Hoc Tap* are intended for the guidance of Party workers. However, since the Party leaders know these articles are translated and read abroad, they are often written so as to carry meanings at different levels, one coded to be understood by Party leaders, another by the Party rank and file, and still another by foreign readers. The message contained in a *Hoc Tap* article will be quite different from a purely propaganda piece broadcast or published in foreign languages, except for those intended for foreign Communists. The broadcasts and publications of the Liberation Front display the same ambivalence: those for foreigners deny any Communist affiliation, but those for inter-

---

[4] "Let Us Step Up the Theory-Formulating Task of the Party," *Hoc Tap*, September, 1966; also broadcast over Radio Hanoi, October 2, 1966. (See Chapter Four for the Indochinese democratic union, and Chapter Five for the Lien Viet Front and the March 6, 1945 accord.)

nal consumption recognize the leadership of the Party. This open and obvious duplicity results from the Communists' confidence in their capacity to deceive the "enemy"—the middle class and the "imperialists."

The publicly stated program of the Liberation Front, announced over the Liberation Radio on February 13 and 14, 1961, called for a government of national and democratic union composed of representatives of all social classes, nationalities, political parties, and religions to achieve independence, democracy, and neutrality for the attainment of "peaceful" reunification.[5] Communist goals and slogans were not mentioned, but the Front program contained buried qualifications. It stated that the new regime would be "largely" liberal and democratic and that "patriotic eminent citizens must take over for the people the control of economic, political, social, and cultural interests." The Viet Minh's use of a two-stage revolution in the North and evidence from captured Communist documents make it clear that if the Viet Cong were victorious, the Communists would be the "patriotic eminent citizens" who would "take over for the people." While a facade of a "largely" democratic government might be created, it would be quickly replaced by a Communist regime, just as it was in the North. Reunification with the North would be the next step, and under the projected circumstances, it would of course be "peaceful."

That the ultimate goal of the DRV is extension of its control over all of Vietnam has been made clear in various statements by DRV leaders and in captured Party directives. These are presented in some detail in Chapter Six. From the Communist viewpoint, Vietnam is a single nation from north to south and only foreign assistance to the South is preventing a reunification under Communist control. This objective was clearly stated in the DRV constitution of 1960, which dedicated the Vietnamese people to reunify the country under Communist party leadership.[6]

The Geographic Setting

While divided Vietnam has ancient roots, the present borders resulted partly from adjustments made during French rule. In the

[5] The Communists usually insert the word "peaceful" in referring to their efforts to achieve reunification. The term applies to the process that is to take place *after* they have overthrown the government in the South by *revolution*. This is quite evident from their many statements with respect to the insurgency.

[6] See "Preamble" to the 1960 constitution in Bernard B. Fall, *The Two Vietnams* (New York, 1963), Appendix I, pp. 399–402.

redrawing of the boundaries, Vietnam lost to Laos some of the mountain territory the Vietnamese had earlier annexed. These were the boundaries used in the postwar settlements by which Laos and Cambodia also regained independence.

Vietnam lies entirely in the tropics, but because of minor variations in the monsoon regimen and in altitudes, the area varies considerably in climate. Overall, the northeast winter monsoon blows cool dry air south from the interior of Asia, giving a dry season with scanty rain from November to April. From late April to August, the southwest summer monsoon brings warm moisture-laden air and abundant rainfall that determines the rice growing patterns. While some of the mountain regions receive the heaviest rainfall, the Hanoi area is drenched with 16 inches monthly during July and August as compared to Saigon's 13.

Hanoi also has the greatest temperature fluctuation, with the mean falling below 70°F. during the four coolest winter months and occasionally dropping as low as 50°. In Saigon the monthly average temperature varies only about three degrees above and below 82. To escape this unrelenting heat, the prosperous take their vacations at Dalat in the nearby highlands. The temperatures and rainfall guarantee a lush tropical growth throughout Vietnam, and stands of hardwood cover some of the mountains.

Geographically, Vietnam has been compared to two rice baskets hanging on a carrying pole. The rice baskets are the deltas of the Red River in the North and the Mekong in the South. The pole is the Annamite mountain chain linking the two ends of the country and crowding the Vietnamese into the series of small deltas and coastal plains of central Vietnam. All the country's deltas and plains together account for only 20 per cent of the land area but are inhabited by over 85 per cent of the population. The Red River delta is small, about 5800 square miles, compared to the southern delta's 14,000. But this ancient homeland of the Vietnamese is one of the most densely populated areas in the world, averaging about 1200 persons per square mile, roughly four times that of the Mekong delta. Even in some strictly rural areas, the population density is over 2500 per square mile. Only in the coastal plain of Quang Nam Province around Danang does the population of South Vietnam reach a comparable density.

The Red River (Song Koi), which formed the Tonkin delta, flows out of China with its major tributaries, the Black and Claire Rivers, in roughly parallel canyons. After emptying into the flatlands, they link into a single channel only 35 miles from Hanoi. Even before reaching Hanoi, the river fans out into numerous interconnected channels, forming a lace-like pattern as they approach the sea. The Red River delta, like the Mekong's, is only a few feet above sea level. At peak flood it carries twice the water volume of the Nile, although it is only 720 miles long. With this flood comes a tremendous load of sediment, which builds natural dikes and gradually raises the river level above the surrounding countryside. The silt carried to the sea is swept down by currents to expand the smaller deltas and round out the coastline south of Tonkin.

Since ancient times, Vietnam's rulers have strengthened and extended the natural dikes to try to prevent the disastrous floods that occur when they break. They are also being further extended to the sea and along the coast to create more land for rice culture. This, in turn, increases the inhabited area that can be devastated by storms or floods. At flood crest the river flows high above the surrounding paddy fields but during the dry season sinks to a third of this height, requiring that water be raised to irrigate the fields. During droughts, to which North Vietnam is subject in the winter monsoon, this variation in level can become disastrous. Widespread double-cropping makes the farmer even more vulnerable to the vagaries of weather, because it pushes the cultivating seasons to the limit.

Double-cropping is less common in the relatively underpopulated Mekong delta, where a rich, fertile land has been built up by the river's many mouths. The heavy sedimentation is expanding the delta southward 250 feet a year. The main delta merges with the smaller and less fertile ones of the Vaico and Saigon Rivers to the north. These rivers, which carry less silt, join to provide a navigable channel fifty miles inland to Saigon, the best port in the far south. Elsewhere, the continuously expanding coastline blocks the entrance of seagoing shipping, except for small ocean freighters which may travel the main channels of the Mekong up to Phnom Penh in Cambodia.

While the Mekong delta is low-lying, its annual flood waters normally spread evenly over a vast area, leaving only the tops of the dikes and the earthen platforms of the villages standing like islands. In the deepest areas, a long-stemmed "floating" rice is grown. The river's main safety valve is the Tonle Sap, a large lake in Cambodia connected to the Mekong by the Tonle Sap River. At flood time, the waters back up the Tonle Sap to fill the great lake. Then, as the waters recede, the current in the Tonle Sap reverses to flow toward the sea, thus maintaining the Mekong at a more constant level than the Red River and sparing the populace the hardships of devastating floods. Only occasionally is there a serious flood, such as that of 1966.

The Red River delta is ringed by the forested mountains of the northern highlands, which extend into China and westward into northern Laos. To the south of the delta, the highlands join with the Annamite Mountains that push down through central Vietnam and eastern Laos. East of the mountains are a series of plateaus dissected by the tributaries of the Mekong, which forms the western border of the highlands. In the mountains and plateaus, tribal peoples cultivate dry crops, including corn and rice, mainly with a shifting slash and burn technique.

Vietnam is thus a land of geographical contrasts. Jungle-clad mountains account for 80 per cent of the land area, but support only about 15 per cent of the total population. It is a tropical land with a long history of intensive cultivation in the North, while relatively "new" and rich fields are barely beginning to be worked in the South.

Cultural Roots[7]

During the ten centuries of direct Chinese rule, the Vietnamese absorbed considerable numbers of Chinese settlers along with significant elements of China's religious and philosophical beliefs, social system, and methods of government. This assimilation of Chinese culture continued throughout Vietnam's nine centuries of independence prior to the French conquest. All of the main social, cultural, economic, and political developments in China were felt eventually in Vietnam. Every Chinese dynastic upheaval sent refugees fleeing to Vietnam, and every Chinese invasion left stragglers to fortify Chinese influence. Vietnamese scholars studied Chinese books, corresponded with Chinese scholars, and often studied in China. Embassies were exchanged regularly and usually included prominent scholars of both countries. Chinese monks brought new religious ideas to preach in Vietnam and sometimes founded new sects.

While absorbing Chinese culture, the Vietnamese adapted it to their own customs, especially in matters of religion. The Chinese form of Mahayana Buddhism, already liberally infused with elements of Taoism, Confucianism, and Chinese spirit worship when it arrived in

[7] Portions of this section are adapted from the author's "The Vietnamese Peasant: His Psychological World and Means of Communication," *Transition*, No. 6 (Washington, D. C., January, 1966), 26-39.

Vietnam, was thoroughly mingled with Vietnam's indigenous animism. All ethnic Vietnamese adopted Confucian ancestor worship with its stress on the collective family. But, for most Vietnamese, the spirits of their ancestors are but a small part of a vast world of spirits, good and bad, that demand attention. These spirits must be humored, propitiated, bribed, threatened, or deceived as the situation requires, but they cannot be ignored. Buddhism has accommodated itself to the spirit and ancestor cults, and Buddhist monks often serve as spirit specialists. But in this field they compete with a variety of other practitioners of the spirit world, such as Taoist priests and astrologers.

Within the Vietnamese home, the most important piece of furniture is the ancestor altar, where offerings of food and drink are made and prayers said to the spirits of the dead. Before this altar, the new bride or the newborn child is introduced to the ancestors, who must be kept informed of all important family events. In strongly Buddhist homes, the same altar may serve a dual purpose, or a separate one may be maintained for Buddhist rites. Catholics say prayers for the souls of the dead before a Christian shrine, which may occupy the place of the usual ancestor altar. Vietnam's eclectic indigenous cults, the Cao Dai and Hoa Hao, which originated in 1919 and 1939 respectively, have also accommodated themselves to the ancestor cult.

Within the village, the cult of the village guardian deity plays an important part in community life. The *dinh,* or cult temple, houses the altar to this deity along with the original government edict that legalized the founding of the village. The *dinh* also serves as a form of community center, and the elective lay priests of the cult are honored notables.

There is no clear statistical picture of Vietnam's religious structure because most Vietnamese practice aspects of Buddhism, Taoism, Confucianism, and animism simultaneously and in varying degrees. They are complementary, not contradictory, for the Vietnamese, who may not clearly separate the religions in his own mind. Thus any tally of the number of Buddhists or Confucianists can be only an estimate. The fact that a Vietnamese may occasionally pray to one or another of the numerous Chinese and Indian deities that have become associated with Vietnamese Mahayana Buddhism does not necessarily mean he considers himself a Buddhist. More than likely he may never have stopped to consider what he is, unless he has specifically been asked. Yet, even a person who denies Buddhist association may be influenced in his ancestor worship by the Buddhist doctrines of karma and reincarnation.

During the long period of independence, Buddhism, Taoism, and Confucianism vied for court favor. Under the last Vietnamese dynasty before the French conquest, Confucianism was the state cult, and there were many national ceremonies led by the emperor and the mandarins. Buddhism and Taoism were persecuted, though not as harshly as Christianity, which first took root in Vietnam in the sixteenth century. Under French rule, Buddhism remained in the shade while Catholicism was favored. Only in the twentieth century did Buddhism begin to regain popularity as a form of nonpolitical expression of Vietnamese nationalism. For much the same reason, the two new eclectic sects, the Cao Dai and reformist Hoa Hao, attracted many adherents. Under Diem, the tendency to officially favor Catholics antagonized non-Catholic Vietnamese. Buddhist monks won a vastly heightened prestige for their part in the overthrow of the Diem government, but this prestige has been dissipated by the continued political agitation of the more militant monks. Active Buddhists may number no more than 3 million with perhaps an equal number of nominal adherents. Catholics number about 1.5 million. Both the Hoa Hao and the Cao Dai claim nearly the same total as the Catholics, but each sect is splintered into several subsects, whose membership claims may be overlapping and exaggerated. Most of the 800,000 mountain tribal peoples are animists.

Before the French conquest, the Vietnamese elite based its right to rule on scholarship, as tested by government examinations founded on a Confucian-oriented body of knowledge. The emperor, however, ruled by "divine right," receiving his mandate from "heaven," usually through inheritance. He was the father of his people and high priest in the Confucian state cult. Theoretically absolute, he exercized his power through scholar-bureaucrats who, like the emperor, were to lead the realm into righteousness by their example. In practice, the antiquarian Confucian philosophy often led to reactionary attitudes and harsh enforcement of arbitrary laws. In general, few but the wealthy could afford the study time for the examinations, yet this did not produce a fixed class structure. A wealthy family that produced no scholars soon declined. Often villagers or family clans would subsidize a poor but bright village boy, for his successes would bring honor to them all.

The Confucian scholar-bureaucrat kept his roots in his village and his family. The family was a close corporation, looking after its own but expecting their foremost allegiance. Within the home, the father was administrator, judge, and high priest of the family cult. Important decisions were made in family council, allowing little individual initiative. The village, too, was governed by a council, its members chosen from among the local elite. A variety of professional, social and self-help associations insured acceptance and security. The system discouraged individual decision-making and minimized personal responsibility, though it produced a strong, somewhat collective village structure. It also created an atmosphere of accommodation and compromise. In any dispute or settlement, neither side must be totally trampled; the loser must be left with "face." The family was accountable for its members and the village for its inhabitants. Religious, political, social, and legal functions were intertwined at all levels, for the state was viewed as an enlarged family, bound together in the cult of the dead, the worship of ancestors and of heroic figures. This link with the past gave the Vietnamese people unity in time, as well as in ethnic geography.

The prestige of the military was low in traditional Vietnam, and the military mandarinate generally remained subordinate to the civil government. The Confucian social scale ranked the scholar first, followed by the farmer and merchant, with the soldier at the bottom. This attitude has not altogether changed and may underlie some of the problems facing the military governments that have ruled since 1963.

Despite the population shifts caused by war and the division of the country, Vietnam remains preponderantly rural. Four out of five Vietnamese still live and work in villages close to the soil, continuing their traditional ways as much as war and revolution permit. Normally, the world of the peasant is small, rarely extending far beyond his village. His loyalties go first to his family, then to his village, and only to a lesser degree to his region and his race. Provincial boundaries have changed so frequently, especially in the South, that they are meaningless to him. He has little awareness of Vietnam as a nation, though he knows he is a Viet as distinct from being a Lao, a Khmer (Cambodian), or a Chinese. In general, however, he considers himself superior to all foreigners. From childhood he has listened to folk stories of Vietnam's heroes—Hung Vuong, legendary founder of the Viet kingdom; the Trung sisters; Le Loi; Tran Hung Dao; and others who defeated the Chinese, the Mongols, the Chams, or the Khmers in past wars. Such stories have fed his sense of race superiority; yet he has little that can be called patriotism or nationalism in the Western sense.

For over a century, no government has given him much reason to commit himself. Traditionally as today, the peasant was rarely involved in the larger affairs of the nation. Within his village, local custom prevailed, with the emperor's law ending at the bamboo hedge that shielded the village from wild animals and bandits. The villager was called upon to serve in the army, to provide corvée, and pay taxes, but otherwise was left to his traditional ways. On occasion, when natural disasters or overly harsh demands from corrupt officials made his life unbearable, he might rise up under the banner of some adventurer claiming descent from a former dynasty. Because of his pattern of obedience, he was relatively easily led into rebellion by one showing power and authority. Otherwise he remained quiescent, expecting little from the central government and giving no more than was necessary. In the face of foreign invasion, however, he could be aroused to defend his country valiantly.

Ethnic Mosaic and Sectional Differences

The valleys, highlands, and plateaus of Vietnam present a complicated ethnic mosaic. In 1966, the population of all Vietnam was about 34 million and was increasing at about a million a year. About 85 per cent were ethnic Vietnamese with a little more than half living in North Vietnam. The ethnic Vietnamese usually inhabit only the lowlands below the 300-foot altitude level. They are found mainly in the two large deltas of the north and south and in the string of smaller deltas and narrow coastal plains stretching between. Only since partition has the flood of refugees sent any considerable number of ethnic Vietnamese to settle in the highlands which traditionally they have feared as dangerous and unhealthy. These highlands are principally the homeland of a variety of tribal peoples.

In the northern highlands the major groups are tribal Thai (T'ai), who number over 700,000 in North Vietnam alone. They might be termed the mountain cousins of the lowland dwellers of neighboring Laos and Thailand. However, they often consider themselves superior to their lowland "relatives" and are generally more sophisticated than the other mountain peoples. The languages of all the Thai groups are, in varying degrees, mutually intelligible. Next in number in North Vietnam are the some 300,000 Muong, apparently ethnic Vietnamese who remained in the hills in a semitribal state. Among other non-Thai groups are the most recent arrivals, the more than 100,000 Man (Yao) who live at the 900- to 3000-foot altitudes, and the equal number of Meo (Miao) who prefer the highest peaks. All of these plus a number of smaller groups extend into China and Laos.

Further south in the plateaus and Annamite Mountains and extending into Laos and Cambodia are large numbers of Indonesian-related tribes. The languages of some of these tribes are of the Malayo-Polynesian family, while others are of the Mon-Khmer group. Collectively, these mountain peoples are commonly known by the French designation *Montagnard*, though the Vietnamese call them *Moi*, which means "savage." Among the earlier inhabitants of Southeast Asia, they form about 25 per cent of the total population of Laos, and about 800,000 live in South Vietnam. Over the centuries, Laos and Vietnam have asserted sometimes conflicting claims to the intervening highlands, where the largely unassimilated Montagnards dwell. Until recently, the Montagnards had little interest in any political organization larger than their own village, though an occasional charismic chieftain was able to inspire a coalition. In both Vietnam and Laos, the ethnic majority has long misused the tribal minorities, creating antagonisms which the Viet Cong and Lao Communists (the Pathet Lao) are exploiting. The nearly half million largely unassimilated Khmers in the delta lands of South Vietnam, which were once part of Cambodia, have caused relatively few problems.

The Chinese represent the largest and certainly the most influential minority in South Vietnam. They have been migrating into Vietnam for more than two thousand years. In the seventeenth century, thousands settled in the southern delta where they helped to found a number of cities, including Saigon and Cholon. Another major migration, totalling nearly a half million, began with Japan's invasion of China and continued until the fall of China to the Communists. Most left the North in 1954, and today there are about a million persons in South Vietnam who identify themselves as Chinese, though over the centuries the majority of the migrants were absorbed.

The Chinese brought their crafts, their industrious way of life, and their gift for trade and commerce, and both the Vietnamese and the French allowed their trading communities considerable autonomy. Ngo Dinh Diem, however, imposed harsh assimilation measures designed to break their grip upon the economy. Chinese born in Vietnam received Vietnamese citizenship, and noncitizens were restricted from a variety of professional and economic activities. Some Chinese evaded the restrictions, but most who were eligible accepted Vietnamese citizenship, though by the laws of both Nationalist and Communist China they remain Chinese citizens also. Sources of friction between the Chinese and Vietnamese are numerous. Vietnamese still fear and resent Chinese economic power. Some complain that the Chinese-Vietnamese evade military conscription and payment of taxes and do not support the war. Others accuse Chinese merchants of buying "protection" from the Viet Cong. The Chinese for their part remain clannish and aloof, tending to feel superior to the Vietnamese. Chinese merchants and Vietnamese officials mutually charge bribery and corruption.

Tensions also arise among the Vietnamese over sectional differences. Geography and history have divided Vietnam into two major population zones, the rice baskets of the North and the South, with the center stretching out as a narrow and relatively thinly-peopled zone between. The North has been cultivated since ancient times and was the historic political center until the beginning of the nineteenth century. In this densely populated area, with its tiny rice fields alternately threatened by drought and flood, the northern farmer works endlessly to scratch out a meager existence. In the more recently developed South, with its rich, well-watered lands, the farmer works at a more leisurely pace for larger rewards. The deltas and small plains of the center range from relatively rich lands to barren sandy soil. Through most of its history, however, the area north of the seventeenth parallel that is now the DRV was the totality of Vietnam. The great southward expansion was only completed in the eighteenth century. At that time, the north and south were ruled by rival Vietnamese kings with capitals in Hue and Hanoi. Real unification of Vietnam in approximately its present total form was not effected until 1802, when Hue in central Vietnam assumed the position of country leadership. This unity lasted only 60 years before the French conquered the Mekong provinces of the south.

Subsequently, the French divided the north and south from the center and created three separately administered divisions. The southernmost, Cochinchina, was annexed to France in 1862 and was most heavily influenced by France. Saigon developed almost as a French city, while Hanoi and Hue had deep Vietnamese cultural roots. Many educated southern Vietnamese preferred to move to France when independence came, rather than give up their prized French passports, though others loyally sought to serve the new Vietnamese regime. For them, Saigon became the new cultural as well as political and economic capital. Tonkin in the north was taken by France some twenty years after Cochinchina, but Hanoi became the seat of the French government and of the first modern university, thus reinforcing its political and cultural prestige. Armed resistance in Tonkin was not broken until just before World War I, and even thereafter the area remained a hotbed of nationalist agitation. Least influenced by France was Annam in the center, where the imperial court maintained nominal rule until 1945. Having fewer resources to exploit, Annam saw fewer Frenchmen. This, combined with the natural insularity of a region geographically divided into many small deltas, kept the center freer of Western ideas and encouraged the retention of the traditional xenophobia.

The most obvious differences among the peoples of the different sections are those of appearance. The Mongolian fold of the eye and the light yellow tinge of the skin are more pronounced in the Tonkinese, while in the center and south, the more frequent rounded eyes and darker skin evidence the admixture of Cham and Khmer. Dialectical variations are also obvious. Like the Chinese, the Vietnamese use tones or differences in pitch to change the meaning of their short monosyllabic words. North Vietnamese use five tones, but southerners slur these off to four, a change which the Northerners ridicule. There are also many variations in vocabulary as well as pronunciation, which may lead to misunderstandings. Temperamental differences are claimed too. Northerners are viewed as more akin to the Chinese in their aggressiveness and zeal for hard work, which "virtues" are resented by the Southerners, who are considered to be less energetic and more easygoing and pleasure-loving. In central Vietnam, where the piractical, aggressive Chams held sway for centuries, there is greater antagonism toward the West and a more rebellious temperament. This area has produced more than its quota of vigorous leaders and rebels, including Ho Chi Minh, Ngo Dinh Diem, and the militant Buddhist Thich Tri Quang.

The 1954 partition of Vietnam complicated the pattern of sectional differences. Nearly a million refugees fled to the South, while perhaps 100,000 moved north. Some of the top leaders of the Communist party and the DRV government are from the South. Similarly, numerous top civil and military figures in South Vietnam are Northerners. Some leading families are represented in the bureaucracies on both sides of the seventeenth parallel. The movement of peoples produced much friction. Many Southerners feared that the Northern elite refugees would squeeze them from the best positions in business and government. Friction also arose among the Communists when Northern political and military cadre came south to take direction of the insurgency. Some observers believe the Hanoi government is concerned that the Viet Cong may develop into a Southern separatist, though still Communist, movement. It has been suggested this was one reason why Hanoi's leaders sent Northern troops into the South before they were clearly needed.

Intellectual and Social Disorientation and the Appeal of Communism[8]

In Vietnam, as in most developing nations, many of the social, economic, and political grievances and problems are so fundamental, so deeply rooted in the culture and society that solution appears to demand fundamental changes. Yet, such changes require the education of new generations to different ways of life. Meanwhile, there continue to be large areas of social dislocation and dissatisfaction that seem inherent to transitional societies. No government, however efficient, can move fast enough to solve all problems at once. The problems are magnified by the lack of honest, technically trained, and motivated personnel. The job of today and the preparation for tomorrow must be done by men trained for yesterday's world. The older personnel that dominate the government are slow to accept new techniques. They tend to cling to their power and prestige, frustrating and embittering younger men who desire to test their new ideas and training. Vietnam's traditional society had limited knowledge of the modern world. Its Confucian tenets discouraged change and rejected the Western concept of progress. Once the door to modernization was cracked open by the French, however, a multitude of new demands was released. The more Western ideas permeated the society, the more changes were demanded. New education further expanded horizons, increasing the desire for change, which in turn created more social dislocation.

Into the family-oriented state of Vietnam, where the individual subjugated himself to the prior demands of society, France injected a philosophy of individualism. The French-educated elite were cut off by their new learning from Vietnam's past. The Confucian literary and historical heritage was locked in Chinese characters which were no longer learned. The new elite too often lost their roots in the family and the village, which had made the world comfortable and meaningful. Without roots they became like smoke drifting over the land.

The chasm between city and village has been widened in South Vietnam by new economic opportunities that have made the rich richer without providing corresponding benefits for the poor. Despite the

[8] Parts of this section are adapted from the author's "The Viet Cong: Communist Party and Cadre," *Transition*, No. 8 (September, 1966), 21-35.

considerable increase in public education facilities, the prosperous continue to have the first chance to receive the higher education which remains the key to prestige, wealth, and political power. Many, disenchanted with Vietnam's facilities and convinced that modernization requires Western techniques, make great sacrifices to send their sons abroad where they spend their formative years in an alien culture. When these young men return, and many do not, they face serious problems of adjusting to their own culture. Though the wealthy enjoy advantages, there are still no strong class barriers in the South, where the extended family may reach across several economic levels. It remains the duty of the prosperous to help their poorer relatives, and it is possible for a poor boy to rise to high position through education and hard work.

Though the cleavage between city and country has been deepened, for most people it is still bridged by the ties of village and family. The city dweller of the South goes back to his village to special family gatherings when he can. Today, however, this may mean crossing into Viet Cong-held zones, for there are few families without members in both camps. For the more than 900,000 who fled from the North, the graves of the ancestors are far away. Millions of others have been uprooted in the South by the strategic hamlet and other regroupment programs or by flight from Viet Cong areas. In the North, the government has forced the movement of a large part of the urban population to rural areas. Moreover, collectives and communes and the massive purges of the traditional elite have disrupted family and village patterns and traditional ties, which the Communists seek to replace by an all demanding loyalty to the Party. The Viet Cong have worked to introduce collectivization into the South, but most Southerners still maintain the family cult, and new villages are still formed, for without these ties the Vietnamese feels himself a homeless wanderer.

The Vietnamese village, traditionally insulated by its communal structure, has been buffeted by many forces and subjected to many alien ideas, particularly since World War II. Its bamboo hedge has been destroyed, literally and figuratively, and its self-sufficient autonomy has been ravaged. The French tampered repeatedly with village government, disrupting patterns of rural leadership. In 1945-46, the Viet Minh introduced Communist-dominated "people's councils," little soviets to replace the councils of the local oligarchy. Countermeasures of the Diem government placed the villages under chiefs appointed by the central government. While this may have eliminated Communist influence from the village leadership, it also completed the destruction of the traditional village structure and eliminated much of its autonomy, which subsequent South Vietnamese governments have sought to restore. Viet Cong and government propagandists compete for the allegiance of the South Vietnamese villager. With large-scale U. S. aid, the government since 1954 has sought to bring more services to the villages. Torn between conflicting promises and caught between rival military forces, the peasant has not known which way to turn. Mostly he wants to be left alone, to till his fields as did his ancestors. But the many promises he has heard have awakened in him a consciousness of a better world. Now the villager expects schools, health services, honest government, and perhaps at least a small say in how that government is to be run.

The Viet Minh were the first to attempt to organize the peasant as an effective political force. They were followed by the Hoa Hao religious sect and, to a lesser degree, the rival Cao Dai. The Diem government also worked to win the villagers but became increasingly less effective as the insurgency mounted and Diem's restrictive rule stifled local and central government initiative. More recently, the Buddhists are exploring this field. Currently, the South Vietnamese government is expending great effort to train and motivate young officials to bring government services into the villages along with security as they are freed from Communist control. There are conflicting reports of the progress of this "social revolution." Charges are made that the government officials move too slowly or not at all, that graft and corruption consume large shares of American economic aid, and that the war against the Viet Cong will be lost despite a military victory, because the South Vietnamese government will not or cannot bring adequate social services, progress, land reform, and security to the villagers. Such charges sometimes have genuine government failures at their base, and certainly a military victory over the Viet Cong means little unless the villagers are won over to government support through a genuine response to their legitimate aspirations for a better life. The South Vietnamese government recognizes this and is attempting to wage both a military and a social war against the insurgents. While some observers report a serious lack of progress in socio-economic areas, others see positive achievements. A social revolution cannot be achieved overnight, however. The experiences of the war on poverty in the United States reveal some of the fundamental problems and pitfalls.

In dealing with the Communist-led insurrection, the government is at a distinct disadvantage, for upon it rests the burden of proving by accomplishment its right and capacity to govern. It must provide those services the people have been led to expect—clinics, education, agricultural services, roads, efficient and responsible administration, and, above all, security, a difficult condition to maintain against guerrilla and terrorist tactics. The more the government provides, the more needs the people recognize, and rising expectations inevitably exceed government capabilities. Moreover, the social changes attendant upon modernization contribute to the reservoir of dislocated and dissatisfied people. In such an environment, the Communist agitator flourishes, enjoying the advantage of revolutionary irresponsibility, isolating the peasants and discrediting the government by destruction and terrorism.

In North Vietnam, the Communists took over an essentially classless society without great extremes of wealth. Most of those few who were wealthy landlords or "capitalists" had fled to the South. Nevertheless, to carry out their "class struggle," the Party dogmatically assigned everyone to classes with minute subdivisions ranging from "comprador capitalist" or "feudal landlord" down to the poorest landless rural worker. Having done this, they inverted the class structure, purging and degrading the former elite elements, including thousands who had been admitted to the Party. At the same time, those who had previously been the poorest farmers and rural workers were theoretically raised to the highest positions, where their inexperience and gratitude made them welcome Party direction. Ironically, the majority of the top Party leaders originated from the old elite group that they purged.

The Vietnamese intellectuals who provide most of the leadership in both North and South Vietnam, Communist and anti-Communist, have been torn between conflicting ideological systems. Dislocated by French rule and education, they could no longer find security or guidances for solving modern problems in the Confucian world of their parents. The Western free-enterprise system was confusing with its uncertain rewards and its demands for individual decision-making, for which they had little training. To many, impatient for quick results, evolutionary processes seemed too slow. Communism, however, offered a planned society to replace their former ordered existence and promised a shortcut to modernization and progress through drastic social and economic revolution. By its all-encompassing demands, the Communist party also provided a substitute for the family and a modern channel for the traditional religious orientation of the Vietnamese. These were potent appeals to the disaffected intellectuals under colonial rule, when

Western democratic ways seemed too closely equated with colonialism. After the colonial rulers departed, the Communists invented "neo-colonialism" as a new symbol around which to teach hatred of Western democracy and its free-enterprise system.

Marxist-Leninist doctrine originally stressed that Communist parties would grow out of the industrial working class, the proletariat. Lenin expanded the concept of the proletariat to include the rural working class, the poor peasant. After early failures to convert the city workers in China and Vietnam, Mao Tse-tung and Ho Chi Minh revised the theory to place primary emphasis upon the peasantry. Communist doctrine, however, has little appeal for most Vietnamese peasants and urban workers. The ultimate goals of communism require the peasant to give up the private farming plot he cherishes and turn it over to a cooperative or state-owned communal farm, where he must work in gangs under Communist party direction. There he must sacrifice his immediate well-being and perhaps that of his children so that the Communist state can build industry out of the fruits of his labor. Ultimately, this industry is supposed to produce goods which will be shared equally by all workers. By the peasant's sacrifice, perhaps his grandchildren may enjoy a better life. Not unnaturally such distant goals are not attractive to most peasants or workers. Their interests are in immediate needs—lower rents and taxes, private ownership of land, a fair price for the products of their labor, reasonably honest and efficient government officials, and such public services as health and education. The peasant and worker want these now, for themselves as well as their grandchildren.

Communism as a doctrine has appealed primarily to a small minority of disoriented intellectuals who have been alienated by the existing government and social system and have fulfilled their personal aspirations and needs by becoming professional revolutionary activists and leaders. A small group of intellectuals, however, can accomplish little without a mass following. Since the Party's doctrines and ultimate goals are alien to the immediate aspirations of the urban workers and peasants, the Communists developed an intricate array of misleading promises and organizational techniques to win their support. During the period of French rule, the Viet Minh harnessed to the Communists' cause the popular desire for independence and democracy. Appealing to nationalism, the Communists blamed the French for all the ailments of the Vietnamese political, social, and economic life. Once the French were defeated and the country achieved independence, the Communists continued to play on nationalist themes in the South by transferring the onus for all evils to the "American imperialists." The independent Diem government was maligned as "the puppet of the Americans," and again the call was issued for the overthrow of "imperialism" and the establishment of "true" independence and democracy. Many South Vietnamese were not satisfied with Diem's brand of democracy, but they preferred it to communism. They considered South Vietnam truly independent and feared reunification with the Communist North. Consequently, the new Communist appeals for revolution aroused little support from the middle class, who had provided much of the leadership in the revolution against France. Also, despite their best efforts, the Communists failed to win significant support among the urban workers in the South.

The Party therefore turned to the villages to cultivate the real or imagined grievances of the poorest peasants, who have the greatest needs, are the most ignorant, and are the most easily led by the promises of free land or low rents. Success with this group is due to the fact that the poorer peasants too often have been neglected by the government and are flattered by the attention the Communists give them. They are relatively isolated from other sources of information and are more vulnerable to the terrorism the Viet Cong have used to increase this isolation. Once within the Communist network, the poor peasant is usually doomed to remain at the lowest Party levels, the wheelhorses who do the hard work and fight the battles. The dissident intellectuals dominate the higher positions, for only they have the education and sophistication to comprehend and manipulate the complicated Communist dogma. The ratio of the different groups within the Viet Cong is probably little different from that described in a North Vietnamese publication in 1955, when, of 1855 responsible positions in the Lao Dong (Communist) Party, only 139 were filled by "workers" and 351 by "peasants," while 1365 were held by "intellectuals." [9]

Economic Realities

When Vietnam was divided in 1954, the North gained slightly more than half of the population, including most of the skilled labor, mineral wealth, and industry. Its major problem was a food deficiency,

[9] Bernard B. Fall, "Power and Pressure Groups in North Viet-Nam," *The China Quarterly*, January–March 1962, pp. 37–46.

for it had long been fed by rice from the South, while exporting coal, tin, cement and other products of its mines and factories. Since partition, which cut trade with the South, the main export has been high-grade coal from the Hon Gay mines near Haiphong, much of which has gone to Japan and continental China.

The Vietnamese have sometimes been called the Japanese of Southeast Asia. Their readiness to learn new skills combined with high energy, ingenuity, and economic aggressiveness gave them a potential for rapid development of their not inconsiderable resources. While the French endeavored to exploit these resources, they discouraged the development of industries that might compete with those of France. Much of what was developed was dismantled by the French as they left the North in 1954. Despite this setback, the Hanoi regime with Communist-bloc aid put many factories back into operation by 1958, including the Haiphong cement plants and the Nam Dinh cotton mills. By 1960, they claimed their production equalled or exceeded that of 1939.

The DRV plans for "socialist construction" aimed to create a collectivized base for further industrialization. To this end, priority was assigned to building of hydroelectric and thermoelectric power plants, which increased production of electricity over 400 per cent by 1964, with more plants coming into operation in 1965 and 1966. A major item in the economic planning was the Thai Nguyen iron-steel complex. While scheduled to begin operation in 1960, its first blast furnace was not fired until December 1963, and it is still believed to have only limited production.

In general, the delay in the Thai Nguyen plant appears to have been paralleled in other industrial fields. Goals have consistently receded and have been reduced. Hanoi publications also complain that the quality of production has been low and there has been excessive waste. Despite strenuous government efforts to increase rice production and expand areas in cultivation, the food deficit has grown, and the majority of the people are subsisting on inadequate rations. The acceleration of the war and the bombing of the North have increased problems in all fields. Great stress has been placed on decentralizing industry by moving it to the hills to develop regional self-sufficiency. Since much of the industrial production is still small-scale, this was possible. However, decentralization places greater strains upon the already inadequate transportation system, which has suffered severely from the bombing. Even before the build up of the war, the DRV gross national product (GNP) was low. The North Vietnamese are now among the poorest people in Asia. To a large degree it is because of this national poverty that, with strong urging from China, North Vietnam has risked the costly attempt to conquer the South. Without South Vietnam's rich rice bowl, North Vietnam can only remain poor, particularly while it effectively isolates itself by pursuing Communist economic policies and adhering to the Communist bloc, thus cutting off most non-Communist foreign assistance and trade.

The South has relatively little industry or known mineral wealth, but it has one of the richest alluvial plains in the world combined with a fairly dependable water supply from the regular flooding of the Mekong. In addition, the South has sizeable rubber plantations, potentially an important source of foreign exchange. There are extensive areas yet unopened suitable for rubber, sugar cane, tea, and other export food crops. The large plateau with its sparse population of Montagnard tribes has a considerable potential for agriculture and cattle raising, and the mountain jungles can provide the basis for a lumber and paper industry.

Because the mineral resources in the north were more accessible and obvious, they were developed first under French rule. The southern mountains have not yet been scientifically explored by geologists. One coal vein near Danang is now being exploited. Iron and aluminum are found nearby and elsewhere are known deposits of tin and copper. These and other resources can be exploited after the war, with the new ports at Chu Lai and Cam Ranh Bay providing shipping facilities hitherto not available. The considerable hydroelectric power potential has been tapped by only one dam built by the Japanese as a reparation payment, but it can supply ample power for industry in Saigon when the country is secure.

With extensive U. S. aid, South Vietnam achieved rapid progress before the DRV stepped up its "war of liberation" in the South. Its GNP is about one-third higher than that of North Vietnam. While this income may be less evenly distributed, ordinarily more is available to the average citizen because less is taken by the state. Apart from the areas most directly hit by the war, only a very small minority of the people in the South have been reduced to the substandard caloric intake of the majority of the people of the North. A greatly increased population together with higher consumption levels caused a decrease in rice exports in the immediate postwar years, and subsequent exports have been disrupted by the accelerating war. Production reached prewar levels of 2.8 million tons by 1957, and in the 1965-66 season had increased to about 5 million tons, despite the war.

A fair portion of this production, however, has been kept from the market by the Viet Cong. Much has been siphoned off as Viet Cong "taxes," part of which reportedly is sold in Cambodia. Some may be carried to the North in the trucks that would otherwise return empty after bringing infiltrators and munitions to the South. As a result of this rice drain and the disruption of transportation by the Viet Cong, the U. S. began to send in grain in 1964. After serious floods destroyed crops and rice stocks in central Vietnam that same year, still larger food shipments were imported. The flow of refugees to government zones has also reduced food production, but the effect may be more serious for the Communist forces who depended upon this source.

Vietnam in Southeast Asia and the World

The global significance of Vietnam is a recent phenomenon. Historically, it has made few important contributions to the West, or even to the East. In earlier centuries, Vietnam was a significant way station for trade between China, India, and Southeast Asia, but with the development of large seagoing vessels and compasses, that function lessened. Vietnam had little to contribute in exports and had few unfulfilled needs to attract Western traders, and those who came made meager profits. No balance sheet for France's colonial venture in Vietnam is available, but certainly Indochina did not bring the wealth in trade and produce French colonists had hoped for. It is not improbable that the total cost of Indochina to France, including the Viet Minh war, exceeded the total economic gain. But nations do not fight wars or take colonies only on the basis of accountants' balance sheets. One important motivating force leading to the French conquest was the zeal of French missionaries who were counting souls, not francs or piastres.

The stakes of the war in Vietnam are far greater than the population, territory, and economic assets of the two Vietnams or even of all Southeast Asia with its some 250 million people. The total American investments and trading interests in Southeast Asia are inconsequential compared to United States' interests in Europe or Latin America. They represent a sum equal to but a fraction of one per cent of the American gross national product. The loss of all of Southeast Asia's tin, rubber, and other products would only temporarily dislocate a small segment of the American economy. There are no direct economic benefits the

U. S. can expect from the area in the foreseeable future that would justify the vast expenditure of American blood and money in Vietnam. But, the U. S. is not fighting in Vietnam for economic gain. The United States and her allies have stated that they are fighting for the rights of small nations to be free of aggression, whether direct aggression, as in Korea, or indirect, as in Vietnam—through subversion and wars of liberation directed and aided by a neighboring state. Vietnam thus has become a testing ground of wills and ideologies between the Communist and the non-Communist worlds. The Sino-Soviet dispute, which divides the Communist world, only makes the struggle more complex and the road to peace more difficult.

In 1959, President Eisenhower defined Vietnam's importance to Southeast Asia and the world:

> Strategically, South Viet-Nam's capture by the Communists would bring their power several hundred miles into a hitherto free region. The remaining countries of Southeast Asia would be menaced by a great flanking movement. . . . The loss of South Viet-Nam would set into motion a crumbling process that could as it progressed have grave consequences for us and for freedom.[10]

This assessment has unfortunately been referred to as the "domino theory." The misnomer unfairly implies that Asian nations have no more self-determination than a row of dominoes. Very few southeast Asians will accept such a pat assumption. Yet, the overwhelming presence of Communist China remains one of the most important facts of life in Asian politics. Asians will fight for their freedom as long as there appears a chance of keeping it, and this seems possible only with U. S. assistance. Once that assistance is no longer assured or is proved inadequate, the small nations of Asia will consider it necessary to accommodate themselves to China. Some critics maintain the United States should not try to prevent such an accommodation to the realities of Chinese power, but others score such logic, saying it would have allowed Eastern Asia to come under the control of imperial Japan and continental Europe to fall under the domination of Hitler.

For more than a thousand years China has viewed itself as the suzerain power of all Southeast Asia. Maps in Communist Chinese textbooks show that the new China still considers all the nations formerly tributary to imperial China to be within her logical sphere of influence. China traditionally was the central kingdom, whose

[10] U. S. Department of State, *Bulletin*, April 27, 1959, p. 579.

emperor received a mandate from heaven to dispense order and the blessings of civilization to the surrounding barbarians. Despite the cataclysmic changes wrought in China, Mao Tse-tung and most of the country's older leaders were steeped in Chinese traditions. They became Marxist but remained Chinese. Even apart from their Communist proselytizing zeal, it seems natural and proper to them that the new China should share her new doctrine with her lesser neighbors. Her demoralizing setbacks of 1965 and 1966 in Asia and Africa have not yet induced China to abandon the imperialistic ambition of expanding her influence through front movements and wars of liberation. If the technique succeeded in South Vietnam as it already has in North Vietnam, their borders would prove no barrier. This has already been shown by the "liberation" movement in northeast Thailand, which, inspired and aided by China and North Vietnam, is following the classic pattern of propaganda, terror, and assassination. Burma is trying to keep China out by keeping everyone out. Cambodia's Prince Sihanouk is struggling to keep his nation free by placating China, and, in line with this, he has sent a son to be educated in Peking. How long these maneuvers would prove effective without the counterbalance of U. S. assistance in Southeast Asia is questionable. Prince Sihanouk, generally a caustic critic of the U. S., wrote to the *New York Times* on June 4, 1965 that he had no illusions about his fate or that of his government "at the hands of the communists . . . after having removed from our region the influence and especially the presence of the 'free world' and the U. S. A. in particular . . ."

Both President Kennedy and President Johnson endorsed the principle involved in the "domino theory." When asked his view of the concept in 1963, President Kennedy replied that he believed it, adding,

China is so large, looms so high beyond the frontiers, that if South Vietnam went, it would not only give them an improved geographic position for a guerrilla assault on Malaya but would also give the impression that the wave of the future in Southeast Asia was China and the Communists.[11]

Vietnam also has an imperialist tradition, a tradition of which both Cambodia and Laos are very actively aware. France annexed these countries on the basis of Vietnam's claims. The Vietnamese Communist interest in Southeast Asia dates back more than three decades, when Ho Chi Minh worked as a Comintern agent under Soviet direction to

[11] Quoted in Kenneth T. Young, "The American Encounter with Vietnam," *Asia*, No. 4 (1966), p. 125.

help organize Communist parties in Malaya, Thailand, and French Indochina. In 1930, he guided the uniting of the Communist factions of Vietnam, Cambodia, and Laos into the Indochinese Communist Party (ICP) which he subsequently headed. In Cambodia, Prince Sihanouk has accused the Vietnamese of trying to subvert his government through the Pracheachon (Revolutionary) party, created by the Viet Minh in 1955, and in 1962, 14 Pracheachon members were sentenced to death. The DRV has been the main instigator and director of the Communist (Pathet Lao) insurrection in Laos, which she has supported with arms, advisers, and whole divisions of North Vietnamese army units. Recently, Hanoi has cooperated with Peking in promoting their "people's war of liberation" in Thailand.

It has been argued that a Communist conquest of Southeast Asia would cut the world in two. India and Pakistan would be flanked and Australia and New Zealand in danger of being cut off. The psychological impact would be enormous among the world's developing nations, such as Venezuela, where incipient liberation wars have been started by local dissidents with outside aid. Opponents of the U. S. commitment in Vietnam contend that the premises underlying it could lead to an endless succession of guerrilla wars. Supporters of the commitment reply that if the U. S. proves that the liberation technique cannot work or is too costly, as was direct aggression in Korea, the Communists will be less likely to pursue it elsewhere. Contrariwise, should allied efforts in Vietnam fail, a succession of guerrilla wars is more certain to occur.

There is ample evidence that the Communists themselves accept this view. North Vietnam's Defense Minister Vo Nguyen Giap explained that South Vietnam is "the model of the national revolutionary movement of our time," and concluded that if the U. S. could be defeated there, "this means it can be defeated everywhere in the world." [12] In a similar vein, Communist China's Premier Chou En-lai told visiting Japanese in essence that a Viet Cong victory is imperative, for if the Viet Cong are defeated, similar movements in other Asian and African countries will be adversely affected. "Without victory," he added, "we will not be believed." [13] Secretary of State Dean Rusk summarized the official U. S. view of this test of wills: "Vietnam presents a clear case of the lawful versus the unlawful use of force.

[12] *Nhan Dan* (Lao Dong Party newspaper), July 19, 1964.
[13] Interview with Chou En-lai on January 7, 1966, quoted in the Japanese monthly *Sekei*, March 1966.

I would agree with General Giap and other Communists that this is a test case for 'wars of liberation.' We intend to meet this test." [14]

The Sino-Soviet dispute has important implications for Vietnam since the disagreement in part concerns the proper tactics for achieving Communist revolutionary objectives in underdeveloped nations. Particularly since 1960, the USSR has supported the thesis that Communist nations should not risk a global or nuclear confrontation to help aggressive liberation movements. The Soviets reason that time is working to the Communists' advantage in their economic race with the West and that victory will eventually be theirs without assuming needless risks. On the other hand, Mao Tse-tung and his followers say the "imperialists" with all their nuclear bombs are only "paper tigers." It is the duty of all Communist nations to aid wars of liberation everywhere. On September 3, 1966, the Communist New China News Agency stated flatly, "All China is the base for the world revolution." Mao believes it is not only inevitable but also desirable that the liberation movements become violent and follow the path of armed struggle as did that of the Chinese Communists. Such struggles, he and his followers maintain, will not lead to nuclear war as the Russians fear, because world public opinion and the lack of suitable targets in an insurgency will prevent use of nuclear weapons. Without always giving Mao due credit, Hanoi's leaders have echoed his belligerent doctrines in radio broadcasts and published statements.

The published evidence would seem to indicate that the Soviets are not enthusiastic over Hanoi's aggressive conduct in South Vietnam. Yet because of hard-line Chinese harassment and the Soviets' worldwide revolutionary interests, Moscow cannot easily abandon Hanoi. It appears she is providing enough material assistance to maintain face, while accusing China of obstructing the passage of that aid. China too is sending considerable assistance but seems to keep it short of a level which might result in war with the United States.

North Vietnam is caught between two giants in the Sino-Soviet dispute, with both sides demanding her support and sometimes obedience. Dependent upon the aid of both for her internal development and the war, North Vietnam has vacillated between the two Communist powers, while trying to keep aid coming from both. Ho Chi Minh's efforts to mediate the dispute have been fruitless. The North Vietnamese increasingly have shown resentment at being pressured

[14] U. S. Department of State, *Bulletin*, May 10, 1965, pp. 697-99.

by both sides. In more or less veiled language, Hanoi has echoed Moscow's charges of "dogmatism and sectarianism" against Peking and Peking's accusations of "revisionism" against Moscow. She has indicated dissatisfaction with the amount of aid from both sides and some bitterness over China's failure to cooperate with Russia in accelerating the shipment of war materials from the Soviet Union. To some degree, Hanoi has declared herself ideologically independent of the other Communist parties, while at the same time continuing to plead for unity in the Communist world.[15] The Lao Dong party leaders have tried to remain aloof from China's violent "cultural revolution," while in mild tones calling for their own version of a cultural revolution by increasing emphasis on education and technical training.

For its part, the United States has declared that it certainly does not want a major confrontation with the Communist powers. The objectives of the U. S. policy in South Vietnam, as officially stated by its leaders, may be summed up as follows: The United States desires an independent South Vietnam whose people are free to choose their own government without fear of external interference and without commitment to the policies of any other nation. The U. S. seeks an end to the fighting in whatever form it takes—whether overt aggression or covert terrorism. The U. S. wishes to prove to the world that it stands by its commitments and to show the Communist bloc that indirect aggression by "wars of liberation" cannot succeed. America seeks no military bases or special position in Vietnam or elsewhere in Southeast Asia. Not only does it not wish to change the Communist government of North Vietnam, but it is also prepared to accept a genuine neutral orientation for South Vietnam. The United States also has expressed its willingness to use its resources for the economic reconstruction of all Southeast Asia, including North Vietnam, and has offered to contribute $1 billion toward this end.

[15] For an illuminating evaluation by North Vietnam of its own revolutionary strategy and its role in the Sino-Soviet dispute, see the previously cited editorial, "Let Us Step Up the Theory-Formulating Task of the Party," *Hoc Tap*, September, 1966.

2: The Sinicization
of the Vietnamese People

Few nations are more acutely conscious of their history than Vietnam. Through the veneration of national and local heroes and heroines in shrines and cults, through the portrayal of historical dramas in villages and cities, and through the recital of legends, national or ethnic history has become an intimate part of Vietnamese life. As the result of their veneration of ancestors, Vietnamese are accustomed to dwelling with the spirits of the dead, who are considered to be part of the living family to be consulted on all matters of importance. Similarly, great heroes of Vietnam's past have the spiritual power to influence today's events. To understand the Vietnamese of today, therefore, one must understand his history.[1]

Legendary Origins

Since Vietnamese origins are obscure, legends freely mingle fact, fancy, and symbolism into rich heroic tales. Some may be the folk recollections of the migrations of the Yüeh or Viet tribes into the Red River valley and their fusion with the region's ethnic Indonesian in-

[1] The author has not attempted to provide detailed footnoting, but where appropriate, some of the more useful books consulted will be noted. The best general history covering the period of Vietnamese national history is Le Thanh Khôi, *Le Viêt-Nam, histoire et civilisation* (Paris, 1955). Also see Nguyen Van Thai and Nguyen Van Mung, *A Short History of Vietnam* (Saigon, 1958) and Joseph Buttinger, *The Smaller Dragon, A Political History of Vietnam* (New York, 1958). A pioneer French work was Adrien Launay, *Histoire ancienne et moderne de l'Annam, Tong-king, et Cochin-Chine depuis l'année 2700 avant l'ère chrétienne* (Paris, 1884). Also see Nguyen Van Que, *Histoire des pays de l'Union Indochinoise* (Saigon, 1932). The author will not attempt to cite in this short history from the large body of monographs and research papers in French on a variety of aspects of Vietnamese history.

habitants. Others were borrowed from China or were invented to match Vietnamese ancestry with China's.

One popular origin myth begins with De Minh, a king descended from the legendary father of Chinese agriculture. De Minh travelled into south China where he married an immortal mountain fairy. From this union came Kinh Duong Vuong (*Vuong* means king), who ruled over Xich Quy (Land of the Red Demons), which included present-day southeast China and Tonkin. He married the daughter of the Dragon Lord of the Sea, and their son became Lac Long Quan, Dragon Lord of the Lac, as his subjects were called. Under his firm government, the Lac became prosperous, but Lac Long Quan tired of governing and went to visit his grandfather, the Dragon Lord of the Sea. Forced to return to repell Chinese invasions, Lac Long Quan cemented a peace by marrying the immortal daughter of the Chinese ruler. The new queen bore a pouch of one hundred eggs from which sprang one hundred sons, who founded the *Bach Viet* or Hundred Viet tribes. Lac Long Quan again grew restless, however, and convinced his wife they must separate because of their different origins. The queen then took half their sons to rule over the mountains, while Lac Long Quan kept the others and ruled the lowlands. His eldest son succeeded him under the name of Hung Vuong, the Gallant King.

The Vietnamese view Hung Vuong as the founder of their nation and of the first Vietnamese dynasty, the Hong Bang. His kingdom of Van Lang, Land of the Tatooed Men, covered an arc of southern China extending into central Vietnam. Legend tells of eighteen kings of the Hong Bang dynasty, who ruled from 2879 to 258 B.C. Their reigns, averaging 150 years apiece, are reminiscent of those of legendary Japanese rulers of the same era, and it has been suggested that seasons were then counted as years. The last Hong Bang king was more devoted to debauchery than to affairs of state. When the ruler of neighboring Thuc asked to marry a Viet princess, he was contemptuously rejected. The embittered suitor passed his grudge to his successor, Thuc Vuong Phan, who invaded Van Lang. On hearing the enemy's victory cries outside his palace, the drunken Hong Bang king drowned himself in a well.

Thuc Vuong Phan united Van Lang and Thuc to form the new state of Au Lac, which he ruled under the name of An Duong Vuong. An Duong built a capital with the supernatural help of Kim Quy, the Golden Turtle. After finishing the task, Kim Quy returned to the sea, leaving An Duong a magic claw. When attached to his bow, this amulet made the king invincible. The magic claw soon proved its power when the Chinese general Trieu Da invaded Au Lac, only to be utterly defeated. Resorting to guile, Trieu Da won An Duong's daughter for his son and then induced the Viet bride to steal her father's amulet. Possessed of the claw, Trieu Da overwhelmed Au Lac. Carrying his daughter behind him on his horse, An Duong fled to the sea to entreat the Golden Turtle for aid. When Kim Quy rose from the waves to reveal the girl's treason, the king angrily beheaded his daughter, then in despair followed the Golden Turtle into the sea.

With the conquest of Au Lac by Trieu Da, legend begins to merge with historical fact.

Factual Evidence and Hypothesis

The facts concerning Vietnamese origins are few and often debatable.[2] By placing together bits of evidence produced by archeologists and anthropologists—artifacts from ancient times and observations of the living races of Southeast Asia—a hypothesis can be derived.

The earliest manlike species found in Southeast Asia is Java man, a short beetle-browed type with a brain two-thirds the size of modern man's. As Java man lived possibly a million years ago, scholars have suggested that some human types may have originated in Southeast Asia. More commonly it is supposed that early man came from the Asian interior, perhaps set into motion by epochal climatic variations.

The earliest human remains in Vietnam were found in caves near Hoa Binh, 35 miles southeast of Hanoi. There the ancient residents tossed aside kitchen refuse and worn tools, building layers of debris over hundreds or thousands of years. The bottom Hoa Binhian layers yielded roughly-chipped stone axes and cutting implements, together with shells and bones of rhinoceros, elephants, and lesser animals. These show early Hoa Binhian man to have been a moderately proficient craftsman. Upper layers provide evidence of improved craftsmanship, with some tools ground almost smooth on the working end. No bone tools were found, though there were bones of a variety of animals.

Implements found near Bac Son, north of the Red River delta, display a higher skill, with differing shapes, finer edges, and more parts ground. Here bone awls appear along with shell implements and

---

[2] See George Maspero, ed., *L'Indochine, Un Empire colonial français*, 2 vols. (Paris, 1929), Vol. 1, pp. 83-92, and H. Mansuy, *La Préhistoire en Indochine* (Paris, 1931).

pottery. The animal bones indicate a varied diet ranging from turtles to wild pigs and rodents. Since all are of types still existing, late Bac Sonian man probably lived only a few thousand years ago. The human bones found with Bac Sonian type tools have been variously associated with the Negrito, the Australian, or the Melanesian (Papuan) species that apparently ranged over vast areas. When the great glaciers impounded huge quantities of water, the seas sank some 300 feet, and men probably could have walked dryshod from the Asian mainland to Java, Sumatra, the Philippines, Taiwan, and Japan. The earliest men to live in Southeast Asia probably were the Negritos, Negroid pigmies who may have arrived 25,000 to 50,000 years ago. Pigmies are still found in the Philippines, Malaya, and the Andaman Islands. Though they long ago disappeared from Vietnam, their characteristics, along with those of the later arriving Australoid and Melanesian types, occasionally may be noted among hill tribesmen.

At a much later date, perhaps only 3000 to 5000 years ago, the ancestors of two Austro-Asian groups still dwelling in Vietnam appeared: the Mon-Khmers and the Malayo-Polynesians. The Mons and Khmers are best known for the Indianized civilizations they created in the lowlands of Cambodia, Thailand, and southern Burma. Among the Malayo-Polynesian speaking peoples were the Chams, who produced the Indianized kingdom of Champa along the coast of central Vietnam, remnants of which survived into the eighteenth century. Both linguistic groups are also represented in numerous seminomadic highland tribes of Laos and South Vietnam. They are brown to light brown in skin color, with wavy black or dark brown hair, rounded eyes, and a high nose bridge. Related linguistic families found throughout Southeast Asia are commonly called "Indonesian," although they are not identical with the present Malay-speaking population of Indonesia. These early Indonesians probably introduced late neolithic and early Bronze Age culture. Remains unearthed at Dong Son in North Vietnam show they were skilled workers and artistic potters. Bronze appeared around 600 B.C. and iron soon afterwards, but stone implements remained important for centuries because iron and bronze were scarce.

The present ethnic Vietnamese arrived long after the Indonesians. Chinese histories tell of tribes known as the Yüeh, who inhabited a large area south of the Yangtze River. Probably members of the Thai family, the Yüeh apparently migrated from central Asia with the ethnic movement that set the Chou tribes on the road to empire in north

China and the Aryans into India and the Middle East. By the tenth century B.C., the Yüeh had created several states in southeast China. While China passed through the classical age that produced Confucius and Lao Tze, the Yüeh gradually fused with the Indonesians. In the fifth century, the most powerful Yüeh state, Tung Yüeh, conquered Wu, its Chinese neighbor north of the Yangtze. This may be the Hong Bang era of Vietnamese folklore.

Archeological evidence indicates that few Viets or Yüeh migrated into the Red River valley before the fourth century B.C. The Chinese conquest of Tung Yüeh in 334 B.C. probably sent a wave of migrants southward, where they merged with the Indonesian populace. Vietnamese legends of the mating of the races of dragons (a sea people) and immortals (mountain dwellers) apparently symbolize this fusion of the Viets and Indonesians. While the dualism of the mountain versus the sea is common to Indonesian mythology throughout Southeast Asia, its presence in Vietnamese folklore evidences clear Indonesian influence in the early development of Vietnamese culture.

Soon after the Viets moved into Tonkin, they were conquered by China. During the more than one thousand years of Chinese rule, there was much racial intermixture. Further Chinese infusion came as Chinese wars sent refugees to the south. Also, since early times, there have been intermittent migrations of tribal peoples into the mountains of Vietnam, among them the Thai, Lao, Man, Meo, and Nung, and many have retained their identity. Moreover, as the Viets expanded southward along the narrow coastal plains and small deltas of central and southern Vietnam, they conquered and largely absorbed the Chams and various Khmer-speaking tribes.

Modern Vietnamese are racially and linguistically the product of this fusion. Physical types vary, depending upon the degree to which Chinese, Cham, Thai, Khmer, or other physical characteristics prevail. The original Viet language was probably a Thai-related dialect, but centuries of fusion have altered it. Much of the common vocabulary, including words for numbers, family relationships, and domestic animals are Khmer, while Thai provides the tonality and many grammatical elements. Chinese words express literary, philosophical, governmental, and military concepts. One is reminded of modern English, whose Anglo-Saxon base is heavily infused with French and Latin.

The only language closely related to Vietnamese is Muong, spoken in the mountains north of the Tonkin delta. The Muong are sometimes viewed as archaic country cousins of the Vietnamese who kept their tribal ways. Most of the numerous Viets who once ruled large areas in south China have been absorbed by the great sponge of Chinese culture. Only the southern Viets, the Vietnamese, retained their national integrity and remain independent, though they still bear the heavy stamp of Chinese culture.

Viet Culture Before the Chinese Invasions

When Trieu Da overthrew the last Thuc king, the Red River delta was very different from the densely cultivated region of today. The site of Hanoi was nearer the sea, for the delta was smaller and was mainly marshland, subject to floods as the river overflowed its natural dikes. The marshes teemed with wild life and virgin jungle covered the surrounding hills and mountains. In the lowlands, the mixed Indonesian-Viet peoples fished and hunted and cultivated wet rice with crudely polished stone hoes. Hunters prized the elephant and rhinoceros, whose valuable tusks and horns they traded for bronze and iron from China. By using the tides that backed up the river waters, the farmers irrigated their rice fields and produced two crops annually.

On the slopes where irrigated rice could not be grown, a destructive *ray* or *swidden* cultivation was practiced to grow dry rice. This system, still used by the Muong and other hill peoples, involves burning off the jungle cover to simultaneously clear and fertilize the land. After two or three crops, the field is allowed to revert to jungle and the process is repeated elsewhere. In a cycle of about twenty years, cultivation is started anew at the first fields. This system hastens erosion and accelerates the building of Vietnam's deltas.

Early Chinese visitors describing ancient Vietnam were struck by the customs of betel-chewing, tatooing, and tooth-blackening. Betel, which played a role in many ceremonies, including marriage rites, is still widely used in Southeast Asia. Many sidewalks in modern market-places are blood-red from the betel juice expectorated by peddlers. Tooth-blackening with a black dye is also seen. Tatooed totemistic designs were used by the Viets for identification by clan and social rank and for frightening evil spirits and dangerous animals. Tatooed dragons writhed on the thighs of Vietnamese kings as late 1293, but tatooing is practiced today by only a few hill tribes. One early Chinese visitor depicted the Viet country as the "Kingdom of the Nude"—indicating that the Viets probably dressed as do some present-day tribal people, with a loincloth for men and a skirt only for women. They tied their long hair in a bun behind the head and seem to have worn turbans similar to those seen today.

The social system was stratified. Viet aristocrats ruled over a substratum of mixed Viets and subordinated Indonesians, not yet totally fused. From the latter, elements of matriarchy prevailed in the strong position enjoyed by women. Tribal chiefs held civil, religious, and military power and were the chief landowners. The king was probably only one of many chiefs, the first of equals. The mass of the people seem to have been virtually serfs on the land held by the chiefs, whose ancestors had founded the villages and cleared the land. Bronze kettle-drums, some of considerable artistic quality, were prized heirlooms of the aristocratic families and were important in rituals. A similar custom is found among many modern tribal people who cherish their ritual gongs.

Bows and arrows and javelins were used in hunting and war. The bows were long, and the bronze or hardened-wood arrowheads were sometimes dipped in poison to quickly fell even the largest animal. A system of tying knots in bundles of strings was used in keeping records. This method, resembling that used by the South American Incas, may have been learned from the Chinese who used a knot system before they developed pictographic writing. Also reminiscent of the Western Hemisphere was the custom of crossing the arms as a sign of respect, as did the Maya Indians of Central America.

Viet religion was largely animistic, emphasizing nature spirits and supernatural beings. Early burial sites indicate belief in the existence after death of the soul or spirit. All of these spirits, particularly those of important persons, required propitiation. Other supernatural forces exacting ritual attention and sacrifice were the spirits of dangerous animals such as tigers and the spirits controlling the waters, the soil, and other facets of nature. The most important festival came at the beginning of spring when the first tilling of the soil was celebrated with abandon and promiscuity.

Such were the Vietnamese when they fell under the sway of China —a people just emerging from the Stone Age, already possessing a mixed culture, race, and language representing centuries of Indonesian and Thai intermixture. Into this composite culture was to be imbedded that of China.

The Chinese Millennium

Throughout its long history, Vietnam has been profoundly influenced by the politics, culture, and economy of China. As noted before, Chinese expansion probably stimulated the Viet colonization of the Red River delta in the fourth century B.C. The conquest of Au Lac a century later was only an aspect of Chinese empire building, and a desire to control the sea trade with Southeast Asia and India inspired the resubjugation of the Viets in the second century. For a thousand years thereafter, Giao Chi, as Au Lac was renamed, was intimately linked with events in the Central Kingdom, reflecting the cycles of renaissance and decay accompanying the rise and fall of Chinese dynasties.[3]

The initial conquest in 214 B.C. came as the great organizer and conqueror Shih Huang-ti (221-210 B.C.) reunited a divided China and expanded its borders in all directions. Following his short but vigorous rule, the Han (206 B.C.-220 A.D.) further extended China's empire over a vast area from central Vietnam to Korea and from the Pacific to the Pamir Mountains. Roughly contemporary with the Roman Empire with perhaps an equal population and area, the Han Dynasty was divided into two periods by the usurpation of Wang Mang (9-23 A.D.) The later Han declined during the second and early third centuries, with their fall being accelerated by barbarian invasions. There followed a period of disunity, known as the Three Kingdoms and Six Dynasties (220-590). Unity was restored under the Sui, who are remembered for their construction of the Grand Canal. After the Sui went down in violence, the T'ang brought three centuries (618-907) of material progress and cultural flowering before they too crumbled before tribal invaders. Thereafter China again suffered disunity during the period of the Five Dynasties and Ten Independent States (907-960), until reunited by the Sung (960-1279). Weakness during China's dynastic upheavals encouraged aggression by the Viets' bellicose southern neighbors, the Chams, and also stimulated revolts in Giao Chi. Thus, during the unrest following the T'ang downfall, the Vietnamese

[3] Through its long history, Vietnam has been known by several names. In addition to Au Lac and Giao Chi, it became Giao Chau, Nam Viet, Van Xuan, Da Nang, Annam, Tinh Hai, Dai Viet, Dai Ngu, Dai Nam and finally Viet-Nam. In early modern times, the term Cochinchina was used by Europeans to describe the south and Tonkin the north. During French rule the center was called Annam.

regained independence, and because of China's continuing weakness for centuries thereafter, they retained that freedom.

When Shih Huang-ti's armies swept southward, they quickly defeated Bach Viet and Man Viet of south China, but the southern Viets stubbornly resisted. General Trieu Da, who then received the Chinese command, advanced slowly over several years, establishing military colonies to hold the land, until he reached the sea at the mouths of the Red River in 214 B.C. The Viet lands were organized into three military districts or commanderies. Au Lac in the south, which became known as Tuong Quan, was left under the rule of Viet chiefs, subject to tribute payments to the Chinese governor. To help populate the conquered lands, Shih Huang-ti deported to them criminals, debtors, and political enemies.

In the scramble for power following Shih Huang-ti's death, Trieu Da proclaimed himself king over the three southern districts, including the areas of modern Kwangsi and Kwantung provinces and North Vietnam. Calling his realm Nam Viet (Southern Viet), he ruled from a capital near modern Canton, adopting Viet customs and identifying himself with his subjects. When the Han reunited China, Trieu Da pledged fealty to the new dynasty and kept his throne. Five kings succeeded Trieu Da in Nam Viet before a clash of interests in 111 B.C. caused it to be annexed to China by the Han Dynasty, beginning a rule that was to last with but brief interruptions until 939 A.D.

Nam Viet, which became Giao Chi province, was divided into several military districts. The three most southerly, covering the present North Vietnam, were Giao Chi in the Red River delta, Cuu Chan on the smaller river deltas of Thanh Hoa to the south, and Nhat Nam stretching down to modern Danang. The early Han made few changes in local administration: Viet chiefs administered their lands and villages under light supervision and paid tribute to Chinese governors who received little attention from the Han court. However, a steady stream of Chinese colonists exerted a growing influence, as they gained lands and married into the local population.

Around the time of Christ, the Han advanced a policy of assimilation, pressing Chinese customs, rites, and institutions upon the Viets. During Wang Mang's usurpation, Giao Chi's governor Si Kuang refused him recognition and gave haven to scholars and officials loyal to the Han. With their aid, Si Kuang opened schools to spread Taoist and Confucian learning and induced the Viets to adopt hats, shoes, and Chinese marriage rites. Agriculture was improved by introducing plows and draft animals. The influx of Chinese officials and colonists with alien customs and rites disturbed many chiefs, who felt their power and prestige and religious leadership were being undermined. Their discontent increased when the restored Han reinforced the assimilation policy.

A serious revolt was touched off in 39 A.D. by the execution of a protesting chief. The dead chief's wife, Trung Trac, and her sister, Trung Nhi, rallied the tribal leaders into full-scale rebellion. The Vietnamese quickly toppled the Chinese strongholds and proclaimed the two amazons queens of a short-lived kingdom called Trieu Quoc. After crushing rebellions elsewhere, the Han sent a disciplined army that crushed the Viet tribal levies in 43 A.D. The spot where legends say the sisters ended their rein by leaping into a river is marked by a temple in which Vietnamese still perform rites to their spirits.

While the Trung sisters provided a symbol for national patriotism, their defeat virtually destroyed the old Viet aristocracy, leaving no buffer to protect the people from the Chinese, and for many years there were no national leaders to inspire revolt. The Chinese used forced labor to exploit the considerable Viet resources—gold and silver mines, ivory, forests, and pearl fisheries. To prevent the rise of a new local elite, education was restricted. Scholars who did study and pass Chinese civil service examinations had difficulty in securing official positions, though gradually these restrictions were relaxed and some Sino-Viet scholars found favor at the Chinese court. Some served as governors and generals in the imperial service, and one became governor of Giao Chi district.

The Han opened a sea trade that brought centuries of prosperity to Giao Chi. Red River ports became important way or terminal stations for a rich Chinese trade with the spice islands, India, and the Near East. Giao Chi, a frontier province, became a cosmopolitan center where traders exchanged their silks, tea, and ceramics for exotic produce of distant lands, and foreign embassies passed en route to the court of China. This was also the period of India's peaceful colonial expansion, when her trade and influence stimulated the growth of Indianized cultures throughout Southeast Asia. Giao Chi became the meeting ground between India and China, influenced by both. With the traders and travellers came Buddhism, which profoundly affected Vietnam's cultural development.

Nhat Nam, Giao Chi's southern district, was most heavily influenced by Indian and Southeast Asian traders. Extending along the narrow coastal plains and scattered small deltas, the sparse Cham population was only lightly touched by Chinese culture. Facing the sea and possessing little good rice land, the Chams became hardy mariners who fished the coastal waters, traded, preyed on the rich sea traffic, and raided their neighbors. As early as 137 A.D., 10,000 Chams are said to have participated in one raid against Giao Chi. Chinese governors established strongholds along the coast to protect trade, but occasionally had to send expeditions to punish the unruly Chams. As Chinese power declined under the later Han, the Chams asserted their independence, apparently led by a native official who took advantage of Chinese weakness to proclaim himself king.

The Chinese called the new kingdom Lin Yi (in Vietnamese, Lam Ap).[4] Cham histories have been destroyed, but inscriptions indicate that the first king was strongly Indianized and possibly was Buddhist. Little is known of his early successors, except that they often plagued Giao Chi with piratical raids. As Champa became alienated from China, Indian influence totally submerged the Chinese. Throughout their more than 1500 years of history, the Chams remained hostile to the Sinicized Viets with whom they maintained a seesaw struggle until they were conquered and absorbed by their northern neighbors.

When the Han Dynasty collapsed in a wave of revolts and barbarian invasions, Giao Chi remained a haven of peace, thanks to a capable and wise governor, Che Hsi (Si Nhiep), who ruled almost independently for 40 years. Giving employment to a new flood of refugee scholars and officials, he fostered Chinese learning and technology. Vietnamese historians call him Si Vuong, "Scholar King." His style was indeed regal. When Si Vuong left his palace to go into the city, musical stone bells chimed, his escort marched to the sound of trumpets and flutes, and dozens of "barbarians" bearing incense burners flanked his chariot.

The upheaval accompanying the Han downfall produced another Viet heroine. To maintain his autonomy and gain local support, Si Vuong encouraged a new class of Sino-Vietnamese notables. When the Chinese state of Wu restored direct Chinese rule after Si Vuong's death, the notables of Cuu Chan district took up arms under the leadership of a fiery young woman, Trieu Au. Though Trieu Au cut a dashing figure mounted on an elephant and flashing a golden sword,

[4] George Maspero, Le royaume de Champa (Paris, 1928) and George Coedès, The Making of Southeast Asia (Berkeley, Cal., 1964).

her small forces were destroyed within six months. In 248 A.D. she, like the Trung sisters, ended her life by drowning.

Wu, the most southerly Chinese state of the Three Kingdoms Period (220-265 A.D.), divided Giao Chi province into two regions. The southern portion, primarily the area of present North Vietnam, became Giao Chau. This separation of Giao Chau drew the basic geographical outlines for the future independent state, though sixteen years later Wu, together with Giao Chau, fell to the state of Ch'in.

While China was weakened by disunity, Lam Ap or Champa grew strong. Sometimes allied with the neighboring Indianized kingdom of Fu Nan, the Chams ravaged the coasts of Giao Chau and south China. When in the fifth century, China fell into dynastic wars, the Cham king audaciously demanded the governorship of Giao Chau. Refused, he sought to achieve his goal by force, only to have his own capital sacked (446 A.D.). The victorious Chinese carried off a spectacular loot, including a golden statue said to have weighed thousands of pounds. This victory brought Giao Chau a century of respite from Cham harassment.

Despite wars and occasional setbacks, Cham wealth increased and her gold, amber, aromatic wood, turtle shells, and perfume became legendary. Chinese visitors also noted a strange plant that produced white balls of downy filament which the Chams spun and wove into cloth that took all colors of dye. The material was worn as sarongs wrapped around the bodies of both men and women. When the king travelled, he was surrounded by flags and shaded by a parasol of the same material, known to the modern world as cotton.

As one ruler toppled the other during the Six Dynasties period (317-590 A.D.), Giao Chau's Chinese governors enjoyed considerable autonomy, but this imposed greater dependence on local resources. China's dynastic wars drained frontier provinces of Chinese troops, forcing governors to recruit locally for border defense and to lean administratively on local landholders and aristocrats, giving them a taste of power. Chinese weakness thus increased possibilities for insurrection. When the Chinese sought to retighten controls, rebellion was almost a certainty, if it had not already occurred. One revolt flared briefly in 484, but more important was that led by Li Bi in 541, which produced another ephemeral Viet kingdom.

Li Bi was a Sino-Vietnamese whose ancestors had arrived in Giao Chau seven generations before. He drove out the Chinese, repelled a

Cham attack and proclaimed himself Ly Nam De, ruler of the kingdom of Van Xuan. Li Bi reigned only three years, however, before Chinese armies drove him into the mountains where he died. According to nationalistic histories and legends, Li Bi's relatives and followers continued a "government in exile," called the kingdom of Danang, but it failed to rally enough strength to challenge the Chinese. Their last leader surrendered in 603.

Meanwhile, China was reunited under the Sui Dynasty (589-607). Before they were succeeded by the T'ang (608-907), the Sui reasserted direct Chinese rule and made administrative reforms to bring the governors under closer court supervision. To the T'ang we are indebted for the earliest population statistics on Giao Chau. Their census showed only 26,778 families or about 108,000 inhabitants in the delta area. This figure, however, probably covered only the Chinese or Sinicized residents of urban centers and omitted the larger population of the villages and surrounding mountains.

Under the T'ang, Giao Chau's sea trade flourished, especially in the eighth and ninth centuries. The use of coinage was also accelerated by the T'ang emphasis on the collection of taxes in cash. The more complete transition to a money economy placed the Viet farmers at the mercy of Chinese rice merchants. The T'ang also sold commercial monopolies of certain products including salt and wine, but collected taxes in kind on such items as ivory, horses, and buffalo. The totality of these demands caused the Vietnamese to remember T'ang rule as particularly burdensome, despite the prosperity the sea trade brought to many.

To strengthen imperial defenses, the T'ang regrouped their frontier provinces under military commands. The northern provinces became An-pei (Pacify the North), while Giao Chau became An-nam (Pacify the South). But the delta did not remain peaceful. A rebellion headed by a Muong leader Mai Thuc Loan (called Hac De, the Black Emperor, by the Vietnamese) flared in 722. Forty years later, Javanese or Malayan sea raiders invaded An-nam and besieged its capital. Thereafter, the fortified city of Dai La was built at the site of modern Hanoi. This construction, plus the war, increased demands for taxes and forced labor, causing new rebellions. Barely was internal peace restored than the Chams again (803) invaded and annexed An-nam's two southern districts. The Chinese, however, soon crushed the Cham armies, forcing them to abandon their conquests and retreat south along the coast.

The next threat came from what is now Yünnan Province of China. During the eighth century, six Thai tribal states were united into the kingdom of Nan Chao. China invested its king, but had cause to regret the action, for Nan Chao was soon seeking an outlet to the sea through An-nam. Many Thai tribes had earlier migrated down the valleys of the Red and Claire Rivers into the frontiers of An-nam. Their problems with Chinese administrators there gave pretext for a series of Thai raids. In 862, the ruler of Nan Chao proclaimed himself emperor and drove the Chinese from the delta, but four years later the Chinese trapped the Thai army when it was busy harvesting rice. Their thorough defeat discouraged the Thai from further encroachment on An-nam during Chinese rule.

These wars cost many lives, especially among the urban Sino-Vietnamese population, but the Chinese rebuilt the war-torn province, constructing fortifications along the frontiers and improving irrigation, roads, and navigation. There followed a period of flourishing trade, prosperity, and cultural flowering sometimes called the Dai La period after the name of the capital. Ironically, this period coincided with the political decline of the T'ang Dynasty. Its fall in 907 ushered in a half century of disunity in China, known as the Five Dynasties period (907-960). In south China, both the states of Ch'u and Nam Han laid claim to An-nam province. During this Chinese disunity, the Vietnamese achieved lasting independence. Driving out an unpopular T'ang governor, they elected Khuc Thua Du, a local Chinese notable, in his stead. The new governor renamed the province Tinh Hai (Quiet Sea), a change which was in a sense a declaration of independence. Khuc Thua Du passed the rule to his son and grandson, who accepted nominal investiture from the state of Ch'u. Nam Han attempted to reestablish Chinese control, but was promptly ousted by a Sino-Vietnamese, Duong Dien Nghe.

When this leader was assassinated, one of his officials Ngo Quyen drove out the murderer and seized the capital. The assassin appealed to the southern Han who sent support by sea. Ngo Quyen's victory over these forces is still celebrated in patriotic songs and stories. Placing iron spikes in the river bottom just below the high water mark, he lured the enemy into a trap by pretending to flee in shallow-draft vessels just as the tide was receding. As the heavy Chinese war junks became impaled on the spikes, Ngo Quyen's men slaughtered the would-be conquerors. Vietnamese hail this victory as the beginning of their independence.

The Synthesis of Cultures

Vietnamese historians tend to view the era of Chinese rule only as a humiliating foreign bondage. It is true that some governors were cruel and greedy, disliked the Viet people, hated the climate, and deemed their stay an unpleasant exile. Yet others became attached to the Viets and made serious efforts to bring to them the benefits of China's rich culture.

The penetration of Chinese civilization was assured by the steady influx of Chinese refugee scholars, discharged officials, deserting soldiers, craftsmen, peddlers, merchants, and laborers. These immigrants and their offspring populated the towns, cities, and seaports and merged with the Viet aristocracy in the rural areas, producing a mixed elite allied with a growing urban merchant group. Many Chinese settlers intermarried with the Viets, adopting the language and customs. At the same time, the Viets became Sinicized. Those who resisted assimilation came athwart Chinese law, which left little room for social and cultural deviation. Even clothing and hairdress were frequently prescribed by law.

The fusion of peoples and cultures was facilitated by the Viet use of Chinese writing. Having no written language of their own, the Viets borrowed that of China, opening vistas into Chinese thought, technology, literature, and art. Some Sino-Viet scholars achieved success in the Chinese bureaucracy. Chinese law generally required that high officials serve outside their own provinces, but within Giao Chau's local administration, lesser Sino-Viet officials held many positions in the graded hierarchy of mandarins, dispensing justice according to Chinese law codes. By the time Ngo Quyen proclaimed independence, the Viets had forgotten any other system and continued Chinese practices with little change, although ancient tribal allegiances still influenced political rivalries.

While Chinese scholars taught Confucian and Taoist precepts, Hindus and Buddhists from India and Indianized Southeast Asia brought the learning and religions of India. Early Indian trading vessels often carried Buddhist monks who served as doctors, priests, and sorcerers. In Giao Chau, they frequently became missionaries. Indian traders and craftsmen settling in Viet ports built temples, spreading their art and architecture as well as their faith.

Buddhism was probably well known in Giao Chau prior to its spread in China.[5] Before the end of the Han, Giao Chi had become an important center for Buddhist study and was a convenient stopping place for Chinese Buddhist pilgrims traveling to India. In Giao Chau, the Chinese could meet Indian and Southeast Asian missionaries with Sino-Viet scholars serving as interpreters. Some of the earliest translations of Buddhist texts into Chinese were made in Giao Chi.

Though various schools of Buddhism reached the Viets, Dhyana or Thien became the most popular. Thien (called Ch'an in China and Zen in Japan) teaches that man returns to his original purity and arrives at the perfect wisdom of Buddhahood by contemplation rather than prayer, rites, or study of sacred texts. One must peel away from one's mind concern for the affairs of the world as one peels away the leaves of the onion until all are gone, leaving nothing. Enlightenment may then come intuitively, bringing perfect calm and goodness. Thien remained the most important Vietnamese Buddhist sect into modern times.

By the end of the seventh century, Buddhist pilgrims came to Annam from many lands. Both the Sui and T'ang fostered Buddhism, building many stupas and pagodas. When the famous Chinese pilgrim I-ching passed through the province in the eighth century, he noted that more than 1000 Buddhist monks were engaged in study and good works there. At an early period, Buddhism seems to have reached down to the lower classes and the rural areas, but there it blended with and by no means supplanted the original animism. Among the educated classes of the cities, Buddhism had to compete with Confucianism and Taoism, which had developed in China about the time Buddha was teaching in India. These three doctrines were to a considerable degree blended in Vietnam to become the syncretic religion of the villager.

The philosophy attributed to Confucius or K'ung-fu-tzu (551-479 B.C.) was essentially a reassertion and organization of what Confucius considered the ethical principles of ancient China. Living in a time when China was divided among many warring states, Confucius taught that kings should rule through virtue and not might. He was concerned not with the supernatural but with the world and with man's relationship to man. He recognized an abstract heaven, but man's relationship with heaven was regulated by the emperor, who received from heaven the mandate to rule on earth. Just as the emperor sought to achieve

[5] Mai Tho Truyen, "Le Bouddhisme au Viêt-Nam," *Présence du Bouddhisme,* (Edition of *France-Asie:* Saigon, February–June, 1958), pp. 801-810.

harmony with heaven by his perfect conduct, so the ordinary man should conform in thought and action to the nature of things on earth, cultivating the human virtues of the gentleman or superior man. Confucius placed great emphasis upon filial piety and rites, which became formalized in the family systems and ancestor veneration of Vietnam and China. As a philosophy, however, Confucianism remained the property of scholars, for whom Confucius became the patron saint because of his stress on learning.

While Confucianism emphasized the group and society, Taoism, first taught by Lao Tzu, an older contemporary of Confucius, was concerned with the individual's search for happiness here and in the hereafter. Confucius pointed to study and learning as a means to harmonizing man's relationship to man in society; Taoism denied the value of scholarship and held that man should seek harmony with the natural order, the *Tao*, through contemplation and nonaction. While Confucianism sought to closely regulate man's conduct within society, Taoism told man to do whatever came naturally. In the hands of Lao Tzu's successors, Taoism became a degenerated mysticism teaching the pursuit of eternal life through dietary rules, breathing exercises, sorcery, and magical practices. In this form it blended with common animistic practices in the Vietnamese village, where the Taoist became an adviser on dealings with the forces of nature.

Vietnamese artistic development was strongly influenced by China. The Viets generally received, but on occasion they also gave. Ceramic replicas of buildings found in Han Dynasty tombs in Giao Chi show that Chinese buildings at that time had roofs with straight lines. However, early Vietnamese wooden buildings had curved and swooping roof lines, which can be traced to Indonesian influence. This style was adopted in south China during the T'ang and passed northward to Korea and Japan. The only surviving buildings of this style in Vietnam are of the Dai La period. Most significant is a 45-foot brick stupa with eleven stories, from the ninth or tenth century A.D.

As for early sculpture, one mutilated ninth-century Buddha and some stone friezes on the remains of a stupa show a strong and voluptuous Indian influence, which, except in Champa, disappeared from later sculpture. The few extant fragments of the early wood sculpture indicate a high level of skill, although it is impossible to ascertain whether the artists were Vietnamese, Chinese, or Indian. Because of the durability and extensive use of ceramics as burial furniture, many whole pieces and fragments of early examples remain. Both the quality and variety of the remains show ceramic production was well developed in Giao Chi as early as the Han period. The early Han pieces evidence strong Chinese influence, but occasional Indonesian designs are seen. One ceramic platter of the second century A.D. is decorated with motifs found on Dongsonian drums, while other pieces show some Indian influences.

Although Chinese cultural developments have continued to influence the Vietnamese people into modern times, by the time they finally achieved independence the blending of the cultures was largely complete. While the Viets were thoroughly Sinicized, they stubbornly retained their spoken language and their sense of separatism. This incipient nationalism was severely tested through the generations of unrest before the Victnamese achieved stability as an independent nation.

Independence and Disunity (939-1010)

The victory of Ngo Quyen brought neither stability nor peace. Instead there followed 70 years of short-lived dynasties troubled by regicides, usurpations, and civil and foreign wars. The principle of hereditary succession was valid only for the strong. A weak or child king was set aside by elections, or a usurper simply seized the crown. This period ended with the election of the first Ly emperor in 1010.

Ngo Quyen appealed to Vietnamese tradition by building his capital at the site of the center of the ancient kingdom of Au Lac. There he established a court and organized his government, but his six-year reign was too short to consolidate royal control. The Sino-Vietnamese notables that he named to govern the provinces built their own power locally as military lords or *su quan*, without developing allegiance to the throne. The 22 years following the reign of Ngo Quyen are called the Period of the Twelve Su Quan. During this time, the *su quan* fought each other and Ngo Quyen's descendants for power, while the Ngo weakened themselves by family squabbling. From the struggle emerged Dinh Bo Linh, a former buffalo tender and mercenary soldier. Not content with the title of king, he proclaimed himself emperor and called his realm Dai Co Viet (Great Viet State). To placate China, he sent tribute to the Sung ruler, who recognized him only as king. The investiture legitimized Dinh for the Viet people who were accustomed to looking to China as the font of civilization and political authority. He, like subsequent Viet rulers, considered triennial tribute cheaper than war with China. This token vassalage which did not impinge on

Vietnamese independence continued with little change for over 900 years, until the conquest of Vietnam by France.

At home, Dinh Bo Linh or Dinh Tien Hoang De (First Emperor Dinh)[6] insured his control by organizing a strong army and issuing new laws, which he harshly enforced. In his audience hall he placed the inscription, "The guilty shall be cooked and eaten." To fortify the threat he kept handy boiling oil and live tigers. His hopes for a lasting dynasty, however, were frustrated by a series of assassinations. The throne fell to a child king, who ruled with the guidance of the queen mother and her lover, General Le Hoan. When the Chinese invaded to capitalize on the situation, Le Hoan, who was proclaimed emperor (Le Dai Hanh) by the army, repelled the attackers. Once victorious, Le Hoan hastened to buy peace with tribute. In return he received recognition as king of An-nam from the Sung, who were facing a Mongol invasion from another quarter.

The Chinese envoy who delivered Le Hoan's insignia and seals of rank provided a colorful if biased description of tenth-century Vietnam. At the gates of the capital, the king offered the Chinese mission betel, which they diplomatically though distastefully accepted. The city contained thousands of straw thatched bamboo huts housing soldiers, lesser officials, and court servants. To Chinese eyes the palace was a dilapidated little house, but the king entertained them at banquet attired in pearl-encrusted red silk with a pearl headdress. In this attire, he waded barefoot into a stream to fish with a bamboo pole. He did not eat with chopsticks, but rolled his rice into a ball and snapped it into his mouth with his fingers. As gifts to his guests, he sent an enormous live python for them to eat and a pair of chained tigers, which they politely declined. The court was guarded by 300 soldiers tatooed with the Chinese characters, "Army of the Son of Heaven." They were armed with spears, crossbows, bucklers, and lances of wood and bamboo. A bodyguard of five eunuchs accompanied the king at all times.

Le Hoan acted with vigor, suppressing rebellions at home and disciplining the Chams who gave sanctuary to a rival and imprisoned a

---

[6] Dinh Bo Linh is a private name. The name he used during his reign was Dinh Thai Binh, while his dynastic title was Dinh Tien Hoang De. Vietnamese reign names were chosen to express the religious or political aspirations of a ruler at his accession and sometimes were later changed. Dynastic titles were given a ruler after death and were not changed. In general, these are used by historians. This practice will be followed here except where an individual was better known by another title or name.

Viet envoy. However, his dynasty survived only the short reigns of two sons, the second being a notorious and cruel degenerate. On his death, the court chose a popular general Le Cong Uan, who as Ly Thai Tho founded the first lasting dynasty. He named his realm Dai Viet, although China continued to call it An-nam. At times, the Vietnamese were also to use An-nam, but to avoid confusion, we will use Dai Viet until the introduction of the name Viet-Nam in the nineteenth century.

While the period of the early dynasties saw violence and disunity, it was an important formative era for the nation. Because the Viet rulers distrusted the Chinese-oriented Confucian scholars, they chose Taoists and Buddhists as counselors, envoys and clerical assistants, and these groups flourished. The Dinh organized the priests of both into hierarchies paralleling that of the government, and the pagodas provided a sanctuary for learning during the troubled years. One visiting Chinese scholar was favorably impressed by his Buddhist escort who matched him in composing Chinese-style poetry. Even the debauched last Le king sent a mission to copy Chinese and Buddhist classics. Such developments paved the way for the maturing of the Viet nation and culture during the long era of the Ly and Tran Dynasties that followed.

3: Independence, Division, and Expansion

With the accession of the Ly, the Vietnamese achieved unity and became masters of their own destinies. They were aware of a national identity separate from, yet not fully independent of, China, whom they viewed as tutor and model as well as suzerain. Through the next eight centuries, Vietnam had only three dynasties—the Ly, the Tran and the Le—aside from the usurping Ho. The last 268 years of the Le saw actual rule fall to powerful families who divided the country. The southern sector consisted mainly of conquests made under the Le as the Vietnamese swept aside or assimilated Chams, Khmers, and tribal peoples in their march south to the Mekong delta. Aggressively expansionist, Dai Viet became itself a suzerain power over Cambodia and the Lao kingdoms.

Meanwhile, whenever strong dynasties won control of China, as under the Mongols and the Ming, they attempted to reassert direct rule over the Vietnamese. Several times Vietnamese armies routed the Chinese, yet respect for the suzerain remained deeply rooted, for however much the Vietnamese might resent the Chinese, they expected their protection and on occasion invited their interference. Within Vietnam, Confucian principles of government and society dominated. Chinese Taoism, Buddhism, and elements of Confucianism mingled with native animism to create a syncretic Vietnamese faith. Like their tutors, Vietnamese scholars venerated learning and closely followed the main trends of thought and literature in the Central Kingdom. At the end of eight centuries of political independence, Vietnamese culture was perhaps a clearer copy of China's than it was at the end of Chinese rule. Withal, Vietnam was no less determinedly Vietnamese.

The First Great Dynasties: the Ly and the Tran

Under two successive dynasties, the Ly and the Tran (1010-1400), Dai Viet developed its own institutions and acquired a high degree of internal stability. In China, this period saw the decline of the Sung, the Mongol conquest and rule, and the rise of the Ming. It was a time of rapid cultural change and progress. The spread of Chu Hsi's neo-Confucianism, the decline of Buddhism, the experiments in state socialism by the Sung minister Wang An-shih, the great increase in world trade under the Mongols—all stimulated corresponding changes in Dai Viet. Meanwhile, in Southeast Asia, Cambodia reached its apogee and began its rapid decline as the Mongol conquest of Nan Chao set off massive migrations of Thai and Lao tribes. The newcomers created their own principalities, disrupted Cambodia's far-flung empire, and brought conflict to Dai Viet. As Cambodia weakened, Champa enjoyed a brief resurgence before an expanding Dai Viet sent it too into sharp decline. By the end of the Tran, the emerging Thai state of Siam was ready to vie with Dai Viet for hegemony in Southeast Asia.

The Ly began their era with four capable and popular rulers who enjoyed reigns totalling 117 years. They consolidated royal power, moved the capital back from the mountains to the vicinity of present-day Hanoi, and implanted loyalty to the new country in the hearts of the people. They also expanded Dai Viet by annexing Champa's northern provinces in punishment for Cham raids and reasserted suzerainty over the mountain tribes. The first three emperors did their work so well that the dynasty could survive the accession of a seven-year-old, Emperor Ly Nhan Tong (1072). Though his mother massacred her late husband's 76 other wives and concubines, mostly daughters of leading families, no revolt occurred. When the Sung sent an army to capitalize on the presumed weakness of this regency, the Viets not only defeated them but temporarily occupied two Chinese provinces.

Toward the end of the twelfth century, the Ly stock deteriorated. Two emperors went insane, and regencies twice weakened royal power. Banditry and rebellions became frequent, and Cambodian armies invaded. After a civil war temporarily unseated one emperor, real power fell to his father-in-law, Tran Thu Do. This ruthless and ambitious man manipulated the crown into his own family by arranging the accession of a seven-year-old Ly princess and marrying her to his nephew, who became Emperor Tran Thai Tong. When the queen produced no heir by the age of 19, Thai Tong was forced to marry her sister, who was already married to his own brother and was, in addition, pregnant. By this total breach of morality, the once powerful and able Ly sank into ignominious oblivion.

Before they too lost their crown to another wily strong man, the Tran vindicated themselves for their unworthy beginnings. Thai Tong soon proved his mettle by repelling attacks from China and Champa. Subsequently, the Tran defeat of the seemingly invincible Mongols provided one of the proudest episodes in Viet history. By 1254, the Mongols had conquered Chin in northern China and Nan Chao on Dai Viet's border. When they requested passage through Dai Viet to attack the Sung in south China, Tran Thai Tong not only refused, but imprisoned the Mongol envoys. The outraged Mongols raided down the river valleys and sacked the Viet capital in 1257 before Thai Tong repulsed them with the aid of his brother, the great General Tran Hung Dao. While Kublai Khan concentrated on Sung China, Thai Tong moved on both diplomatic and military fronts, sending tribute to the Mongol court while building up Vietnamese defenses. To avoid succession problems during a war, Thai Tong raised his son Thanh Tong to the throne as co-ruler, while retaining control as a senior emperor. When Thai Tong died, Thanh Tong in turn made his son, Nhan Tong, co-ruler, thereby making it difficult to distinguish responsibility.

After the Mongols completed the conquest of China, they again demanded passage through Dai Viet to punish the unruly Chams who had aroused Kublai's anger. Suspecting a trap for themselves, the Tran again refused. A vast Mongol and Chinese force then swept through Dai Viet in 1284. The Mongols installed a puppet king, but the Vietnamese refused to accept defeat. General Tran Hung Dao recruited and trained new armies and welded the people into a truly national resistance. Harassed by guerrilla warfare and debilitated by tropical climate and disease, only remnants of Kublai's invasion force of possibly 500,000 men straggled back to China. Humiliated and challenged, Kublai ordered another major offensive. Again General Tran Hung Dao drove off the Mongols, destroying an entire fleet of 400 vessels in the process. Kublai's death in 1294 stopped a third Mongol invasion, and his successor chose to accept Viet peace overtures.

The struggle left Dai Viet weakened and devastated. Recovery was delayed by insurrections among the mountain tribes and Cham raids. Following the accession of Che Bong Nha to the Cham throne in the mid-fourteenth century, Champa terrorized the Viets for three decades, looting cities and enslaving thousands. Hanoi was twice pillaged, one large Viet army was ambushed and destroyed, and the emperor Due Tong was killed. Not until Che Bong Nha's death did the Viets regain the offensive; thereafter, Champa struggled unsuccessfully against Viet expansion.

During the last 70 years of Tran rule, through the reigns of seven monarchs, two successive "retired" emperors, Minh Tong and Nghe Tong, dominated state policies. Both were men of letters who encouraged scholarship but neglected administrative and military affairs. Corruption and sale of offices undermined the civil service system. Nghe Tong had to fight for his throne when his predecessor died without naming a co-ruler. Though he appointed a series of co-rulers, Nghe Tong fell increasingly under the sway of a shrewd prime minister, Le Qui Li. On his deathbed in 1394, Nghe Tong named Le Qui Li regent for the child king, thus bestowing on him virtually complete power.

Le Qui Li effectively cut off the aristocracy by moving the capital to Thanh Hoa province and gradually eliminated potential opposition, including even the most able generals though they were needed in the Cham wars. After a plot on his life in 1399, Le Qui Li executed 370 prominent court figures. He then exiled the boy ruler and proclaimed himself emperor under the name of Ho Qui Li, taking the family name —Ho—of his Chinese ancestors. Ho initiated many needed reforms, but these combined with his usurpation only alienated the people. When a Tran heir requested Chinese aid, the expansionist Ming Dynasty, which had displaced the Mongols about 40 years earlier, sent an army in 1406. Ho could not rally the nation, especially since the Chinese purported only to be aiding the legitimate Trans. But when the Tran claimant was killed during the war, the victorious Ming generals declared the dynasty extinct, and Dai Viet again became a Chinese province.

Evolving of a Vietnamese Society and Government

The long Ly rule (1010-1225) brought stability and a sense of nationhood to Dai Viet. Upon this foundation the early Tran built well, strengthening Viet national character and institutions in time to enable the country to survive and even repel the Mongol onslaughts.

The Ly government was modelled after that of the Chinese. Confucian ethics and ceremonials dominated government activities, although Buddhism and Taoism vied for honors. The Ly showed many favors to Buddhism: Missions were sent to China for Buddhist and other scholarly texts which were housed in new libraries, and monks were honored as astrologers, doctors, and teachers. Under the later Ly, however, Taoist influences led many Buddhists into the study of magic. Superstitious practices influenced the court, and together with a growing corruption, hastened the decline of the Ly. With one exception, the early Tran also fostered Buddhism. Tran Thai Tong wrote essays on Thien, while Nhan Tong founded the Bamboo Forest sect, which flourished briefly. Despite royal patronage, the corruption of Buddhism continued as elements of Lamaism brought further infusions of sorcery and magic.

Accelerating this decline was the rise of neo-Confucianism. This Confucian revival, led by Chu Hsi in Sung China, greatly influenced the Vietnamese scholars who staffed the bureaucracy. Even while favoring Buddhism, both the Ly and the Tran cultivated Confucianism which strongly supported royal rule. The third and fourth Ly emperors were noted as scholars. Ly Thanh Tong built the first Confucian temple of literature and extended the Confucian spring and autumn rites to the provinces. Ly Nhan Tong began regular civil service examinations based on Confucian classics and founded a college to train royal princes and sons of high officials. The Tran broadened the examinations to include Taoist and Buddhist studies, added a third degree (the equivalent of the Ph.D.), and set up new schools to train officials.

Vietnamese government became thoroughly Confucian in concept. The ruler's power, received as a mandate from heaven, was theoretically absolute, but in practice was exercized through and with the advice of the scholar officials. As the father of his people, the emperor had paternal responsibilities: He was expected to provide an example of virtue for his officials who in turn were models for the subjects. The emperor's person was sacred, but if plague, flood, famine, or other misfortune befell his people, he must accept blame, seek his error within his conscience, and acknowledge his guilt to heaven. This Confucian pattern of authority and responsibility permeated Viet society. It stressed filial piety, mutual responsibility, and authority through five relationships: ruler to minister or subject, father to son, husband to wife, elder brother to younger brother, and friend to friend. The state was viewed as an enlargement of the family.

Like the family, the state had religious responsibilities. The emperor was the high priest and his officials lesser priests. State ceremonials were based mainly on Chinese court rites, but with a liberal admixture of local ingredients. The emperor led the nation in the important planting and harvest rites of spring and autumn. Ruler and subject shared in celebrating Tet, the lunar new year, when Taoist and Buddhist priests assisted in the essentially Confucian ceremonies to the ancestral spirits. Further evidence of the eclecticism of Viet religion and of the endurance of Indian influence was the emperor's first ceremony during Tet—a visit to a temple dedicated to the Indian deity Indra.

Both the early Ly and early Tran displayed the reforming zeal common to new dynasties, invigorating the economy, the government, and the military. Conversely, the later rulers of both dynasties showed symptoms of dynastic decay. Rulers neglected their duties, offices were sold, officials misused power, and the people suffered. In general, however, there was a shift of emphasis from landholding as the basis for power to scholarship and the ability to pass civil service examinations. While the examinations were limited primarily to those whose wealth and position afforded them the required years of study, they were the only route to power. Official position gave opportunities to improve wealth and acquire land, but lacking primogeniture, estates were soon broken up and descent to the peasantry followed for a family that could not produce new successful scholars. On the other hand, wealth alone did not guarantee prestige or official position. Successful merchants invested their fortunes in land to disguise its source so that their sons might be able, through scholarship, to merge with the landed scholar-gentry. Opportunities for the poor were few, although an unusually brilliant boy might be adopted by a declining or childless gentry family in an effort to restore the family's fortunes through his success in the bureaucracy.

Requirements for the military mandarinate were lower. A poor scholar with a strong back might hope for success, although military life was downgraded by Confucian tradition. Military candidates were examined for physical strength, mastery of weapons, and military history and tactics, plus some knowledge of government and history. The Ly introduced a universal military conscription adapted to the needs of agriculture. In preparation for the Mongol wars, the Tran raised an army of 200,000 as well as a large navy. When not engaged in war, half the army tilled the soil, while the other remained on active duty. This peasant force fought well and loyally, and military mandarins presented no threat to royal power under the Ly and Tran.

Until the Mongol invasions, Dai Viet enjoyed prosperity. The coming of independence perhaps cut off some share of the China trade, a trend that may have been increased by the introduction of the compass in the twelfth century and the construction of larger sea vessels. Still, many ships hugged the coasts and stopped at Vietnamese ports en route between China and southern Asia. The great expansion of trade under the Sung, the Mongols, and early Ming inevitably spilled some profits into Vietnamese coffers. Both Le Hoan and the Ly rulers minted Vietnamese coins, but Chinese cash remained popular in both internal and foreign trade, despite the Sung's prohibition of the export of cash. The first paper money, backed by royal lands, was issued by Le Qui Li to finance his government. Taxes on agricultural and other produce such as fish, salt, and betel were often collected in kind rather than cash.

Agriculture was, as it is today, the main occupation for most Vietnamese. A fast growing rice introduced from Champa during the eleventh century contributed to the prosperity and encouraged population growth. The Ly constructed dikes along the Red River to expand rice culture. The Tran extended them and named a commission to supervise dikes and waterways. Since only the emperor could organize sufficient labor to control the rivers and assure a dependable water supply for irrigation, the hydraulic works contributed to royal power and government stability. At the same time, the emperor became more dependent upon the bureaucrats whose knowledge included such practical subjects as hydraulic engineering, while the peasant who worked the land and maintained the dikes was kept in semiserfdom.

According to Chinese principles, the land belonged to the ruler, who divided it among his subjects. This principle was never fully adopted in Dai Viet, but some land was dispensed by the king to provide salaries of officials. As a dynasty weakened, ownership of such lands tended to become hereditary. Both the Ly and the Tran donated lands to maintain the pagodas and their numerous monks. The Buddhist tendency to retreat from society and civic duty combined with the alienation of land from the tax rolls antagonized the Confucian bureaucrats. Particularly during the late Tran Dynasty, the neo-Confucianists attacked the Buddhist monks as antisocial and sought to reduce the holdings and privileges of the pagodas.

The growth of the scholar-bureaucrat class stimulated literary production, though it developed slowly and was at first largely in the Chinese tradition and language. It is from the Tran era that the earliest important works have survived. These include histories, annals, and biographies, plus numerous patriotic treatises inspired by the victory over the Mongols. Under the Tran, *chu nom*, a system of writing Vietnamese using the phonetic values of Chinese characters, was developed. *Chu nom* was scorned by scholars until it was fostered by an eminent minister of justice, Nguyen Thuyen, whose vernacular poetry became widely imitated. Under the Tran, too, the first dramas were introduced by Chinese actors captured from the invading Mongol armies.

Traditionally, justice was dispensed harshly according to Chinese-inspired laws. Penalties were severe: a thief might lose fingers, hands, or feet. Buddhism gradually lessened the earlier tendency toward brutality and bloodshed, and both the Ly and Tran reformed the law codes. The Ly set up a bell which anyone might ring to receive immediate justice. Ly Thai Tong pardoned a rebel under circumstances in which earlier rulers might have massacred his entire family, and the Tran were lenient toward those who had cooperated with the Mongols.

The court developed a refinement far above that of Le Hoan's. The four-story palace was surrounded by numerous large buildings with massive, colorfully glazed tiled roofs, whose graceful curves might be decorated with carved and brightly painted dragons. The supporting framework and rows of pillars were deeply carved with storks, dragons, and divinities, painted in gold and red lacquers. Mingled with these motifs were Chinese characters expressing lofty sentiments. Encompassing the palace were well-organized and restful gardens. Except for the pagodas, which reached a height of twelve stories and about 130 feet, the overall impression of court architecture was one of earthbound horizontal lines. In this resplendent setting, the emperor held court dressed in a long robe of yellow silk, topped by a purple tunic. Officials wore tunics and robes of black with spiral-shaped hats of woven bamboo threads on their topknots. All carried ceremonial fans and bore symbols of their rank. The women dressed in green robes with straight long sleeves that fluttered daintily as they walked; showing through the slit sides were undergarments of black. Only the emperor rode in a carriage, and it was pulled by men, while officials travelled in simple palanquins.

Decorating the tables and the altars of the court and the homes of the wealthy was a variety of fine pottery and brass and bronze ware. This was the great period of Vietnamese ceramics. Celedon bowls, jars, and vases in pale blue and green shades were sometimes decorated in low relief with Chinese-style motifs, especially water lilies, lotus flowers, and birds. Statuary and stone carving also generally followed Chinese trends. Some surviving pieces may have been the work of Chinese craftsmen, but much is clearly Vietnamese and is testimony to the steady improvement of native skill and artistry. Many luxury items, however, were still imported from China, a situation symbolic of Dai Viet's continued cultural dependence upon her Chinese neighbors, who remained both tutors and suzerains.

The Chinese Return and Unity Under the Le

The Ming conquest dealt a crushing blow to the Viet people. Ming armies systematically ravaged the country, carrying off to China the Viet fleet, soldiers, horses and war elephants, plus thousands of craftsmen and scholars and even many Viet books, such as those on history and military subjects. Chinese garrisons were spotted at strategic locations. When few Vietnamese would serve them, Chinese were imported to staff the bureaucracy at all levels and a rigid assimilation was imposed. Vietnamese were required to learn to speak Chinese, to adopt Chinese costume, hairdress, religious practices, ceremonies, and customs. Tattooing, tooth-blackening, and betel chewing were prohibited. Following a general census, identity cards were required to assure that no man escaped military draft. Heavy taxes were imposed, and the mines and forests were exploited with forced labor.

Revolution against the Ming was delayed in part by the blood bath perpetrated by the Ho in their rise to power, and in part by the slaughter and deportation of potential leaders by the Ming. The deposed Tran were the first to rally support. Though the Ming had declared their dynasty defunct, a new Tran claimant was proclaimed emperor by a rebel group, but he alienated his followers by murdering most of his surviving relatives and his best generals. The reinforced Chinese soon put down the rebels, ending the episode called the Second Tran Period.

Le Loi, who led the Viets to independence, was a scholar and former minor official from a wealthy family of Thanh Hoa province. He early inspired legends about his courage, kindness, and integrity, though some were said to have been cultivated for his own propaganda purposes. Legends recount that Le Loi drew a sword from a lake while fishing and was fired with the belief that he was divinely ordained to lead his country to freedom. After victory, he returned to the lake and cast the sword into the waters. With a clap of thunder, it leapt from its scabbard and was transformed into a dragon before it disappeared.

At this lake, known as the Lake of the Sword, a cult was consecrated to the hero who restored Vietnamese independence and founded the Le Dynasty, under which Dai Viet achieved greatness.

Le Loi began his ten-year struggle in 1418. Several times he suffered setbacks but always rallied. At one time he was supported by the neighboring Lao, only to have them desert to the Chinese. After gradually winning the southern provinces of Nghe An and Thanh Hoa, Le Loi challenged the Chinese in the delta in 1425. As he marched northward, recruits flocked to his ranks. He quickly overwhelmed the Chinese garrisons and took Hanoi.

When victory appeared certain, Le Loi sought peace through diplomacy. By raising a Tran descendant to the throne under the name of Tran Cao, he provided a face-saver for the Chinese who had claimed to enter Dai Viet to restore the Tran. This move also gave a rallying point for the divided Vietnamese. After seeming to accept the solution, the Chinese launched new battles but were decisively defeated. Le Loi generously permitted the Chinese soldiers, officials, and merchants to return home and granted amnesty to their Vietnamese collaborators. His official proclamation of victory is considered one of Vietnam's literary masterpieces.

Le Loi requested and received investiture for Tran Cao from the Ming, but his officers demanded that he take the throne himself. Though Tran Cao fled, he was subsequently poisoned. Le Loi then assumed the crown under the name of Le Thai To (1428-33), founding the (later) Le Dynasty[1] which was to reign though not always rule for three and a half centuries.

Renaissance Under the Le

The brilliant initial period of Le rule produced three outstanding monarchs: the founder, Le Thai To (1428-33); the fourth emperor, Le Thanh Tong (1460-97); and his son, Le Hien Tong (1497-1504). Between the first and the fourth were two long minority reigns in which Thai To's policies were continued by regents. Thus Dai Viet enjoyed three-quarters of a century of strong, orderly government, internal peace, prosperity, and an intellectual and spiritual renaissance. Dai Viet grew both in size and stature. While cultivating good relations with China by rich and regular tribute, the Le continued the

---

[1] The short-lived dynasty founded by Le Hoan is sometimes referred to as the early Le.

march southward at the cost of the troublesome Chams, who provided provocation by raiding the Viet seacoast.

The Le divided their realm first into five then, after conquests of portions of Champa, thirteen provinces. Each was headed by a military and a civil governor and a chief judge, except for certain border provinces directed by viceroys. The central government in Dong Kinh (Tonkin), the capital established by Le Thai To at the site of modern Hanoi, was headed by two chief ministers of the left and the right (so named for their position by the emperor at court), under whom were six functional ministries. A board of censors sent roving inspectors to check on provincial administrators. A host of mandarins and clerks carried out routine affairs. These were recruited mainly from among scholars who passed the civil service examinations. The village chief was the highest non-degree holder, ranking below the nine official grades, though after six years of successful administration he could be promoted to the bottom step of the mandarinate. Officials were paid from the revenues of lands reserved for this purpose. Top officials retired at the age of 65 and lower ones at 60, both with pensions. Penalties for officials convicted of bribery or falsehood were severe.

Le Thai To required all lower mandarins to take new civil service examinations, which he revised and expanded. He reorganized the National College and added new provincial schools open to the poor as well as the rich. Scholars winning the coveted doctor's degree in examinations held at the capital every six years had their names inscribed on stone steles. Thanh Tong, himself a poet and scholar, personally supervised these examinations. He created an additional college, built dormitories and new libraries, and founded a literary academy to honor leading scholars.

Much effort was required to reconstitute the Vietnamese literary and historical works taken by the Ming. Despite this, under the Le, Vietnamese literature, both in classical Chinese and in the Vietnamese chu nom, truly reached maturity. Notable compilations of national legends, poetry, and other literature were produced, in addition to numerous works in geography and history. The annals of Dai Viet begun under the Tran were brought up to date, and the legendary Hong Bang period was added along with historical criticisms. Le Thanh Tong mapped the provinces, giving special attention to sites related to historical and legendary events. He also created a royal printing establishment.

With neo-Confucianism the popular philosophy of the scholars,

Buddhism and Taoism now enjoyed only limited favor. Le Thai To ordered all lower Buddhist monks and Taoist priests to complete examinations on the doctrines of those cults. Although the Le built the Pagoda of the Sword, they discouraged young men from becoming monks and priests and restricted construction of new religious buildings to check the development of what the Confucian scholars considered superstitions. Thanh Tong simplified marriage and funeral ceremonies and published twenty-four articles emphasizing Confucian-type moral behavior which were to be read on all official occasions. On the other hand, neo-Confucianism, while encouraging scholarly endeavors, had the long-range effect of stultifying scholarship. Because of its retrospective outlook, neo-Confucianism in Vietnam, as in China, led scholars into a sterile, antiquarian narrow-mindedness and a nit-picking sort of argumentation that rejected new ideas and slowed progress. This trend among the bureaucrats hastened the decline of the Le.

Among the greatest achievements of the Le were their legal reforms. Thanh Tong published the Hong Duc code, which remained in effect until the nineteenth century. Based on a much earlier T'ang dynasty code of China which stressed Confucian morality, the Hong Duc was adapted to Vietnamese customs and was notably humane for the period. The powers of officials were limited. While the code assigned fixed, graduated punishments for crimes, it decreed many exceptions for the aged, infirm, and descendants of those who had performed great services to the country. Women received nearly equal legal rights with men.

Le Thai To assumed rule over a country devastated by war. Since large areas had been depopulated, Thai To ordered a broad land redistribution following a general census. Everyone inscribed on the tax registers received land on the basis of rank. Officers and soldiers who had fought for independence were rewarded with lands taken from traitors, but loyal persons retained their properties. Village lands were redistributed according to population needs. Orphans, widows, and the aged were provided for by communal village plots, and victims of flood and other natural disasters received aid from public granaries.

The large army of 250,000 was reduced by 100,000 after the expulsion of the Chinese. These were divided into five parts which rotated on active duty, leaving as many men as possible free for farming. Le Thanh Tong took great interest in military and naval affairs as well as in scholarship. He fostered cults to military and national heroes and gave special care to national monuments to stimulate patriotism and a fighting spirit in the people.

Le Thai To so successfully reasserted Viet suzerainty over various tributary tribal peoples of the neighboring mountain regions that no revolts occurred during the reigns of his immediate successors. He did not attempt to punish the Lao kingdom of Lan Xang for the treachery of its army, but during Thanh Tong's conquest of Champa, a quarrel over a sacred white elephant provoked a Vietnamese invasion of the Lao state. Though the capital was taken, the Lao resorted to guerrilla war until a combination of battle losses and disease forced the Viet army to retreat. The old Lao ruler died shortly afterward and his son renewed friendly relations with the Vietnamese by sending tribute. Thereafter, Dai Viet claimed suzerainty over much of Laos.

Under the first two Le kings, the long quarrel with Champa was quiescent, although in 1407 the Chams had reclaimed provinces lost to Dai Viet under Ho Qui Li. After 1441, when Champa renewed the offensive during a minority reign, the forces of child emperor Nhan Tong took the Cham capital and installed a more cooperative king. His successor continued regular tribute, but the next Cham sovereign chose to test his strength against Le Thanh Tong, who raised an army of 650,000 to eliminate his troublesome neighbor. The Cham forces were quickly swept aside and their capital taken, with 60,000 Chams dead in the onslaught.

This defeat virtually ended Cham independence. The Vietnamese annexed all of Champa north of Cape Varella and established military colonies in the conquered areas to provide a self-supporting army of occupation. The remainder of Champa was divided among three Cham princes, who became vassals of Dai Viet. Under the later Le even these three remnants of the once great Champa fell to the Vietnamese and Cham identity was lost. They either evacuated in advance of the Vietnamese or were absorbed by harsh assimilation measures similar to those the Ming had imposed upon the Viets. Today, only about 30,000 persons in Vietnam are still recognizable as Chams. Little remains of Champa's former glory apart from a number of brick towers housing multi-armed Hindu gods behind carved stone portals, where some modern Vietnamese still burn incense and pray.

Usurpation and Division

The fortunes of the Le declined rapidly after Hien Tong's death in 1504, and for nearly two centuries, Dai Viet was torn by almost perpetual strife as rival families fought for power. During the first 23 years after Hien Tong, five emperors reigned but with little power, and only the first died of natural causes. The second was blown from a cannon after a six-year reign of terror. The next three were murdered during the struggle among three powerful families—the Nguyen, the Mac, and the Trinh. As puppet emperors passed between rivals, the oppressed peasantry rebelled repeatedly. One group led by a monk claiming to be a descendant of the Tran and a reincarnation of Buddha sacked the capital. As usual in a time of Vietnamese weakness, the Chinese interfered and effectively encouraged continued strife by sanctioning a division of the country.

The military mandarin Mac Dang Dung gained ascendancy in 1527 and proclaimed himself emperor, founding the short-lived Mac Dynasty. The Mac won control of Hanoi and the north, but failed to crush the Nguyen and the Trinh. Mac Dang Dung and his successor, whom he appointed co-ruler, sought to bring order and prosperity within the framework organized by the Le. To their chagrin and despite sending rich tribute and ceding six Viet districts to China, the Ming named the Mac "governor-general" rather than king. The Viet people were even more reluctant to accept the Mac. The popular affection for the descendants of Le Loi made them excellent tools first for the Nguyen and then the Trinh, who led frequent revolts. For a time, however, the Mac seemed victorious. Nguyen Kim, head of the Nguyen family, fled to Laos, and one Le claimant was executed. But soon afterward, Nguyen Kim won Thanh Hoa province to the south and proclaimed another Le emperor. When the Ming sent an army to support the Le, Mac Dang Dung bought off the Chinese, who compromised by recognizing both the Mac and Le as governor-generals.

This action left Dai Viet divided between the contestants, but neither would accept the resolution. When Nguyen Kim died in 1545, his army was taken over by his son-in-law, Trinh Kiem, because Kim's sons were too young. Thus fortunes in the south swung to the Trinh family. For nearly fifty years, the adherents of a succession of Mac and Le "emperors" intermittently fought for sole power. When the Trinh took Hanoi in 1592, the Mac partisans founded a small kingdom at Cao Bang near the Chinese border. Three successive Mac rulers of Cao Bang harassed the Trinh who wielded the power of the helpless Le emperors over most of Dai Viet.

As Mac power declined, Nguyen descendants gained strength in the south. For his assistance to the Trinh, Nguyen Hoang, Nguyen Kim's able son, had been appointed governor of the former Cham provinces south of Hue. He utilized his exile from the center of power to build his own position. By governing well, he won his subjects' allegiance so solidly that at his death in 1613 his domain passed almost as a kingdom to his son, Sai Vuong.

Hemmed in by the Mac to the north and the Nguyen to the south, the Trinh dared not usurp the throne, taking instead the title of "chau" (lord), hereditary chief of the government. The emperor reigned and the Trinh ruled, but over a troubled realm. The Nguyen recognized Le sovereignty, but ignored Trinh pretensions. In Tonkin, the Trinh faced rebellions led by Mac and Le partisans. Wearying of the struggle, the aging Trinh chau abdicated in favor of his two sons who fell to fighting, leaving their father to die alone by a roadside. After Trinh Tran defeated his brother, he launched a campaign to enlarge his influence, first attacking the Mac and then moving against the Nguyen. A bitter war tore Dai Viet for nearly half a century until a truce in 1672 divided the Trinh and Nguyen domains at about the seventeenth parallel.

Three years after this truce, the Trinh drove out the last of the Macs. Only then did China's new dynasty, the Manchu, raise the Le to the status of kings. Within Dai Viet, the Le were still called emperors, while the Trinh elevated themselves to the rank of "king of the east," as they sat on the east side of the emperor. One later Trinh ruler called himself Thuong Vuong, "Super King." In a war of titles, the Nguyen adopted first the rank of chau and later that of king.

With one emperor and two kings, three costly courts were maintained. The palaces in Hanoi were vast, with covered galleries connecting the many buildings. Each of the several royal wives had a private house and garden. The Trinh court was guarded by 12,000 men with 500 elephants. When the Trinh and Le rulers travelled together for the spring and autumn ceremonies, their entourage included 40,000 soldiers. At Hue the Nguyen imitated this royal style on a lesser scale. Both north and south of the seventeenth parallel, peasant, craftsman, and merchant bent under a staggering burden of taxes, forced labor, and military duty.

Particularly before the Nguyen's absorption of Champa and annexation of the Mekong provinces from Cambodia, the Trinh realm was far the more populous. Exhibiting the expansionist drive typical of strong Viet rulers, the Trinh claimed suzerainty over numerous mountain tribes, and after 1696 asserted protection over the Lao kingdom of Vientiane. The Trinh capital impressed European visitors with its large population and broad paved streets. The boats on the river were report-

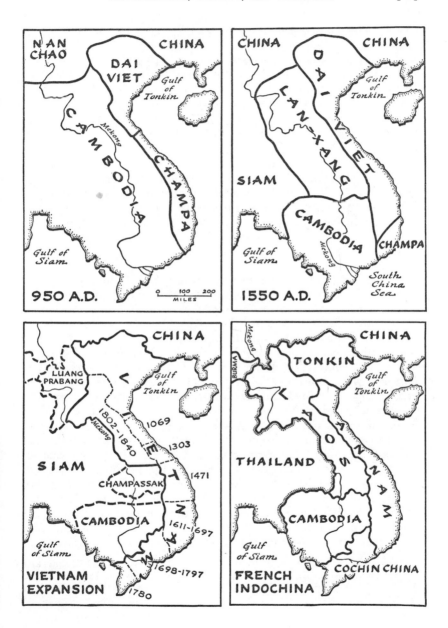

edly more numerous than those in Venice, while traders from many lands thronged the ports.

Significant European contacts date from this period. Portuguese traders began to frequent Trinh ports in the sixteenth century, but the Dutch gained favor in 1637 with the presentation of a cannon. Though they opened a post at Pho Yen, the inadequacy of Dutch aid in the war with the Nguyen soured relations, and by 1700 the Dutch had abandoned their unprofitable post. English and French efforts were even less successful.[2] Aside from military supplies which were in small demand after the truce, European trade offerings were mainly luxuries with few goods suitable for general consumption. Another limiting factor was the Vietnamese insistence on treating foreign trade as a government monopoly. This gave considerable power to the mandarins, whose Confucian training made them disdain trade and traders. Their petty interference with business transactions and their efforts at extortion made trading a trying and not always profitable process for Europeans.

While the Trinh had resources, they also had liabilities and problems. In addition to their troubles with the Mac and Le adherents, they had to quell frequent tribal uprisings and contend with a number of strong noble families who ruled considerable areas as feudal lords. Recurrent droughts and floods drove many starving peasants to desert their lands to become virtual serfs of the rural lords or to join brigand and pirate bands. The Trinh attempted periodically to reform the bureaucracy by demoting officials who failed re-examinations, but decay and corruption eroded the administration. Some of the most able scholars migrated to Nguyen lands to escape the turmoil of Tonkin.

In the south, the Nguyen labored to create a strong government, military organization, and economy. From their original base, they too expanded, pressing southward at the cost of the Chams and Cambodians. Even before Champa was swallowed up, the Vietnamese were colonizing the southern delta. As Siam rose, the great Khmer empire of Kambuja crumbled, and by the seventeenth century, Cambodia's existence depended on a balance between the ambitions of the Thai and those of the Nguyen. The latter dabbled in the troubled Cambodian court, supporting rival claimants to the weak throne, gaining as

[2] For early French contacts consult Thomas E. Ennis, *French Policy and Developments in Indochina* (Chicago, 1936) and Herbert I. Priestly, *France Overseas Through the Old Regime, A Study of European Expansion* (New York, 1939).

"reward" one Cambodian province after another. The last annexation in 1758 rounded out the present delta provinces except for Soc Trang, which was added in 1840. The Nguyen were on the verge of annexing all Cambodia when the Tayson brothers launched their rebellion.

To settle the conquered lands, the Nguyen followed Le Thanh Tong's pattern of creating self-sufficient villages in which peasant cultivators were also soldiers for self-defense. War veterans especially were rewarded with lands in such military colonies. Other colonists were welcomed from Tonkin and China. The fall of the Ming in the mid-seventeenth century sent a wave of Chinese refugees. One fleet under the Chinese General Mac Cuu was directed by the Nguyen into Cambodian lands in the far south. There they settled at Ha Tien, Rach Gia, Ca Mau and Phu Quoc Island, where they were joined by Malays, Cambodians, and Vietnamese. Attacked by the Thai, Mac Cuu requested Nguyen protection and was named governor of Ha Tien province. Though Mac Cuu passed the position to his son, the Nguyen gradually increased their direct control. These settlements and others at Baria (Phuoc Le), Bien Hoa, and Gia Dinh accelerated the Nguyen occupation of eastern Cambodia. Later the support of these regions was a decisive factor in the Nguyen reunification of all Vietnam.

The Nguyen were little more hospitable to European trade than the Trinh. Under them a stronger merchant class developed, but officials still obstructed both foreign and domestic commerce. Despite this, Nguyen ports received ships of many nations. This trade helped pay the costs of the large and well-trained army and navy and brought better guns. A Portuguese adventurer assisted in constructing an arsenal at Hue in 1614, but a trade center opened in 1637 closed after four years. Portuguese military supplies played a crucial role in Nguyen defenses against the Trinh, but after the truce their trade declined. Dutch aid to the Trinh made them suspect in the south, although they traded there occasionally. The first English trader was killed by villagers in 1612, and subsequent English and French visitors enjoyed scant success. As in the north, the chief deterrent apart from official attitude was the lack of European trade goods which the Viets needed or wanted.

Religious and Cultural Trends Under the Nguyen and Trinh

Aside from the remarkable territorial expansion during these years, perhaps the most significant national developments occurred in religion.[3] A Buddhist revival formalized the syncretic faith of modern Vietnam, and Christianity introduced new international tensions. The Buddhist resurgence also stimulated art and architecture after several unproductive centuries when neo-Confucianism stifled both the religion and the artistic production which it inspires. Moreover, the century of peace following the truce brought renewed intellectual activity for which the scholarly emphasis of the early Le had laid a foundation.

Buddhism, which mixed with Taoist, Tantric, and animistic elements, had gained strength among the people despite the lack of Le support, returned to official favor under the Nguyen and Trinh during the sixteenth century. Though Confucian patterns prevailed in the bureaucracy, neo-Confucianism had lost its virility and much Confucian scholarship was reduced to historical compilation and petty disputation. Into this environment came revitalizing Buddhist currents from China. Tao-dong, a Thien sect introduced in the south in 1633 by a Chinese monk, was popularized by his Vietnamese disciples. Later in the century, another Thien sect, the Lieu-ton, was founded near Hanoi. Lieu-ton advocated faith as important to achieving Buddhahood, while Tao-dong stressed understanding. Lieu-ton was favored by the Trinh who fostered the collecting and printing of Buddhist texts and the building or reconstruction of pagodas and stupas. The early Nguyen also liberally supported the erection of pagodas and collection of cult objects. Among the Chinese refugees after the fall of the Ming was the founder of the Lam Te sect of Thien, which is still popular in central Vietnam.

The temporary decline of Confucianism and revival of Buddhism led many scholars to seek refuge from the troubled world in the pagoda. Bringing with them into Buddhism their knowledge of Confucianism and Taoism, some further mingled the three doctrines by evolving theories that all had common origins and content. It was this period especially that developed the syncretic and confusing blend of Buddhism, Confucianism, Taoism, and animism found in modern Vietnam.

At the same time, Christianity took root in Dai Viet. The first Portuguese adventurer who visited the country in 1516 was followed eleven years later by a Portuguese Dominican missionary. Two Domin-

[3] For general information on religion in Vietnam, see Léopold Cadière, *Croyances et pratiques religieuses des annamites* (Hanoi, 1944), and, more briefly, Kenneth P. Landon, *Southeast Asia, Crossroad of Religion* (Chicago, 1949).

icans began working in Ha Tien in the far south in 1585, but not until 1596 was a mission founded in central Dai Viet, at the Nguyen port of Fai Fo. Probably the most outstanding missionary was the French Jesuit Alexandre de Rhodes who not only worked zealously among the Vietnamese but also stimulated European interest in the country. Arriving in Fai Fo in 1615, he quickly mastered the language and wrote a Vietnamese catechism and a Portuguese-Vietnamese-Latin dictionary. He also perfected *quoc ngu,* a Romanized alphabet for Vietnamese developed earlier by Portuguese and Italian Jesuits. Father Rhodes' most effective preaching followed his transfer to Hanoi. In three years he claimed to have baptized 6700 persons, including members of the royal family. Perhaps because of his success, he was expelled by the Trinh for undermining filial piety, ancestor veneration, and the state cult to heaven.

Father Rhodes later propagandized the mission in Europe, particularly in France. To gain financial backing, he dangled the prospect of quick wealth by combining trade and missionary work. His efforts resulted in the creation of the Paris Society of Foreign Missions, which was to link the forces of trade and religion in Indochina. With the backing of the French king, the society trained missionaries, supported the development of a native clergy, which Father Rhodes urged as essential to lasting success, and sent missionary bishops to strengthen their work. Merchants contributed to the costs of missionary work in return for assistance in their trading activities. Some clergymen regularly mixed trade and proselytizing, and the first French traders up the Red River were missionaries in disguise.

Whatever their European origins, missionaries and traders alike usually looked after their governments' interests and equally sought their aid and protection. This mingling of religion, trade, and politics antagonized the Confucian mandarins of Dai Viet. Highly ethnocentric, they looked upon Europeans as barbarians and especially despised merchants. They believed Christianity challenged the foundations of Dai Viet's government and moral and social order, and viewed the missionaries as spies and agents of foreign governments. Contributing to this belief was the papal division of Dai Viet into spheres of activity for missionaries of different orders and nationalities, in an effort to reduce their bickering.

Aside from Father Rhodes' early successes, neither missionaries nor traders achieved notable results. Both the Nugyen and Trinh considered Christianity a threat to the traditional way of life and government. Both sporadically expelled priests and forbade their subjects to become Christians. Partly because of official laxity and partly because the missionaries repeatedly risked their lives, the edicts were never totally effective. The first serious persecution occurred in 1662 when, during a temporary Confucian revival, the Trinh outlawed the books of Buddhism, Taoism, and "false doctrines." Christian missionaries and some of their converts were killed. The Nguyen embarked on similar persecutions, though some Jesuits had personally found favor at the Nguyen court as doctors, mathematicians, and astronomers. Bishop Pigneau de Behaine of the Paris Society established a seminary in Cochinchina in 1769, but it was soon destroyed.

Despite the wars and division, the later Le saw some cultural progress. The revival of Buddhism stimulated the production of masterpieces in art and architecture, particularly in the numerous pagodas constructed by both the Nguyen and the Trinh. Sculpture reached its peak at this time. The Ninh Phuc temple built by the Trinh has two fine examples of seventeenth-century wood statues, one a sensual multi-armed figure of Kuan-yin, the other an emaciated Buddha showing a high order of realism. At the same temple are 26 bas-reliefs of highly animated mythological scenes. Several other statues of the period attest to the high level of skill in casting, as do the ritual urns at the palace of Hue. Numerous extant stone steles are decorated with phoenixes, unicorns and dragons, though the later stone carving shows increasing use of geometric patterns.

The troubled years of the Nguyen and Trinh wars discouraged scholarship, but the following century of peace was more productive. Contributing to the spread of learning was the increased use of woodblock printing which the Viets had been slow to adopt. To encourage printers, the Trinh forbade the import of Chinese texts. Historical studies were stimulated by the commissioning of a complete revision and updating of the chronicles of Dai Viet. The resulting 24 volumes printed in 1697 became the basic historical works on the country. The major scholars were generalists. Ly Quy Don, a child prodigy, ambassador and statesman, competed in poetry composition with the best scholars in China, wrote essays on virtually all fields, and compiled anthologies of prose and poetry. While most of the scholarly writing and record-keeping in Tonkin was still done in classical Chinese, writing in *chu nom* increased. Perhaps because the Nguyen were more concerned with building a new country than encouraging scholarship, *chu nom* was more popular in the south and was promoted by its use in government administrative orders. Probably the most popular literary form in both the north and south was the lyric poem expressing social criticism.

Upheaval of the Tayson Rebellion (1772-1802)

In 1772, the long truce was shattered by the Tayson Rebellion, which eliminated the Trinh and the Le and temporarily displaced the Nguyen.[4] Beginning as a revolt against an oppressive Nguyen government under a regency, it ultimately involved the Thai, the Chinese and the French. While the Tayson leaders only briefly controlled all Dai Viet, their rebellion furnished the foundation for reunification of the country under one ruler in 1802.

The rebellion was named after the village of Tay Son in central Dai Viet, which was the home of its three leaders, the brothers Nguyen Hue, Nhac, and Lu. Their family, which had adopted the rulers' name on moving into the Nguyen domain, were said to be merchants, and early support for the rebels came from the merchant class, whose activities were continually frustrated by the anti-business mandarins. By attacking rich landlords and officials and sharing the spoils with the poor, the Tayson gained a Robin Hood-type image. They taught a doctrine of equality and justice and claimed to be fighting against the tyranny of the mandarins. Because one of the brothers was a monk, Buddhist and Taoist support was rallied, and their claim to be descendants of Cham kings gained for the brothers Cham and Montagnard backing.

Tayson success was rapid. Having won considerable strength fighting the Nguyen, they allied themselves with the Trinh to secure their rear. The important port of Qui Nhon was taken by Tayson trickery, while Hue fell soon afterward to the Trinh armies. After the young Nguyen king was captured and killed with his son in 1777, Nhac, the eldest of the rebel leaders, proclaimed himself king at Chabon, a former Cham capital, and divided the Nguyen domain with his brothers.

The rebels had yet to reckon with Nguyen Anh, a nephew of the murdered southern king, who had escaped to the far south. There he raised loyal forces and drove the Tayson back to Qui Nhon. Although

[4] Nguyen Phut Tan, *A Modern History of Viet-Nam, 1802-1954* (Saigon, 1964) contains useful details on the Tayson and early Nguyen dynasty period, particularly on the missionary role. For a Marxist view, see Jean Chesneaux, *Contribution à l'histoire de la nation vietnamienne* (Paris, 1955).

Ahn was proclaimed king in 1780, his forces were overwhelmed and the Tayson regained all the south. Anh escaped to Phu Quoc Island where he was befriended by the French missionary Pigneau de Behaine, Bishop of Adran and Apostolic Vicar of Cochinchina. After failing to recover the delta with forces sent by Siam, Anh was persuaded to authorize the bishop to seek French assistance. De Behaine then sailed west, taking with him Prince Canh, Anh's eldest son.

At Pondichéry in India, de Behaine was rebuffed by the French governor-general, who thought the intervention would overextend the strained resources of a France then on the eve of revolution. Next the bishop moved to Paris, where in 1787 his persistent lobbying secured a treaty and promise of aid from a reluctant but weak King Louis XVI. The treaty called on France to provide military and naval aid in return for a trade monopoly and cession of Tourane (Danang) and Poulo Condore. When he reached Pondichéry to pick up the promised forces and supplies, de Behaine found opponents at court had sent ahead a cancellation of the order. Nevertheless, he managed with private aid to fit out two ships with guns, munitions, and some twenty volunteer officers. The year was then 1789.

Meanwhile in Dai Viet, a Trinh quarrel over succession permitted the second and most brilliant of the Tayson brothers, Hue, to move into Tonkin and take Hanoi in 1786 as the protector of the Le. Hue attempted to restore power to the Le emperor, but barely had he returned south than another Trinh was dictating to the weak monarch. While the brothers Nhac and Hue fell to quarrelling, a Tayson general drove out the last Trinh and attempted to seize power, but Hue stormed north and executed the traitor. The foolish Le ruler appealed for aid from China which sent a force of 200,000 men. The Chinese briefly took Hanoi, but Hue, who had proclaimed himself Emperor Quang Trung, regained the offensive. After utterly defeating the invaders, Hue followed the traditional course by sending tribute to China with a request for recognition of his rule. The Chinese, as they had done in the past when challenged by real Vietnamese strength, accepted the situation and in 1789 recognized Hue as king of Annam. Soon thereafter, the last Le ruler died in China, ending a dynasty that had seen more glory and degradation than any of its predecessors. Hue as Quang Trung ruled over Tonkin until his death in 1792, while Nhac maintained sway over the central provinces and Lu over the south. Hue was succeeded by his son, who reigned for ten years before Nguyen Anh ended the Tayson Dynasty.

Most Vietnamese histories of the Tayson period are biased inasmuch as they were written under the Nguyen who viewed the Tayson only as rebels and usurpers. Yet even from these it is clear the Tayson represented a truly popular uprising. The early Tayson government was vigorous and effective. The Tayson briefly brought the country under the rule of one family, ending the long Nguyen-Trinh split. Former mandarins were well treated. Abandoned lands were surveyed and the landless resettled. New markets were opened, and internal and foreign trade was encouraged. Banks were established, new coins minted, and taxation regularized. While Nguyen Hue is remembered as a military genius, he was much concerned with education, founding schools at all levels and recruiting officials through examinations. He made chu nom the official language and ordered the translation of Chinese classics. Under his encouragement, a number of outstanding poets and scholars emerged. Hue was on his way to open a library when he died prematurely at the age of 40. Because he was tolerant toward religion, Catholics enjoyed new freedom. Hue made efforts to raise the quality of the numerous but generally ignorant Buddhist monks, forcing the least able to become laymen. Nguyen Hue's ambitions extended beyond Dai Viet. He built a strong army and employed pirates to harass the coasts of China. Just before his death, he requested marriage with a Manchu princess and demanded the cession of Kwang-si and Kwang-tung provinces on the grounds that they had belonged to ancient Nam Viet.

Since Hue's successor was only fourteen years old, a regency followed, and factions soon were competing for power. As the old-school mandarins reasserted their influence, government gradually sank to former levels. Again the peasants were oppressed and the merchants harassed. Meanwhile, Nguyen Anh was challenging the Tayson in the south. In 1786, after having served the Siamese king for several years, Nguyen Anh rejoined his partisans in Cochinchina where Lu, weakest of the Tayson leaders, had neglected defenses. Aided by Chinese, Cambodians, and Tayson deserters, Anh defeated Lu and in 1788 seized the Gia-Dinh-Saigon area, where he organized a government. The following year he was joined by de Behaine, Prince Canh, and their little force of French adventurers.

Now older and more cautious, Nguyen Anh made careful plans for conquering Dai Viet. With the guidance and assistance of de Behaine and his officers, soldiers were trained, fortifications and ships built, and the government placed on a sound basis to support these activities.

Anh destroyed the Tayson fleet at Qui Nhon in 1792, but ten years of campaigning followed before his victory march into Hanoi. By this time, all three Tayson brothers had died. Anh's triumph was saddened, however, by the deaths of both de Behaine and Prince Canh.

A few months before entering Hanoi in 1802, Anh proclaimed himself Emperor Gia Long. To commemorate his victory, he changed the name of his empire to Nam Viet (South Viet). The Chinese acceded to his investment, but reversed the name to Viet Nam, to avoid any suggestion that Kwang-si and Kwang-tung might be Viet provinces as the Tayson had claimed.[5] The Chinese thus accepted a *fait accompli*. Having failed in direct interference, they had permitted internal forces to reach their own adjustment. Though Gia Long and his successors functioned as independent sovereigns, their return to Confucian conservatism, their policy of isolation, and their hostility to the West and persecution of Christians, which invited the French encroachment, all reflected a similar disastrous pattern in Manchu China.

[5] Though Gia Long accepted this name change, his successors subsequently adopted Dai Nam (Great South), which had more imperial connotations. This was used internally until 1945, when the Viet Minh revived Viet Nam for their Democratic Republic of Viet Nam. The French in the meantime complicated matters by calling the entire country variously Cochinchina, Annam, and Tonkin, before settling on these as geographic and political terms for the south, center, and north respectively. This history will henceforth use Vietnam, the modern name.

4: French Conquest and Rule

Gia Long and his successors gave Vietnam a half century of unity before France began her piecemeal conquest. The Nguyen were hard-working and conscientious rulers, who improved and centralized the government, encouraged scholarship, and ruled through scholar-officials. Like their Chinese suzerain, they tried vainly to shut out the new forces from the West, which their reactionary Confucian philosophy prevented them from understanding. The French conquered and ruled without consistent plan or direction. The result was a thorough-going domination and exploitation. When even Vietnamese efforts to win a relaxation of French control by collaboration were harshly repressed, nationalism was channeled into revolutionary activities. World War II and the Japanese occupation paved the way for the Viet Minh uprising under Communist leadership.

The Nguyen Dynasty and Traditionalism

Gia Long (1802-1820) regained the throne less by brilliance than by energy, courage, and persistence, and by attracting able men to his court.[1] Though his formal education was neglected, he read widely. He studied Western military techniques, but remained a Confucian to the end, convinced that all important learning was already known in the East. While he honored the French advisers who stayed after victory, their influence remained primarily in military realms. He became increasingly suspicious of Christianity, which he believed would undermine Vietnam's government and society. In deference to the dead de Behaine, he did not bar missionary work, but neither did he interfere with the petty harassment of missionaries by his officials. He chose as his successor a concubine's son, Minh Mang, who was hostile to Christianity and all Western influences. In so doing, he ignored the

---

[1] Nguyen Phut Tan, *A Modern History of Viet-Nam* (Saigon, 1964) presents a Vietnamese view of the reign of Gia Long and his successors.

son of Crown Prince Canh, who had been partly educated by Christian missionaries.

In the traditional sense, Minh Mang (1820-1841) was a good ruler. He worked hard, consulted his officials, and kept informed on state affairs. A poet and scholar who wrote political essays, he was truly a philosopher king. If his vision was narrow, it was partly because his Confucianist philosophy no longer suited a changing world. When war, plague, and famine disrupted his land, Minh Mang as father of his people assumed responsibility for their sufferings before the altar of heaven, but he took few practical steps to cope with the new forces encroaching upon Vietnam. Most of his subjects loyally supported him and bestowed upon him the posthumous title of "The Saintly and Humane Emperor."

Thieu Tri, who succeeded Minh Mang, had only a six-year reign. Some have said he inherited the faults but not the virtues of his father. Nevertheless, both Thieu Tri and his son Tu Duc were poets and continued Minh Mang's scholarly tradition. Though only 18 when he assumed rule, Tu Duc (1847-1883) became one of the foremost scholars of his realm and, like Minh Mang, was devoted to duty. Unfortunately, his education had ignored the new currents of Western thought, and he found incomprehensible the brutal directness of the Europeans who were encroaching upon his domain.

Perhaps the most striking feature of Nguyen rule was governmental centralization. For centuries under the later Le, the country had been divided. Even within the two major divisions, provincial governors had exercised considerable autonomy, and central control was further diluted by the power of wealthy noble families. The Tayson epoch disrupted the large landholdings, and the Nguyen eliminated them. Mandarins were no longer paid by land grants, but received fixed pay in rice and cash. Despite official housing and other emoluments of office, the salary could not maintain the living standard expected of officials. Consequently, corruption of a wide variety became generally accepted. Titles of nobility were still granted, but they carried no office or power, and the land grants once accompanying them were reduced to sites for family tombs under Thieu Tri and to small cash stipends under Tu Duc.

Gia Long organized the country into three sections or *ky* along the lines of the Tayson division. Viceroys governed Tonkin and Cochinchina, while the center, Annam, fell under direct imperial rule with Hue as the capital. To link the country more closely, the Mandarin

Way was constructed from China to Cambodia, with 98 relay stations and inns. Gia Long also built or improved many canals, bridges, and public granaries, and enlarged the seaports. In major political centers, strong Vauban-type fortifications were erected.

The Nguyen financed their conquests and numerous public works by a combination of taxation and corvée. A census every five years registered persons from 18 to 59 years of age who were required to pay personal taxes. Each village kept registers of its rice lands, which were taxed in kind according to their productivity. Other products of the land, sea, and forests and virtually all stages of commerce were also taxed. Additional government revenues came from such royal reserves as mines and the salt monopoly. Trade and industry, which could have increased state revenues, were discouraged. Except for a limited commerce in Asian products largely dominated by Chinese, foreign trade was feared because it brought unsettling ideas. Domestic merchants were harassed by petty taxes and regulations, licenses, and mandarinal corruption, and were hampered by inadequate internal transportation. The Mandarin Way, a mere footpath, had more political than economic value. Vietnamese desiring to introduce new industrial techniques could not get an audience at court. As a result, the economy remained simple and highly self-sufficient.

Legal and judicial reforms were hardly more enlightened. The Gia Long code, an adaptation of the reactionary codes of Manchu China, was designed to support royal absolutism. In contrast to the religious toleration of the Tayson, the Gia Long code restricted Buddhism, Taoism, and the spirit cults, although these had become part of Vietnamese life. Many of the provisions which restored outmoded customs were ignored by the judicial mandarins.

At Hue, Gia Long created a great citadel, with walls six miles around enclosing a complex of luxurious palaces and official buildings —a small copy of the Manchu court at Peking. This formidable fortification insulated the Nguyen emperors from reality, and Hue's geographic position midway between the major population centers of the north and south increased the isolation. The north, long the most important center, resented its loss of stature, and the southern frontier area was far removed from the cloistered court in spirit. The emperors were also separated from their subjects by a screen of courtiers and officials, who, while competing ruthlessly among themselves, cooperated to exclude disruptive intellectual currents.

Gia Long's successors extended his centralizing efforts. Minh Mang for a time abolished the vice-royalties, reorganized provincial boundaries, and brought the governors directly under Hue. The provinces were further subdivided into *tongs* formed by several villages, and the *tong* chief was selected by village delegates. Officials above this level were part of the mandarinate, responsible ultimately to Hue. Minh Mang's zeal for centralization antagonized both the north and south, and, combined with his spiteful acts against the sons of Crown Prince Canh, aroused open revolt. Most serious perhaps was that of Le Van Khoi, who secured Siam's assistance and briefly controlled Cochinchina (1833-35). In retribution, Minh Mang executed Khoi's seven-year-old son and a Catholic missionary.

Thieu Tri's short reign was relatively peaceful, but Tu Duc's succession touched off a rebellion by adherents of an older brother who sought the throne. In addition, various Le pretenders fomented uprisings. That of Le Phung, a native Catholic, prevented Tu Duc from devoting his full resources to resist the first French invasion. Later, Chinese brigands, backwash from the Taiping and Muslim rebellions, plagued Tonkin. Natural disasters added to the misery of the people; dams and dikes failed, flooding large areas. At the same time, forced labor was used extensively on the palaces and fortifications. Contemporary accounts abound with stories of peasant suffering and of some literally worked to death on royal projects.

The Nguyen followed divergent policies toward foreign states. With China, they were submissive, presenting the traditional triennial tribute of elephant tusks, rhinoceros horns, cinnamon, silk, gold, and silver. Toward Laos and Cambodia, the Nguyen were aggressive, demanding tribute and interfering in internal affairs, thereby causing hostilities with Siam, including a Thai invasion of central Vietnam in 1831. Through much of the century, Vietnam vied with Siam for control of Cambodia, which briefly became a virtual Vietnamese province before the two powers established joint suzerainty. Vietnam also competed with Siam for the Lao principalities, directly annexing much Lao territory and exerting suzerainty over the rest. With the Europeans, the Nguyen pursued a hostile policy of isolation. This, combined with internal persecution of Christians, brought conflict and eventual loss of independence.

Vietnam on the Eve of Conquest

In the mid-nineteenth century, Vietnam was a mature country, aware and proud of its long history. Its sophisticated government ruled with fair success and managed to dominate its smaller neighbors. A self-sufficient though exploited peasantry lived in the security of centuries-old customs. The only fundamentally disruptive innovations had come with Christianity and the socio-political ideology of the Tayson.

The Nguyen bureaucracy, though altered in detail and more centralized, followed the Confucianist patterns established 800 years earlier by the Ly.[2] The theoretically absolute emperor who ruled by a mandate from heaven was father and mother to his people, high priest, law giver, chief justice, commander-in-chief, and administrator of the state. To accomplish this staggering assignment, the emperor delegated duties to a bureaucracy of scholars, the mandarinate, which was divided into nine grades of two classes each. The only legitimate route into this bureaucracy was successful competition in state examinations, which tested a candidate's mastery of all that Vietnamese scholars conceived to be important in human knowledge. Although they overemphasized learning by rote much impractical or even invalid knowledge, the examinations did test insight and reasoning power. Having passed the examination and obtained an office, a mandarin ordinarily rose through the ranks on the basis of proven ability.

The mandarinate enjoyed the highest status, and there was no true hereditary nobility. The five grades of semihereditary titles granted to the royal family and to persons who performed outstanding services gave social prerogatives and certain tax exemptions but no official position. Since succeeding generations received the next lower title, descendants of the highest nobility passed into the commonality. From the emperor to the poorest peasant, status was clearly defined by sumptuary laws fixing living standards for all levels—the kind of housing, conveyances, attire, and property each could have according to station or rank.

The Nguyen maintained their armed forces through conscription, with provinces considered the most loyal furnishing the most recruits. The 16,000-man navy guarded the coast with war junks, galleys, and a few locally constructed European-type vessels. Both army and navy suffered from nonexistent paper recruits, for whom corrupt officers collected pay. Graft also reduced the quality of arms and munitions. When the French invaded, the Vietnamese forces were undermanned, inadequately trained, poorly equipped, and badly led.

At the base of the government was and still is the village, which

---

[2] See Do Xuan Sang, *Les juridictions mandarinales* (Paris, 1938).

in Vietnam tends to be a cluster of hamlets, each of which is by American standards a village.[3] An economic, social, political and religious unit, the village became an almost autonomous state, collectively responsible for the behavior and well-being of its members. Without his village, the Vietnamese was rootless, unstable and, in Vietnamese eyes, immoral. The village was dominated by a council of notables, elected according to local customs from among the oligarchy of the more prosperous and prestigious residents. The notables enforced local law, kept the tax registers, assessed taxes, and designated army and forced labor recruits. They also assigned the rental of the common lands held to support village communal activities and supervised the maintenance of the dikes and canals vital to the wet-rice culture. These powers were often abused by notables who favored family interests and manipulated tax and land registers for personal gain, victimizing the poor peasant.

Religion was woven into all Vietnamese institutions. The *dinh,* which housed the altar to the protecting deity of the village, also served as a social and administrative center. The deity provided a religious bond for the village, as the ancestors did for the family. So important were these deities that Nguyen officials in Hue reviewed their claims, promoting, demoting, or replacing as merited. The *dinh* and the common lands set aside for its maintenance were attended by notables who served as priests of the village tutelary cult.

While most villages engaged in agriculture or fishing, some specialized in handcrafts. One might shape pottery while another painted or glazed it. Still others wove baskets or silk, or made fans or parasols. Within the villages, the peasants or craftsmen might belong to one or more of a variety of associations. Some provided mutual assistance for funerals, house-building, or other special occasions; others were professional or social. Each had its protecting spirit and so had elements of a cult. These interlocking groups helped maintain the conservatism of the village, providing for nearly all needs, but made integration of newcomers difficult.

The basic building block of Vietnamese society was the family.[4] A man owed allegiance first to his family, then to his village, and finally to the nation. The village was a collection of families, the nation a

---

[3] Two outstanding early works on the Vietnamese village are P. Ory, *Commune annamite au Tonkin* (Paris, 1894) and Éliacin Luro, *Le pays d'Annam; étude sur l'organisation politique et sociale des annamites* (Paris, 1897).

[4] See Tran Van Trai, *La famille patriarcale annamite* (Paris, 1942).

collection of villages of the Bach Viet, the legendary hundred Viet families. The individual without a family was a virtual outcast. Exile from one's village was a terrible punishment, but banishment from the family consigned one's soul to wander homeless and unattended through eternity. The Vietnamese family, like the Chinese, has been compared to a tree, the father the trunk, living descendants the branches, and the ancestors the roots. A wife is a branch grafted onto the husband's tree. In theory all with the same name shared a common ancient ancestor, but conquered Chams and others were required to adopt standard Vietnamese names. The administrator, judge, and high priest of the extended family was the oldest male of the direct line. He was legally and morally responsible for the well-being, education, and conduct of the family, though in practice important decisions were reached in family council, and his wife was the family business manager. He could inflict serious corporal punishment even on adult male descendants, who remained his wards as long as he lived. Each family looked after its own: if one member prospered, his family shared; if one needed money, the family helped. Family loyalty cut across all other loyalties, inevitably encouraging nepotism.

Toward older relatives children owed a sacred duty of filial piety. A mother surviving her husband was a true matriarch, although legally the eldest son became family head. Children must put the welfare of their elders before their own. The older the parents, the more they were pampered. A dutiful daughter might not marry if there was no son to tend the parents, but a son had a sacred obligation to provide children to perpetuate the ancestor cult. Polygamy was common among the prosperous, partly to assure descendants, but also to display one's opulence. The first wife, however, remained the legal mother of all her husband's children. The ancestor cult was the cement binding the family.[5] The dead required devotion just as did living elders, and for most Vietnamese the cult of the dead was a religion. Ancestors' spirits had power to do good and evil and had to be propitiated, just as were the spirits of nature. They also had to be informed of all family affairs. Brides and new babies were presented to them in solemn ceremony.

All scholars from emperor to the most lowly literate notable were adherents of the cult of Confucius, which venerated the master and virtually worshipped learning in the temples to Confucius. A village

---

[5] See Léopold Cadière, *Croyances et pratiques religieuses des annamites* (Hanoi, 1944).

might also maintain shrines dedicated to historical figures, famous mountains or rivers, or deities concerned with agriculture, fishing, or local crafts. Most Vietnamese, particularly the women, made occasional offerings and prayed in the Mahayana Buddhist pagodas, where they found an emotional satisfaction lacking in Confucianism. Serving the popular needs were also various necromancers and spirit specialists, some of whom practiced as Taoist priests. At this level, religion merged imperceptibly with the animism or spirit worship that permeated the whole society. Because of the Nguyen hostility to Buddhism and Taoism, there was little organized training of monks or priests, who therefore tended to be both uninformed and steeped in the popular superstitions.

Vietnamese Christians retained and adapted many parts of their earlier beliefs with relatively little intellectual wrench. Ancestors were honored and prayed for. Christian saints replaced household and village protecting genii, while Christ supplanted Confucius or Buddha. Names and images changed more readily than basic attitudes. One important difference, however, was the Christians' intolerance of other faiths and deities. By denying the worship of state gods, Christians struck at the roots of the state and were therefore persecuted for treason as well as heresy.

Justice in old Vietnam was communal in outlook and was intertwined with religious life.[6] The end of the law was moral, to teach man the path of righteousness, but the protection of public interests and the peace of society were also considerations. Though punishments were severe, their aim was to correct and rehabilitate. Having paid his penalty, the culprit received moral and legal absolution, for the mandarin as delegate of the son of heaven was priest as well as judge, legislator, and administrator. Any man could seek justice by beating a drum outside the mandarin's door, but this step was not taken lightly. In every case someone had to be found guilty and punished. There were no lawyers: no intermediaries could stand between the litigants and the judge. Justice was supposed to be free, but laws forbidding gifts to magistrates were commonly ignored. Custom regulated the size of gifts, and "corrupt" magistrates were those demanding more. However, reports by visiting Europeans tell of the rapacity of officials who bankrupted both sides in a case before rendering a decision. In practice, most disputes were settled by arbitration within the village,

---

[6] See Tran Van Chong, *Essai sur l'esprit du droit sino-annamite* (Paris, 1922).

with the notables offering resolutions based on custom and equity. Under a series of scholar-rulers, learning and literature should have flourished, but as in contemporary China the emphasis was upon a backward-looking Confucianism that rejected new ideas and new literary forms. While there were some scholars in most villages and about 20,000 schools throughout the country, the difficulty of learning the alien and cumbersome Chinese ideograms required in state examinations made real literacy and advanced learning a fairly closely held monopoly. Several valuable historical compilations were produced in Chinese, but in general the literature in Chinese was sterile, alien in language and spirit to most Vietnamese. The most creative literary works were in *chu nom*, in which scholars could escape the confining intellectual bounds of Confucianism, to enter the realm of emotions and metaphysics. Most influential was Nguyen Du's romantic narrative poem *Kim Van Kieu*, which still arouses deep emotions in old and young in Vietnam.

The downgrading of Buddhism and Taoism by the Nguyen had a dampening influence on the arts. While some scholars dabbled in painting, serious work was limited. Such traditional crafts as embroidery, lacquerware, mother-of-pear inlay, wood carving, and casting of ritual ware were maintained at a high but not spectacular level.

Such was Vietnam on the eve of the French conquest, a country steeped in a Confucian tradition, which it refused to adjust to modern ideas and technology at a time when European nations were building Asian empires.

Piecemeal Conquest by France

France has for centuries been divided on the subject of colonialism, uncertain whether French destinies lie purely on the European continent or in overseas expansion.[7] This indecision characterized official French behavior toward Indochina, and the final conquest resulted more from individual French initiative in the field than from calculated national policy.

When Bishop de Behaine visited Paris on behalf of Nguyen Anh,

[7] John Cady, *The Roots of French Imperialism in Eastern Asia* (Ithaca, N. Y., 1954) makes good use of French archival sources on the development of French policies. For a Vietnamese view of the French conquest and the struggle of early nationalist leaders, see Nguyen Phut Tan, *op. cit.*

anti-colonial sentiments prevailed inasmuch as eighteenth-century wars had reduced French overseas holdings. Napoleon's defeat cost most of the remaining. Under the restored Bourbon government, however, many nobles and former colonials sought to recoup revolutionary losses by new colonial exploits. Coincidentally, missionary interests supported by the French clergy revived the Paris Society of Foreign Missions. Bordeaux shippers were encouraged to explore trade possibilities in East Asia, particularly Cochinchina. A first visit in 1817 was well received, thanks to the efforts of Chaigneau and Vannier, former companions of de Behaine who still served Gia Long in Hue. Two years later Bordeaux ships profitably exchanged their cargo of silver and sugar for Vietnamese goods, although meanwhile Gia Long had rejected French diplomatic overtures.

Serious tensions developed between Vietnam and France under Minh Mang, who was determined to prevent the spread of Western influence and especially of Christianity while French missionaries were equally resolved to expand their activities. When Chaigneau was named French consul, Minh Mang refused to recognize his diplomatic mission. After a French merchant vessel smuggled in a Catholic missionary, Minh Mang ordered closer surveillance of foreign ships. The involvement of native Catholics and foreign missionaries in Khoi's revolt revived active persecution. Between 1833 and 1840, ten foreign missionaries were killed and thousands of Vietnamese Catholics were executed or exiled, but missionaries still clandestinely entered Vietnam. In 1840, Minh Mang sent an embassy to Paris to protest what he considered French efforts to inspire his subjects to treason. Influenced by the Pope and by the Paris Society of Foreign Missions, the French court refused even to receive the Viet envoys.

Under Thieu Tri, relations with France worsened, largely because of missionary violation of Vietnamese prohibitions. While he executed no missionaries, Thieu Tri jailed all he could seize. With the Church pressing the French government to intervene, warships twice threatened force to secure the release of imprisoned missionaries. Some of those rescued returned secretly to Vietnam, still further straining relations. After France extracted commercial privileges and freedom to preach Christianity in China following the British victory in the first Opium War, two French warships entered Tourane harbor (Danang) in 1847 to negotiate similar advantages in Vietnam. A clash ensued in which the French destroyed a Viet fleet. In retaliation, Tu Duc, who ascended the throne a few months later, ordered execution of all foreign missionaries, the exiling of Vietnamese Catholic leaders, and prohibition of trade with Westerners.

Tu Duc's harsh policy toward his approximately 400,000 Christian subjects was the single most important factor in Vietnam's loss of independence. To pro-colonial Frenchmen, it provided moral justification for their encroachments. France's preoccupation with the revolution of 1848 only delayed the reckoning. When Napoleon III became emperor, French interest in Asia was revived, stimulated in part by concern over Britain's second annexation in Burma in 1852 and her subsequent conclusion of a commercial treaty with Siam. In France, aggressive commercial and missionary groups pressed for action before the opportunity was lost. At Napoleon's court, Empress Eugenie's missionary sympathies made her a useful ally.

In 1856, France engaged in a general diplomatic offensive in Southeast Asia, and also joined with the British in the short "Arrow War" against China. A treaty was concluded with Siam, but diplomatic efforts at Tourane ended with the French commander destroying the port's fortifications. The infuriated Vietnamese rejected a second French envoy and accelerated persecution of Christians. Missionary interests in Paris increased their agitation for protection, at the same time stressing the great profits to be gained by opening Vietnam to trade. Missionaries in Vietnam sent military intelligence, and some promised that French forces would be welcomed as liberators by the Vietnamese Catholics.

Despite strong opposition on both moral and military grounds, Napoleon decided upon invasion. The execution of a Spanish missionary brought Spain's participation, giving the invasion the appearance of an international crusade. When Napoleon ordered the expedition on Tourane in 1857, his goals were limited and vague. There appears to have been no expectation of large territorial annexations, but rather of the establishment of a base for trade and for favorable negotiations to protect the missionaries. The expedition, however, set in motion a series of actions that ended only with the capitulation of all Vietnam, Laos, and Cambodia.

The conquest of Vietnam required about 26 years and was punctuated by five campaigns and five treaties, while Paris wavered between expansionist and anticolonialist stances. The first campaign had unexpected results. When Tourane, attacked in 1858, failed to fall easily, the mixed French and Spanish force turned southward. Despite stiff resistance, France annexed three provinces around Saigon. Recognizing that France was concerned with more than missionaries, the Spanish withdrew. Tu Duc stubbornly fought on until the need for troops to quell Le Phung's revolt forced him in June 1862 to sign a humiliating treaty with France. In addition to losing the three French-occupied provinces and Poulo Condore, Tu Duc paid a heavy indemnity, promised freedom for Catholic missionary activity, opened trade to France and Spain in Tourane and other ports, agreed not to cede territory to any other foreign power, and relinquished to France his suzerainty claims over Cambodia. Tu Duc's subsequent diplomatic efforts for retrocession of the lost provinces almost succeeded because of a swing of French sympathies against overseas expansion, but pro-imperialist forces in Paris prevailed. France not only rejected retrocession but, in 1867, annexed three adjoining provinces because they were bases for guerrilla bands harassing the French in the conquered areas.

French intervention in the north followed explorations by a naval lieutenant, Francis Garnier, who discovered that while the Mekong River was not navigable into China, the Red River through Tonkin was. Garnier strongly advocated that France gain control of this route, and the local situation seemed propitious. Black Flag and Yellow Flag bandits ravaged the Tonkin countryside, and a Muslim rebellion occupied the authorities in south China. Partly through Garnier's machinations, a French merchant, Jean Dupuis, contracted with the Chinese governor of Yunnan to deliver arms and munitions up the Red River. Outraged by Dupuis' brazen disregard of their protests, the Vietnamese appealed to the French in Saigon. Lt. Garnier who answered this call joined forces with Dupuis. While Garnier's instructions were vague, he considered it his mission to establish a French protectorate over Tonkin, though without calling on Paris for support. When negotiations broke down, Garnier seized Hanoi with a force of only 300 men, many of them Chinese mercenaries. He quickly overran the major delta cities, enlarging his force by recruiting native Christians. When the shocked Vietnamese called on China for aid, a contingent of the Black Flags, who were sometimes employed by the government, moved into Tonkin. There they ambushed and killed Garnier in December, 1873.

Philastre, who succeeded Garnier, concluded a new treaty in March 1874. Tu Duc now recognized the loss of all lower Cochinchina, opened Hanoi, Haiphong, and Qui Nhon to trade, gave French citizens extensive privileges, and effectively accepted a French protectorate over Vietnam. Though both powers ratified the treaty, neither was satisfied. As the French evacuated conquered areas, Vietnamese officials launched bloody reprisals against the Christians who had aided them, refused to accept a French resident at Hue, and covertly encouraged the Black Flags to attack the foreigners. Meanwhile, French colonial aspirations were fed by the discovery of coal and minerals in Tonkin and by rumors that Germany and Great Britain might gain concessions from Tu Duc. Moreover, as Vietnam's traditional suzerain, China challenged France by sending forces into Tonkin.

In 1881, the French government authorized action. Though the governor of Cochinchina instructed him to enforce the 1874 treaty by peaceful means, Navy Commander Henri Rivière repeated the exploits of Garnier by seizing Hanoi and even being ambushed and killed at the same spot. This time French forces remained in Tonkin, Tourane was taken, and the Vietnamese were forced to sign another treaty making many additional concessions. But the Vietnamese had not truly capitulated even though the old Emperor Tu Duc had died just before the armistice. However, the Chinese forces sent to their aid failed to provide much protection. After the French carried the undeclared war into China, the humbled Chinese signed a treaty in June 1884, agreeing to withdraw from Tonkin, accept the Franco-Vietnamese treaty, and abandon their ancient suzerainty claims over Vietnam. The following month a second treaty of Hue tightened the French protectorate over Vietnam.

Thus, by a series of military actions and treaties, France gradually annexed Cochinchina, gained administrative control over Tonkin and Annam, acquired Vietnamese suzerainty claims over Cambodia and Laos, and severed Vietnam's tributary status to China. Christians gained religious freedom, Vietnam was opened to French commerce, and Frenchmen received extraterritoriality. In return, France guaranteed Vietnam's internal and external security and promised to assist her modernization and provide military and naval guidance and weapons.

French Colonial Rule and Its Impact

Just as France had no master plan for creating an Asian empire, so she lacked a blueprint for ruling one.[8] The pendulum swung between direct and indirect rule. Those advocating the direct approach assumed the conquered region could become one with the home country and

[8] The material on French colonial rule is drawn from the author's doctoral dissertation (The American University), *A History of Viet-Nam from the French Penetration to 1939* (University Microfilms, Ann Arbor, Michigan, 1956). Also see Stephen Roberts, *History of French Colonial Policy 1870-1925*, 2 vols. (London, 1929).

its culture. Those favoring indirect rule believed the Indochinese were too different in culture and tradition to be assimilated and therefore France should rule indirectly in "association" with the native governing class. Had the latter policy prevailed, France might have led Vietnam into the twentieth century better equipped to deal with its pressures and problems.

Because of persistent Vietnamese resistance in Cochinchina, direct rule and assimilation early became fixed, though there were intermittent efforts to bring Vietnamese into the government. Assuming the peasants hated the mandarins as the missionaries had claimed, Admiral Charner, the first of a series of admirals to govern Cochinchina, ordered his officers to erase all trace of the former administrators. The mandarins had not waited to be eliminated but had destroyed official records and tax rolls and fled almost to a man. The French therefore found government virtually nonexistent above the village level.

The Vietnamese people, moreover, were not grateful to their "liberators," nor did most spring to the defense of Christianity. Rather they cooperated with the refugee officials who returned clandestinely with secret encouragement from Hue to collect taxes and organize guerrilla warfare. Military colonists and discharged soldiers formed partisan bands which took reprisals against collaborating Catholics and plagued the French for years, long after resistance was hopeless.

In 1879, Cochinchina was transferred to the Ministry of Colonies. As a colony it sent a delegate to the French National Assembly and elected its own local assembly, the Colonial Council. Both, however, were chosen by only about 2000 French citizens, who were mainly government employees. A few Vietnamese earned French citizenship by complete subservience, but the mass of the people remained disfranchised subjects. To accelerate assimilation, the French established schools and colleges for the few Vietnamese who won their trust. By encouraging the use of *quoc ngu* script to replace Chinese and *chu nom*, literacy was made easier but its use cut off the young from their heritage of traditional Vietnamese literature that was not translated into the Roman script.

There was more vacillation of administrative approach in Tonkin and Annam, though the framework was established by 1900. In 1887, Cochinchina, Annam, Tonkin, and Cambodia (Laos and the French leasehold of Kwangchow in China were added later) were placed as separate units under a governor general with headquarters in Tonkin, which he directly administered. Tonkin became a separate protectorate, cut off from even the nominal jurisdiction of the emperor in Hue. In Annam, the emperor maintained the forms of rule without the substance. A French superior resident, assisted by a council and a French-dominated bureaucracy, ran the government. Native Consultative Assemblies were created but without legislative powers. Each protectorate was divided into residencies or provinces, headed by French residents aided by provincial councils. The governor general exercized nearly dictatorial powers and was assisted by a secretary general, a Council of Government, and a large bureaucracy. The capital migrated semiannually between Hanoi and Saigon, though few of the politically appointed, short-term governor generals proved strong enough to subordinate the willful and entrenched bureaucracy of the "assimilated" colony of Cochinchina.

The French penetrated even into the traditionally autonomous village. By attempting to strengthen the elective principle in the council of notables, they caused the influential oligarchy to withdraw. The new councils, forced to levy ever heavier taxes and fill the large quotas set for the government monopolies, became discredited tools of the French. Subsequent efforts to restore the old system met with suspicions.

The basic outlines of French administration were established by Paul Doumer, who became governor general in 1897. He reversed the "associationist" policy of Governor General Jean de Lanessan (1891-94) who tried to revive the emperor's authority and to develop Western-trained mandarins responsible to the people. Doumer's centralized system proved so stifling to native authority and local initiative that some relaxation followed. Albert Sarraut, twice governor general (1911-14 and 1917-19) and later minister of colonies, again fostered "association." He pruned the bloated bureaucracy of Frenchmen, named more Vietnamese officials, expanded the schools, and increased Vietnamese participation in the Cochinchinese Council. In 1928, the Council of Government was paralleled by a more representative Great Council of Economic and Financial Interests, which included Indochinese members after 1931.

Any assessment of the economic results of French rule is difficult. We cannot know what might have happened to a colony had it ruled itself. The experience of neighboring Thailand, however, suggests that Vietnam might have developed more rapidly without foreign domination but with foreign cooperation and assistance. After discovering that Vietnam could not provide a lucrative trade route into China, the French determined to exploit Indochina for itself. To this end, Doumer and his successors undertook large public works and development programs. Their accomplishments make impressive statistics—1800 miles of railway, 12,000 miles of paved roads, 6000 miles of telephone and 12,000 miles of telegraph lines. Vietnamese claimed the improvements chiefly benefited the French, while the Vietnamese paid for them. Withal, much of the internal traffic still moved on the vast network of navigable waterways. No railroad and only two unpaved highways reached Laos. On a unit-area basis, Indochina had only one-fourth the railroad mileage of British India. While cultivated areas in Cochinchina quadrupled by 1937 with a comparable expansion in foodstuffs, kapok, and cotton, large landholdings by a few companies and individuals increased to the detriment of the peasant. Rubber plantations, which the French developed at a terrible cost in human life, often occupied the land of upland tribal peoples in violation of their traditional rights.

The improvements were paid for by oppressive taxation and ruthless exploitation of the former royal monopolies on salt, opium, and alcohol. In only three years under Doumer, salt monopoly revenues spiraled 3000 per cent. This hurt not only fishermen but all Vietnamese who used salt as a preservative, especially for their fish sauce, *nuoc mam*. When the villagers resisted or evaded the taxes, the French imposed consumption quotas of salt and alcohol. By 1942, the monopolies provided 16.8 per cent of government revenues, with more than half derived from the sale of opium, reflecting a growing addiction throughout the country.

Many Frenchmen stressed France's "civilizing mission," and cited such scientific and cultural innovations as the Pasteur Institute and the French School of the Far East as evidence of success. Vietnamese, however, criticized these efforts as too little and too French. Scholarly research was all in French, and French-operated schools ignored Vietnamese history and culture. In 1939, only 15 per cent of Vietnam's school-aged children were receiving any schooling, and about 80 per cent of the population was illiterate. Many provinces had no secondary school and one university with 631 students served a country of 20 million people. The main purpose of education was to provide interpreters, clerks, and petty bureaucrats for French businesses and government.

The French introduced modern medical facilities on a modest scale. In 1939, however, there were only two Western-type doctors for each 100,000 inhabitants, as compared to 25 in the Philippines and 76 in

Japan. Most people still patronized traditional herb doctors. Mortality rates were 24 per thousand, as compared to 21 in India and 19 in the Philippines.

Most influenced by French culture were the urban elite, but discontent grew among them as the French left few responsible posts for Vietnamese. The villagers, constituting 85 per cent of the population, remained relatively unaffected. The peasant toiled in the paddy fields as he had a century before. He wore the same somber clothes, lived in the same hut, and ate the same foods, though a little less of them. French laws loosened the legal hold of the village and the family, but these remained the basic institutions. The state cult to heaven and the imperial majesty became hollow shells, although the tie to the family elders and the ancestor cult continued strong. The council of notables survived in weakened form. The *dinh* was still the focal point of village life, which continued to be linked together by a network of associations and mutual aid societies. For the multitudes who rarely saw a Frenchman, the spirit world of the immediate present was more real than distant France.

Very real, however, were the miserable conditions of both urban and rural labor. Actual wages declined between 1912 and 1923 and dropped sharply during the depression. The mines and the rubber plantations particularly exploited their workers. Having been enticed by promises of high wages, the laborer, if he survived the years of hard work, poor food and inadequate medical care, sometimes found he lacked even the fare home.

Despite the inadequacies and inequities of the government and society, Vietnam in 1939 was for France more prosperous than it had been since the 1920s. It was a profitable colony with large exports of raw materials. Colonial officials liked to view it as an ideal colony, ignoring or underestimating the simmering political unrest.

Resistance Movements and Nationalism

The French conquest aroused an intense awareness of national identity among Vietnamese intellectuals.[9] This produced a variety of nationalist activities to which the French replied with sharp punitive measures, executing and imprisoning thousands of Vietnamese during the ninety odd years of their rule. By wrecking generation after genera-

[9] Nguyen Phut Tan, *op. cit.*, contains excellent material on the major nationalist leaders and on several minor resistance movements. Also see Ellen J. Hammer, *The Struggle for Indochina* (Stanford, 1954).

tion of potential leaders with their thorough repressions, they contributed considerably to Vietnam's present political problems.

The initial reaction to French encroachments produced efforts to forcibly eject the foreigners and restore the imperial power with its traditional bureaucracy. Nationalist horizons broadened with Japan's victory over Russia (1904-5) and the Chinese revolution (1911), which stimulated a consciousness of Asian potential and provided new sanctuaries and training grounds for Vietnamese nationalists. A recognition of the failure of conservative Confucianism led many to work for independence through dissemination of Western learning and techniques. Of these, some believed that foreign aid would be necessary to oust the French. More moderate reformers hoped to regain national sovereignty through collaboration with France and reform of Vietnamese institutions. As disillusionment with collaboration grew, revolutionary and Communist groups gained strength. Paralleling and allied to the various movements was a religious revival with nationalistic implications.

The initial stubborn resistance in Cochinchina set the pattern for the Monarchist Movement or Scholars' Revolt by mandarins who refused to accept the protectorate treaties. Their leader, Ton That Tuyet, who had established the "Scholars' Party" in 1874 during the first French invasion of Tonkin, dominated the regency in Hue following Tu Duc's death. This group "removed" three emperors in 1883 and 1884, two meeting death after the signing of the new degrading treaties. Though the French had themselves invested Ham Nghi, Tu Duc's fourth successor, the young monarch was immediately involved in a plan to massacre not only the French but also their Vietnamese Christian allies. The attack on the French miscarried, but some 20,000 Christians in dozens of villages perished in the first months of the Scholars' Revolt. The royal family escaped to the mountains where Ham Nghi and his followers continued guerrilla warfare until he was betrayed and exiled, while Tuyet sought aid in China. The French meanwhile had enthroned the more cooperative Dong Khanh, who worked with them against the rebels. The Scholars' new leader, Phan Dinh Phung, aided by General Cao Thang, organized a brilliant but futile campaign. The French steadily increased their strength by recruiting Vietnamese or tribal auxilliaries, pitting Vietnamese against Vietnamese in the divide-and-rule tactics which they employed throughout their regime.

The death of Cao Thang in 1893 and of Phan Dinh Phung in 1896 ended the Scholars' Revolt in Annam, though intermittent armed resistance by the part-bandit forces of De Tham (Hoang Hoa Tham) occupied French forces until 1913 in Tonkin. It was to frustrate De Tham that Colonel Gallieni, one of de Lannessan's aids, instituted his "drop of oil" technique for creating pacified centers out of which peace would spread. De Tham submitted to the French in 1901, but, inspired by Japan's victory over Russia, he was involved in an abortive attack on Hanoi in 1908 that was to include mass poisoning of the French garrison there. After his reported assassination in 1913, his harassment of the French ended.

Other contemporaries pressed for modernization as the route to independence. Among these was the brilliant Phan Boi Chau who directed Vietnamese nationalism into progressive channels. He learned from his experience as Phan Dinh Phung's lieutenant leading a Youth Resistance Movement, that successful revolution required modern weapons and organization, and, if possible, foreign aid, for which he looked particularly to Japan. To train future leaders Chau arranged for young Vietnamese to study in Japanese universities and, later, at the Whampoa Political and Military Academy in Canton. Deeply impressed by both the Japanese and the Chinese, Chau contacted leading political figures in both countries. In 1906 in Japan, he founded the Vietnam Modernization Association (*Viet Nam Duy Tan Hoi*) advocating independence under a constitutional monarchy headed by Prince Cong De, a descendant of Gia Long. Subsequently Chau joined with other Asian revolutionaries in a League of Asian Peoples, more generally known as the *Dong Du* or Pan Asian Movement.

After conversion to republicanism by the Chinese, in 1912 Chau formed the Vietnam Restoration Association (*Viet Nam Phuc Quoc Hoi*) after the example of Sun Yat-sen's Kuomintang. While the Phuc Quoc was too conservative to attract broad support, it trained militant revolutionaries within Vietnam, proclaimed a government in exile, and participated in several Vietnamese uprisings between 1913 and 1940, including Emperor Duy Tan's futile effort during World War I to repeat Ham Nghi's exploit. Phan Boi Chau's revolutionary activities were ended in 1925 when he was literally sold to the French by the Communist leader Nguyen Ai Quoc (Ho Chi Minh).[10] Though Phan

[10] According to Hoang Van Chi, *From Colonialism to Communism* (New York, 1964), pp. 33-4, Ho gave as his reason for this treachery that Phan was too old to be of further use to the revolution, that his arrest and trial would stimulate Vietnamese patriotism, and that the money paid by the French would

Boi Chau was sentenced to death, a wave of popular protest induced French leniency. He remained under house arrest in Hue until his death in 1940.

While Phan Boi Chau urged revolution with foreign aid, others worked for a democratic and republican Vietnam through evolutionary methods by collaborating with the French and educating young Vietnamese to Western ways. To this end in 1907, the eminent scholar Phan Chu Trinh helped organize the Tonkin Free School in Hanoi, which encouraged the founding of similar schools elsewhere. Paralleling this movement was a modernist society called "Hair Cutters," after the symbolic cutting of the traditional queue. This group urged social reform and popular education. Both the school and the society were suppressed in 1908 as part of the harsh French reaction to nationalist agitation and De Tham's attempted poisoning of the Hanoi garrison. Trinh was imprisoned until 1911, when he moved to Paris. There he taught revolutionary doctrines to young Vietnamese, including the future Ho Chi Minh. Trinh returned to Saigon with the Socialist Governor General Varenne in 1925. His death the following year triggered a country-wide mourning strike which in turn incited another French repression.

The brilliant journalist Pham Quynh also urged reform under French protection. One of his disciples was Emperor Khai Dinh, who sent his son Bao Dai to France to be educated. Khai Dinh's petition for genuine implementation of the protectorate treaties only brought further French restrictions after he died in 1925. Nonetheless, in 1932, following two terrible years of revolution and bloody French reprisals, young Emperor Bao Dai returned to Vietnam, hoping that a modernized imperial government might induce the French to institute a true protectorate. He named a young liberal mandarin Ngo Dinh Diem to head a reform commission. Through French influence, Pham Quynh was appointed minister of education and cabinet director, though Bao Dai considered him too conservative. A series of reforming edicts produced few changes, as the old mandarins resorted to intrigue and slander to block them. Diem found himself frustrated by Quynh, while French and Vietnamese bureaucrats closed ranks against the reformers. After four months, Diem resigned in disgust, and Bao Dai, unable to stand alone, retired to a life of pleasure.

---

be used to further the cause of the revolution. Nguyen Phut Tan, *op. cit.*, pp. 322-25, states that Ho Chih Minh had implied falsely that Phan Boi Chau had offered to sacrifice himself. It would appear that one major objective was to eliminate Phan, whose influence was a barrier to Communist aspirations.

The French had also temporarily silenced the revolutionaries. Following Phan Boi Chau's arrest, revolutionary nationalism was dominated by the Vietnam Nationalist Party or *Viet Nam Quoc Dan Dang* (vnqdd) and the Communists. Their ranks were swelled by Vietnamese outraged by Governor General Varenne's failure to fulfill his progressive promises. Modelled after the revamped Kuomintang, the vnqdd was moderately Socialist, but non-Communist. By 1929, the party, led by a former teacher, Nguyen Thai Hoc, had 120 cells with 1500 members—mainly soldiers, teachers, and lower officials. An ambitious but poorly organized revolt in 1930 miscarried when a mutiny of the Vietnamese garrison at Yen Bay failed and other planned uprisings aborted. Though the French executed Nguyen Thai Hoc and many of his colleagues, a weakened vnqdd survived, thanks to Kuomintang support.

Capitalizing on this turmoil and the acute economic distress caused by successive crop failures, the Communists incited mass demonstrations, strikes, and peasant uprisings, known by the French as the "Red Terror." The brutal retaliation, called the "White Terror" by the Communists, claimed the lives of thousands, including many moderate nationalists. The Communists received a further setback when the British in Hong Kong jailed Nguyen Ai Quoc, the party's link with the Communist International.

The most successful revolutionary movement, however, proved to be that of the Communist party, organized and led by Nguyen Ai Quoc, best known by the last of his many aliases, Ho Chi Minh.[11] Though many details of Ho's life are vague, certain facts emerge. He was born of a scholar family about 1890 in Nghe An Province, which has produced many revolutionaries. Just prior to World War I, Ho toured the world as a cabin boy before settling in Paris to study revolutionary doctrines. He joined in socialist agitation for freeing the colonies and participated in the founding of the French Communist party and the Third International. After study in Moscow, Ho reappeared in Asia in 1925, ostensibly as a translator for the Russian Borodin mission, sent to advise the Kuomintang during the period when the Chinese Nationalists and Communists were cooperating. His real task, however, was to build a Southeast Asian Communist movement.

In Canton, Ho organized the Association of Vietnamese Revolu-

---

[11] I. Milton Sacks, "Marxism in Viet Nam," in *Marxism in Southeast Asia,* ed. Frank Trager (Stanford, 1959) is probably the best study in English on the rise of the Communist party in Vietnam. Also see Ellen Hammer, *op. cit.*

tionary Youth, a Communist front, generally referred to as the *Thanh Nien*, which proselyted young Vietnamese nationalists studying at the Whampoa Military Academy. Youths who rejected communism were betrayed to the French police on returning to Vietnam. Among the recruits sent for training in Moscow was Pham Van Dong, later prime minister of North Vietnam. Following Chiang Kai-shek's break with the Communists in 1927, Ho fled to Moscow and the *Thanh Nien* moved its headquarters to Hong Kong. By 1929, it claimed 1000 members with 200 working in Vietnam and had become an overt Communist organization. Although most were young professionals, intellectuals and students, largely from mandarin or landlord families, their promises of reform and independence won a following among the peasants and workers. The *Thanh Nien*, however, was refused membership in the Communist International as too bourgeois. Thereafter Ho was returned to Southeast Asia, and in 1930 helped to unite the *Thanh Nien* remnants with two rival Communist groups into what became the Indochinese Communist Party (ICP), which was admitted to the Comintern.

After the "White Terror" repressions, links between the ICP and Moscow were tenuous until 1932 when Moscow-trained Tran Van Giau returned to Cochinchina to rebuild the party and re-establish contacts with leaders in China. In Saigon, Giau and his followers cooperated with a rival Trotskyite Marxist group to win election of some of its members to the Saigon Council in 1932 and 1937. In 1935, in response to the Comintern's new line of "popular fronts" against Fascism, the ICP joined with liberal groups in the Indochinese Democratic Front led by Pham Van Dong and Vo Nguyen Giap. A similar coalition, the Popular Front, won the 1935 elections in France.

This victory and the appointment of a Socialist minister of colonies aroused hope among Vietnamese nationalist leaders until it became apparent that neither the Socialists nor the Communists in Paris intended to free the colonies. Fearful of alienating French public opinion, the Soviets even discouraged the Vietnamese from advocating independence. This posture reduced the ICP's popularity, while the Trotskyites, by pressing for independence, grew stronger until they won 80 per cent of the vote in the 1939 elections for the Saigon Council.

The Trotskyite victory was short-lived. With the signing of the Stalin-Hitler pact and the outbreak of war in Europe, the Comintern reverted to an anti-war, anti-imperialist line aimed to sabotage French war efforts. In November, the ICP conformed to the new line by calling for the formation of a United Front of Anti-Imperialist Indochinese People to overthrow French colonialists and "native feudalists." With the help of the USSR, the front was to fight for independence and the creation of a democratic republic of Indochina. This line caused the French to ban all Communist parties. The wave of arrests that followed in Indochina caught most of the Trotskyite leaders. Many ICP members were arrested, but the top figures escaped to China to direct the ICP from abroad. Having built a solid underground with 3000 members in Cochinchina alone, the ICP could carry on despite weakened communications between cells in Vietnam and the central committee in China.

Some Vietnamese found a nationalist outlet in religion. Though under the restrictive laws of the Nguyen Buddhism had declined in strength and prestige, Buddhists loyally supported the early resistance to French encroachment. Subsequently as the French tendency to favor Catholics alienated and isolated the pagodas, Buddhists continued their moral support to nationalist movements. Many non-political nationalists found Buddhism a safe expression of Vietnamese cultural values. During the 1920s and 1930s, as part of a general Asian Buddhist resurgence, study associations grew throughout Vietnam to foster Buddhism, publish Buddhist literature, and spread literacy in *quoc ngu* among the common people.

The same intellectual and cultural ferment led other Vietnamese to religious experimentation. After 1919, Nguyen Van Chieu attracted a following with his eclectic cult called *Cao Dai,* his term for the universal god. *Cao Dai* borrowed from religions of both East and West and modelled its organization after the Church of Rome. In the mid-twenties, Le Van Trung, a Saigon merchant, assumed leadership. Converts so multiplied that by 1939 the sect claimed one million faithful, although a schism had divided their ranks. Pham Cong, who became Pope in 1934, secretly cooperated with pro-Japanese nationalists. Later to emerge was the Hoa Hao cult, founded by Huyn Phu So as a reform of Buddhism. Within a year after its initiation in 1939, So's reputed miraculous cures swelled his following to 100,000. Hoa Hao eliminated elaborate and costly rites and funerals, approving only simple prayers and offerings to Buddha, one's ancestors, and national heroes. Hoa Hao rapidly became an important force in Cochinchina and early evidenced nationalist overtones.

French Eclipse Under Japan

In World War II, the Vietnamese were confronted with another alien force, the expanding power of Japan. The net effect, apart from the economic drain, was a strengthening of Vietnamese nationalism as a result of rival French and Japanese efforts to win Vietnamese support. Many nationalists who had looked to Japan for guidance and aid welcomed the new force, despite its recent history of conquest in China and announced intent to create a New Order in Eastern Asia.

Japanese control of the major cities of China and much of its coast left only Burma and Tonkin as supply routes for American and other aid to reach the Kuomintang government in Chungking. After the fall of France in 1940, Japan forced the closing of the Tonkin-Chinese border. Barely had the Pétain government sent Admiral Decoux to replace the pro-Allied General Catroux than Japan demanded transit rights and air fields. A compromise opened Indochina to Japanese trade and planes but confirmed French sovereignty. Before this agreement could be publicized, a premature Japanese invasion from South China set off a rebellion by the pro-Japanese *Phuc Quoc*. However, the expected Japanese aid failed to arrive and the rebels were soon defeated. The French ordered mass executions of those who did not escape to China. Sympathetic uprisings of various elements under Communist leadership in Annam and Cochinchina in late 1940 brought an equally severe French reaction, further damaging the Communist network.

During 1941, Japan tightened her grip over Indochina. She rewarded Thailand's cooperation by forcing France to cede to the Thai disputed Lao and Cambodian provinces. The French were compelled to accept Japanese "partnership" in the defense of Indochina. Japanese troops landed in Vietnam in mid-1941, and a November agreement placed Indochina's economy at Japan's disposal. President Roosevelt was attempting negotiations for Indochina's neutralization when Japan attacked Pearl Harbor and the Philippines on December 7.

Since France cooperated with Japan, French civil administration was continued with relatively few Japanese occupation forces, while the Indochinese economy was heavily tapped. The Vietnamese exchanged rice, rubber, and other raw materials for yen which were useless since few Japanese goods were available for purchase. French rule became more authoritarian under Fascist influence. Numerous publications were banned. Prisons were filled not only with Vietnamese nationalists and Communists but also with French liberals and Jews. Paradoxically, however, Vietnamese nationalism was stimulated by French competition with Japan's Greater East Asia propaganda. Decoux doubled Vietnamese participation in the lower and middle government ranks, equalized pay, made vague promises of future autonomy, created 5000 new rural schools and doubled school enrollments. A youth movement (headed by a covert Communist) taught initiative and discipline and instilled a new patriotism. Cut off from foreign trade, Vietnamese had to learn techniques and develop industries hitherto discouraged by France.

Even while they permitted the French to continue their colonial rule, the Japanese worked to undermine it. A virtual underground war developed between the French secret police (sûreté) and their Japanese counterparts of the kempeitai. Although nominally acting as security police, the kempeitai actively assisted pro-Japanese nationalists whom the sûreté tried to suppress. They released Cao Dai and Hoa Hao leaders whom the French had imprisoned and aided them to reorganize their sects. Similar aid went to the Phuc Quoc, whose pro-Japanese leader Prince Cong De aspired to Bao Dai's throne. Pro-Japanese nationalist groups such as the Dai Viet Quoc Dan Hoi or Dai Viet (National Party of Greater Viet Nam) were organized in Tonkin. By these maneuvers, the Japanese cultivated groups that might oust the French should Japan be defeated or could staff a government under Japanese tutelage after their victory.

While the Pétain government promised not to hinder the Japanese war effort, many Frenchmen in Indochina secretly collaborated with the Allies and some, including General Catroux, escaped to join the de Gaullist forces. After France was freed, de Gaulle sent General Mordant to head the resistance movement in Indochina. Leaders and military supplies were parachuted during 1944-45 and French units trained secretly. The Japanese, though aware of these activities, did not move until March, 1945, when an Allied landing seemed likely. Overnight they rounded up and interned the entire French civil and military organization.

On Japanese advice, Bao Dai proclaimed independence for Annam and Tonkin. He earnestly tried to organize an effective government. After Ngo Dinh Diem refused the premiership, a moderate nationalist leader Tran Trong Kim organized a cabinet that won the support of many moderate and right-wing nationalist groups, including the Phuc Quoc and Dai Viet. Strong reform measures were promulgated. But

Bao Dai soon learned he had merely changed masters. Cochinchina remained under direct Japanese rule and Japanese "advisers" dominated the administration of Tonkin and Annam. Not until too late did the Japanese accede to Tran Trong Kim's urgent pleas to return Cochinchina and give real powers to the Vietnamese. Most damaging to Bao Dai's government, however, was the Japanese refusal to distribute their hoarded rice stores to alleviate the terrible famine in Annam and Tonkin. Political prisoners released by Japan added to the confusion as did the new Communist front, the Viet Minh. Few Vietnamese understood the need for patient work, skill, and cooperation in running the government. Too many miracles had been promised by revolutionary agitators. When Japan capitulated in mid-August 1945, Bao Dai's government had lost the initiative to the Viet Minh.

5: Independence and Disunity
in Vietnam

As Bao Dai lost his struggle to create an independent monarchist Vietnam, Allied forces prepared for the Japanese surrender in Indochina. The Allies agreed at Potsdam that the Chinese and British would move in north and south of the sixteenth parallel respectively. For their return, the French planned to establish an Indochinese Federation within an undefined "French Union," permitting increased native participation. But France miscalculated the strength of Vietnamese nationalism and the effectiveness of Communist strategy.

The Viet Minh and the DRV

The creation of the Democratic Republic of Vietnam (DRV) and its conquest of North Vietnam present a classic example of the takeover of a country by a small, well-organized Communist party through the techniques of the "united front" or "national liberation front," a protracted "war of liberation," and a two-stage revolution.[1] As noted in Chapter One, the united front involves a strategy of deception to secure temporary cooperation from the middle class and the landlords. These elements Lenin termed "deaf mutes" because their "bourgeois morality" prevented their comprehending the Communists' cynical use of fronts, deception, and fellow travellers in their nontraditional warfare. This warfare mingles psychological, cultural, economic, and political tactics with violence. Peaceful techniques are used when produc-

[1] For an analysis of the united front technique and its relationship to the two-stage revolution, see James D. Atkinson, *The Politics of Struggle, The Communist Front and Political Warfare* (Chicago, 1966); Robert Strausz Hupé et al., *Protracted Conflict* (New York, 1963); and Cyril E. Black and Thomas P. Thornton, eds., *Communism and Revolution: The Strategic Uses of Political Violence* (Princeton, N. J., 1964).

tive but are backed by armed propaganda, terrorism, guerrilla fighting, and conventional warfare as required for victory. Coordinated with violence are nonviolent demonstrations, propaganda, and psychological warfare on the scene of conflict and world-wide—through interconnected Communist fronts and fellow-traveller networks. By these tactics, the Communists aim to divide their opponents, whom they call the "enemy," and to turn world opinion against them by making their cause and actions appear "unjust" or "immoral."

The war strategy of the Indochinese Communist Party (ICP), developed by Vo Nguyen Giap, a former history professor and long-time Communist, was based on Mao Tse-tung's "protracted war" in three phases.[2] During the liberal-democratic revolutionary stage, the Party organizes a coalition or front of workers, peasants and "patriotic" bourgeois and landlords to fight the "feudalists" and "imperialists." In phase one, front groups are formed, secure bases are developed in isolated areas, and guerrillas and propagandists are trained and infiltrated into government-held areas. In phase two, control is extended over the rural population by propaganda, political struggle, terrorism, and sabotage of government services. Arms are secured from abroad and from raids on government posts. When a regular force is ready and the government weakened, phase three, the general offensive, is launched to seize political power. Throughout, Giap stressed, the revolutionaries must: (1) maintain "absolute moral superiority" by indoctrination and thought control, (2) create a favorable international climate by propaganda aided by Communists world-wide, and (3) maintain strong discipline and unity while promoting division among the enemy.

The ICP launched their first revolutionary stage during World War II. After the 1940 Communist uprisings in Indochina failed, Ho Chi Minh (then Nguyen Ai Quoc) was called to Moscow.[3] Returning to South China with new instructions in early 1941, Ho convened the ICP Central Committee which adopted a united front policy and formed the League for Vietnamese Independence (*Viet Nam Doc Lap*

---

[2] See Vo Nguyen Giap, *People's War, People's Army* (Hanoi, 1961) and George K. Tanham, *Communist Revolutionary Warfare: The Viet Minh in Indochina* (New York, 1961), pp. 1-32. Truong Chinh, Secretary General of the ICP, may have introduced Mao's doctrines in Vietnam. See his *The Resistance Will Win* (Hanoi, 1960), originally published in 1947.

[3] Nguyen Ai Quoc's activities from 1932 to 1941 are uncertain. Some Vietnamese believed he had died in 1933. Other reports placed him in various countries. Hoang Van Chi, who knew Ho, tells of the Moscow trip in *From Colonialism to Communism* (New York, 1964), pp. 66-67.

Dong Minh), best known as the Viet Minh front.[4] Viet Minh propagandists later called this a meeting of Vietnamese nationalists. The front's announced objective was to unite Vietnamese of all classes, groups, and nationalist parties to defeat the Japanese and French and to establish a postwar independent liberal-democratic republic. While the ICP organized and directed the Viet Minh, the Party concealed its Communist goals in order to use other nationalist groups to oust their common enemies.[5] Another unannounced objective—the securing of Nationalist Chinese aid—was achieved. The governor of Kwangsi Province, Nationalist General Chang Fa-k'uei, who had served with Ho under Borodin, subsidized the Viet Minh as a resistance movement and a source of intelligence in the enemy territory and, hopefully, as a tool for establishing a pro-Chinese republic in postwar Vietnam.

Utilizing the ICP network, the Viet Minh built a solid underground in Vietnam. Although they provided the desired intelligence, Nguyen Ai Quoc's known Communist orientation caused the Chungking government to order his imprisonment in 1942. General Chang Fa-K'uei then sponsored a convention of 700 Vietnamese revolutionaries, including VNQDD, Dai Viet, Phuoc Quoc, and other nationalist representatives, along with some Viet Minh. This congress formed the League of Vietnamese Revolutionary Parties or Dong Minh Hoi, which advocated independence with Nationalist Chinese aid. When the Dong Minh Hoi failed to provide adequate intelligence, General Chang released Nguyen Ai Quoc with the understanding that he would fill the need. To deceive Chungking, Nguyen Ai Quoc assumed a new identity as Ho Chi Minh (Ho, the Enlightened), a non-Communist nationalist. As a member of the Dong Minh Hoi's central committee, Ho used Chinese subsidies to strengthen the ICP and the Viet Minh, while the Dong Minh Hoi languished. Disturbed by the Communist gains, in March 1944, General Chang called another Vietnamese congress in which the Viet Minh were in the minority. Under VNQDD leadership, this group proclaimed a republican government-in-exile. The Viet Minh remained in the Dong Minh Hoi and Ho received a minor "government" post, but the two organizations remained deadly rivals.

Thereafter, Ho Chi Minh returned to Vietnam to direct Viet Minh ac-

---

[4] Giap, *op. cit.*, pp. 74-7. Also see I. Milton Sack's "Marxism in Viet Nam" in *Marxism in Southeast Asia,* ed. Frank Trager (Stanford, 1959).

[5] Truong Chinh explains the strategy of deception in *The August Revolution* (Hanoi, 1962), pp. 21-2 (facsimile edition, Bernard B. Fall, ed., *Primer for Revolt: The Communist Takeover in Viet-Nam* [New York, 1963]).

tivities and to frustrate Kuomintang designs for a pro-Chinese republic. In May 1944, the Party Central Committee drew up plans for a general insurrection during the confusion expected at the end of the war. They also stated the Party principle—to eliminate their enemies by playing one against the other and to exploit others while not being themselves exploited.[6] The Viet Minh then claimed over 200,000 members in Tonkin, including guerrilla and propaganda units, and had proclaimed its first "liberated zone." By 1945, Vo Nguyen Giap had trained an army of 10,000 men, many recruited among the mountain tribes by exploiting traditional ethnic antagonisms. Although surprised by the internment of the French in March 1945, the Viet Minh rapidly adjusted their plans. Mounting a large-scale guerrilla movement, they appropriated much of the north as a "liberated zone," capturing considerable Japanese military equipment. In the liberated areas, the Viet Minh replaced the traditional councils with people's revolutionary committees, which attracted popular favor by abolishing taxes and distributing Japanese and French- owned properties to the poor, although most of the taxes were later to be reintroduced and the lands distributed were to be reclaimed by the state to form collectives and communes. Throughout Vietnam, the Communists accelerated their propaganda, including "armed propaganda," i.e., armed demonstrations and psychologically-directed terrorism such as involving whole communities in the public "trial" and "execution" of local leaders. On July 1, the Viet Minh called for the overthrow of both the Japanese and Bao Dai and for the creation of a republic. Recognizing the Viet Minh could not simultaneously fight the Chinese-supported nationalists and the French, Ho adopted a temporary policy of compromise with the French. But, although he offered cooperation to the Free French in return for a promise of future independence, no French officials were willing or able to negotiate.[7]

After the first atomic bombing of Japan, the Party moved rapidly. On August 7, a Party congress activated the steps planned the previous year. The guerrilla forces were proclaimed a "liberation army," the last ties were broken with the Chinese-sponsored provisional government, and plans were announced for a democratic republic of Vietnam. On August 13, Ho called for general insurrection and asked the Japanese to surrender to the Viet Minh. The strategy aimed to estab-

---

[6] See the Party circular of August 6, 1944, quoted in Philippe Devillers, *Histoire du Viêt-Nam de 1940 à 1952* (Paris, 1952), pp. 110-11.

[7] These maneuvers are discussed in Devillers, *op. cit.*, pp. 132-35.

lish a Viet Minh-directed coalition government over all Vietnam before the Allied arrival. This required popular support and the appearance of unity among the anti-French forces. To create a united front facade, a congress of nationalists of all parties and classes was hastily convened. This congress met in a Communist-dominated "lightning" session on August 16, with only 60 of the 100 invited delegates present. Many of these knew neither the Viet Minh nor their leader Ho, who had kept himself in the background. However, the congress created a People's Liberation Committee under Ho's chairmanship. Though it had a substantial majority of Viet Minh members, its program avoided mention of Communist objectives. The Party's policy at this time was later described in *Hoc Tap*:

Our party cleverly applied its tactics. On the one hand it cleverly took advantage of the regional and temporary contradictions of the enemy to sow division among them. On the other hand it united with anyone who could be won over, neutralized anyone who could be neutralized, completely isolated the imperialists and their most dangerous lackeys and concentrated the spearhead of the attacks to overthrow them.[8]

Meanwhile, on August 14, the Viet Minh had seized public buildings and military supplies and had flown the Viet Minh flag over Hanoi. A burst of enthusiasm swept the land, steered by Viet Minh cells. Through the confusion moved Communist assassination squads, eliminating many nationalist opponents as "counter-revolutionaries" and "collaborators." Communist leader Truong Chinh later complained that this policy of "sweeping away reactionaries" was not adequately executed because the Party was sometimes "conciliatory to the point of weakness," forgetting Lenin's dictum that "a victorious power must be dictatorial."[9]

The rival Dong Minh Hoi and other nationalist groups moving into Vietnam with the Chinese occupation forces were unprepared to contest this massive bid for power. As the Chinese pushed slowly southward, Bao Dai futilely invited the Viet Minh to form a government under the crown. Seeing no alternative, on August 25 in Hue, Bao Dai abdicated in favor of the newly established provisional government and was given the title of Supreme Adviser. In effect, Bao Dai transferred

---

[8] "Let Us Step Up the Theory-Formulating Task of the Party," *Hoc Tap*, September 1966. Both Truong Chinh, *The August Revolution* and Giap, *op. cit.*, are good Communist sources on this period.

[9] Truong Chinh, *August Revolution*, pp. 39-40.

the "mandate of heaven" to the Democratic Republic of Vietnam, which Ho Chi Minh proclaimed in Hanoi on September 2.

Breakdown of Negotiations

Thereafter, the Viet Minh proceeded cautiously. A Chinese occupation army of 185,000 exerted strong influence in the north, while French forces reoccupied Cochinchina in the south. Having no desire to restore French rule, the Chinese permitted Vietnamese, including the Viet Minh, to retain weapons, while disarming Frenchmen along with the Japanese, and would not permit the French flag to fly at the Japanese surrender ceremonies. Still, the Chinese distrusted the Viet Minh because of their Communist leadership and favored rival nationalist groups that were pro-Kuomintang. While strong in organization, the Viet Minh was weak in numbers compared to competing political groups, most of which violently opposed a French return. The Trotskyites re-emerged as a strong though divided ultraradical force in both the north and south. The VNQDD had split from the Dong Minh Hoi, but both groups, with Chinese support, seized domains in the north and demanded a role in the DRV government. Other parties also had considerable collective strength.

The Communists took steps to disarm and weaken the nationalist opposition. In November 1945, they officially dissolved the Indochinese Communist Party, which functioned thereafter as a "Marxist Study Association." [10] Elections were scheduled for a national assembly and seventy "free seats" were promised the Dong Minh Hoi and VNQDD. People's Councils replaced the old bureaucracy at all levels, neutralizing the anti-Communist traditional oligarchies. Vo Nguyen Giap, as interior minister, shortened working hours, abolished unpopular taxes, and initiated a literacy program. Respect for religion was proclaimed. Something was offered to virtually all segments of the population to draw on the broadest possible support.

The assembly elected under close Viet Minh control in January 1946, represented all parties and factions, but had a safe Communist Viet Minh majority. Most of the electorate, however, had cast their ballots for independence and democracy, not for communism, which was not discussed. Though impressed by Ho's personal resounding victory in Hanoi, the Chinese pressured him into increasing Dong Minh Hoi and VNQDD representation in his government. The Dong

---

[10] Sacks, op. cit., pp. 158-9, quotes the ICP communique.

Minh Hoi head became vice-president and nationalists replaced leading Communist ministers though by reshuffling duties the Communists retained decisive power. Concurrently, they combined terror and propaganda to destroy the opposition and win popular support for Ho and the Viet Minh. Assassination squads moved against nationalist leaders, while People's Councils and courts tried the local elite on charges of collaboration, fascism, or anti-revolutionary activities. Among the victims were the founder of the Hoa Hao cult and a brother of Ngo Dinh Diem. Attacks upon Catholics led some dioceses to organize self-defense units. The nationalist parties retaliated by attacking Communists.

Meanwhile in Cochinchina, where Viet Minh influence was weakest, the French quickly reasserted control. At the war's end, the Cao Dai and Hoa Hao held nearly independent states with strong paramilitary forces. These and numerous other political groups formed a United National Front which with Japanese approval virtually ruled the south in Bao Dai's name. Led by Moscow-trained Tran Van Giau, the Viet Minh's Committee of the South (Committee of Nambo) secured United National Front support of the DRV despite their distrust of the Viet Minh's conciliatory policy toward France. This uneasy alliance collapsed with the assassination of a pro-Vietnamese French priest during the independence day celebration in Saigon on September 2, 1945. Blaming French youths, Vietnamese groups killed four more Frenchmen, injured scores, and looted hundreds of French homes and stores. When Tran Van Giau used Japanese forces as police, ordered Vietnamese to turn in their weapons, and banned inflamatory political activities, most Vietnamese felt betrayed. Suspecting the Viet Minh of plotting to reinstate French rule, the United Front refused cooperation. The countryside degenerated into chaos, with serious clashes between the Viet Minh and the rival groups. British General Gracey, who arrived with Indian troops on September 13, restored order by rearming interned French soldiers, who drove both factions from Saigon. French reinforcements under General LeClerc landed in Saigon October 5. By February, the Japanese were disarmed, the British had departed and the main delta cities were in French hands. Governing the reconquered area proved more difficult. The colonial bureaucracy, minus the top Vichy collaborators, returned to their desks, but few able Vietnamese would serve them. Many Vietnamese civil servants joined the dissidents, who controlled much of the countryside.

French penetration of the north was blocked by the Chinese and the DRV. Faced with growing DRV control, the French made major concessions to secure Chinese withdrawal. The Franco-Chinese agreement led the DRV to accept a compromise short of total independence with a view to using the French against the anti-French, anti-Communist nationalists. On March 6, France recognized Vietnam as a "free state" within an undefined Indochinese federation and French Union. Cochinchina, Annam, and Tonkin were to be reunified pending a referendum. In return, 15,000 French troops could replace the Chinese. The agreement recognized the weakness of both sides. The DRV's economic situation was desperate and their political and military positions were still insecure, while France lacked the forces to recapture the north. Each side bought time to build up forces to defeat the other. Many knotty problems remained for future negotiations.

The truce was short-lived. It satisfied few Frenchmen and Vietnamese nationalists charged Ho Chi Minh with betrayal. Paris reluctantly confirmed the compromise, but High Commissioner d'Argenlieu, a de Gaulle appointee of imperialist convictions, chose to destroy it. Playing on regional rivalries, he induced the French-dominated Saigon government to proclaim Cochinchina a "free republic," ignoring the referendum agreement. In May, he set up a separate administration for the Montagnards of central Vietnam. In such an atmosphere, negotiations at Dalat and in France for a more precise definition of Vietnamese independence proved futile. While playing divide and rule in Vietnam, the French in Paris were split over colonial policy. Ho Chi Minh, under Moscow's orders not to embarrass the French Communists in forthcoming elections, was willing to compromise.[11] But his fellow delegates returned home when France refused full independence. On September 14, Ho signed a *modus vivendi* that only postponed the reckoning.

Following the March 6 agreement, Ho had organized the Lien Viet or National Allied Front to broaden popular support, but the nationalists were not mollified. While Ho was in Paris, French troops joined the Viet Minh to crush the nationalists, whose strongholds were turned over to the Viet Minh. Many nationalist leaders were killed. Others, including the DRV vice-president and acting president, fled to China, where Bao Dai had earlier taken refuge. On Ho's return, he doubled the number of Communists in his cabinet, and further purges pro-

[11] These orders issued through the French Communist party's agents in Saigon were seen by Harold Isaacs, *No Peace in Asia* (New York, 1948), pp. 173-74.

ceeded the second session of the National Constituent Assembly on October 28, 1946. With many members dead or absent due to terrorism, the Assembly met under complete Communist control. It prepared a democratic constitution designed to attract naive nationalists and to present the Viet Minh in a favorable light abroad. An elective unicameral People's Parliament would elect a president, who would appoint a premier. A Permanent Committee, empowered to act when the legislature was not in session, provided the legal cover for Communist domination since the Parliament rarely met. Actually, the democratic provisions and rights of this constitution were ignored. No elections were held for 16 years, while the 1946 Assembly nominally continued to exist.

The French progressively encroached upon Vietnamese "independence." Finding himself a French puppet, the president of the Cochin-chinese Republic hanged himself. When France's arbitrary tax collections and seizure of customs collections in Haiphong cut off funds, the Viet Minh replied with armed resistance. With the authorization of Premier Bidault in Paris, the French bombarded the city on November 23. Estimates of the death toll, chiefly unarmed men, women and children, ranged as high as 20,000. This action rallied the remaining nationalists behind the DRV and ended hopes for peace. Tensions mounted as the French seized Tourane. While still pressing for negotiations, the DRV rounded up pro-French Vietnamese and built barricades.

Though Socialist Leon Blum, a critic of French colonialism, became premier December 16, war began three days later when a French order to disband the Viet Minh militia caused the Vietnamese to attack the French in Hanoi. When the French took Hanoi, the DRV leaders retreated into the hills. A mission sent by Blum asserted that a military decision must precede negotiations. Both sides charged the other with bad faith, both with justification, because each had used the other. The climax came when the French felt able to re-establish their authority and when the Viet Minh believed the French had become more dangerous than useful.

Two Governments and Formal Partition

While the Viet Minh initiated the December 19 attack, the French refusal to grant genuine independence precluded a workable peace and practically insured Communist control over the DRV. At the time of the March 6 agreement, the DRV leadership represented a coalition of nationalists over whom the Communists exercised a precarious control. Many observers believed the French might have swung control to non-Communist nationalists, or at least have fostered a Tito-like neutralism.[12] Instead, they helped destroy the nationalist parties and drove many nationalists into the Communist camp.

Overshadowed militarily and unable then to secure foreign assistance, the DRV appealed for a peace based on unity and independence in return for respect of French economic and cultural interests. Ho Chi Minh took measures to broaden internal and external support, naming more non-Communists to his cabinet and spreading the fiction that neither he nor the other Viet Minh leaders were Communists.[13] Only after 1951 was it admitted the Party had "continued to lead the administration and the people." The French, deluded by their quick conquest of the Tonkin delta, demanded virtually unconditional surrender. Though some early recognized that only a massive expeditionary force could completely reconquer Vietnam, by November 1947, the French high command believed they had defeated the Viet Minh. In fact, Giap had only withdrawn into the mountains and paddy fields to harass the French with guerrilla attacks.

In the spring of 1947, a "third force" of nationalists, including the VNQDD, Dong Minh Hoi, Cao Dai, and Hoa Hao, formed a coalition that aimed to create an independent government opposed to the Communist-dominated Viet Minh. While they distrusted the French, they cooperated with them to achieve their objective. As a rallying point, they looked to Bao Dai, then still in Hong Kong. In May 1948, this movement organized a provisional government reuniting Cochinchina, Annam, and Tonkin, and a year later, Bao Dai returned to head the State of Vietnam. By agreements in 1949 and 1950, France granted Vietnam, Laos, and Cambodia limited independence within the French Union. Though the independence was far from complete, it won diplomatic recognition for the new states from Great Britain, the United States, and over 30 other non-Communist nations.

[12] This thesis is developed by Robert Shaplen, *The Lost Revolution* (New York, revised 1966). However, the writings of such Communist leaders as Truong Chinh and Vo Nguyen Giap make this appear highly improbable.

[13] Although during this period Ho usually denied his identity as Nguyen Ai Quoc, he was so identified by several people, among them Harold Isaacs who had known him in 1930-31; see "Indochina: The Fight for Freedom," *New Republic*, February 3, 1947, p. 16.

Bao Dai's return and the arrival of the victorious Chinese Communists at Vietnam's border altered the external and internal policies of the Viet Minh. To receive Red Chinese aid, the Viet Minh had to follow Mao Tse-tung's hard line.[14] Dropping pretenses, the DRV admitted its Communist orientation and tightened Party control over the government and all front organizations. In January 1950, Ho proclaimed the DRV the only legitimate Vietnamese government and invited diplomatic recognition. The Peking regime was the first to respond, but was quickly followed by the USSR and other Communist countries. With Chinese guidance and books, the Viet Minh intensified political indoctrination throughout their front organizations, jungle factories, and army. Training schools for Vietnamese officers were established in China and thousands of Chinese advisers came to Vietnam. These were joined by several hundred Soviet technicians. In March 1951, the ICP surfaced as the Lao Dong or Workers' party, and the Viet Minh merged with the Lien Viet Front, which still claimed to represent a broad following of all classes.

Beginning in 1950, large-scale military aid from Communist China and the Soviet Union permitted the DRV to undertake major offensives. The French rallied with the appointment as commander-in-chief of the outstanding General de Lattre de Tassigny, who received full military and civil powers. The strengthened French Union forces inflicted heavy casualties on Giap's main forces, but permitted the survivors to retreat to the jungle. Before his death in 1952, De Lattre ordered a network of concrete defense works to be built in and around the Tonkin delta. This defense perimeter proved a sieve through which DRV units filtered almost at will, tying French forces to their forts and the cities, while the Viet Minh ruled the villages. French morale sank steadily.

At Vietnam's insistence, France transferred additional services and created a Vietnamese army with units from the French Union forces. But the French refused to grant the true independence which would have attracted enough popular support to defeat the Viet Minh, despite the urging of the United States, which by 1953 was paying 80 per cent of the war's cost. Many Vietnamese recruits and officers deserted, some defecting to the Viet Minh. Circumscribed by the French, Bao Dai's government accomplished little. In 1953 Premier Nguyen Van Tam

[14] The Chinese regime first indicated its intention to push a militant Communist line in Southeast Asia at the Australasian Trade Union Conference in Peking in November 1949 (Oliver E. Clubb, Jr., *The United States and the Sino-Soviet Bloc in Southeast Asia* [Washington, 1962], p. 16.).

tried to invigorate it by holding elections and forming a national assembly. But Bao Dai proved little credit to his country, remaining aloof from the government except to block a too-strong premier.

A French attempt to recapture the initiative in 1953 by the appointment of General Navarre, failed when he chose to make a stand at an isolated outpost at Dien Bien Phu. After twice overrunning parts of Laos to divert French forces, DRV troops under Vo Nguyen Giap began a siege in March 1954 during the rainy season. The fortress capitulated with 16,000 troops on May 7, one day before the opening of the major Geneva Indochina discussions, which aimed to end the Vietnam war. The loss of Dien Bien Phu alone was not decisive, but it was an important psychological victory for the Viet Minh. It came as a French Socialist government sought a way out of the unpopular Indochina War. Giap's victory cost some 23,000 main force Viet Minh killed or wounded, but bought a stronger voice at the conference for the DRV delegate Pham Van Dong.

Preliminary peace negotiations had begun early in 1953, by which time the Vietnamese and Korean Wars had merged with the global East-West struggle. French Union forces depended heavily on the United States, while the DRV could hardly have survived without Chinese and Communist bloc support. The Geneva discussions covered both Korea and Indochina. The sessions devoted to Indochina included representatives of France, the USSR, Communist China, Great Britain, and the Indochinese countries, with the U. S. sitting as an observer. Before the conference opened, Great Britain had settled upon division of Vietnam as the best solution. The U. S. reluctantly agreed when France accepted the proposal, but warned partition would offer the Communists a respite.

Pham Van Dong, who also represented the small Communist-led rebel movements of Laos and Cambodia, proved a capable though truculent negotiator. He made extravagant demands but, when China withheld support, bargained on the basis of Vietnam's temporary partition, subject to national elections in two years. Bao Dai's delegate rejected even provisional partition and insisted any elections must be completely free and supervised by the United Nations. He refused to be bound by conference decisions when these terms were ignored.

Two principal documents recorded the Geneva accords of July 1954—a ceasefire agreement, which was signed, and an unsigned Final Declaration. Separate documents dealt with Laos and Cambodia.

Vietnam was divided along the seventeenth parallel, with the DRV and State of Vietnam administering the north and south respectively. Within 300 days, hostile forces were to regroup within these boundaries, and civilians could move from one zone to another. Neither side was to introduce new troops or military equipment or to permit the establishment of foreign bases. An International Control Commission (ICC) with inspection teams composed of equal numbers of representatives of Canada, India, and Poland was to supervise the execution of the agreements. The Final Declaration emphasized that the military demarcation was provisional and that general elections would be held in July 1956 under ICC supervision with preliminary consultations to begin after July 1955.[15]

Neither Bao Dai's government nor the U. S. accepted the agreements, but both promised not to use force to oppose their implementation. The American representative, General Walter Bedell Smith, made clear that the U. S. would consider any renewal of aggression in violation of the agreements a threat to international peace and security. The U. S. also supported the South Vietnamese insistence on United Nations supervision of reunification elections.

Thus one phase of the Vietnamese struggle ended and the conditions were set for a long, bitter contest between the two Vietnams, both of which claimed sole sovereignty over the whole.

Diem and the Republic of Vietnam

On June 4, 1954, as the Geneva conferees were dividing the country, France granted Vietnam full independence, without reference to the division. At this juncture, Ngo Dinh Diem accepted the premiership of Bao Dai's government, after being guaranteed nearly absolute powers. Diem was from a central Vietnamese mandarin family that had been Catholic for 300 years. After displaying unusual ability as a provincial governor, he assisted Bao Dai's 1932 reform effort. Thereafter, he remained in retirement but in contact with other nationalists. Though captured by the Communists in 1945, Diem was released despite his rejection of a DRV cabinet post. After refusing to lead Bao Dai's government in 1949 because Vietnam's independence was limited, Diem lectured in the United States, where he met Cardinal Spellman

[15] For the text of the Geneva agreements, see Marvin E. Gettleman, *Viet Nam, History, Documents and Opinions on a Major World Crisis* (Greenwich, Conn., 1965), pp. 137-59.

and other prominent Americans, including Senators Mike Mansfield and John F. Kennedy.[16]

Diem's new assignment appeared overwhelming. The economy was in chaos, the countryside was war-damaged, and government services were nonexistent where Viet Minh guerrillas had roamed. The Cao Dai, Hoa Hao, and Catholic paramilitary sects held nearly autonomous areas. Dozens of splintered political groups were led by inexperienced intellectuals. The Binh Xuyen gangsters, who reportedly paid tribute to Bao Dai, policed Saigon-Cholon, while Chief of Staff Nguyen Van Hinh, who wanted Diem's post, dominated the army. In subordinating these forces, Diem was backed by the United States, which continued large-scale assistance. General Hinh was outmaneuvered in November 1954 by a compromise with other army leaders, and Diem effectively divided the sects by giving them cabinet posts and inducing portions of their troops to support the government. The Binh Xuyen attacked Diem's palace when he choked off their income by closing their gambling concessions, but loyal forces drove them from the city and later finally crushed them. The remaining Hoa Hao and Cao Dai opposition then crumbled. Diem's victory gained new respect from Washington, which had been concerned over the unrest.[17]

Meanwhile, Diem's brother Ngo Dinh Nhu was building a political machine based on the National Revolutionary Movement (NRM). Government officials headed its branches down to village levels, where militant cadre organized an extensive propaganda network. Its confused ideology, derived from the French Catholic philosophy of Personalism, aimed at a compromise between Marxist collectivism and Western individualistic capitalism, while stressing Vietnamese values. Through the overlapping Civil Servants League, Nhu mobilized government employees for such activities as providing demonstrations or bringing out the vote. Both the League and the NRM were personally controlled by Nhu and were infiltrated by Can Lao members. Organized in 1956, the Can Lao or Revolutionary Personalist Workers' Party had a secret membership, mainly trusted officials, who infiltrated other parties and served as an intelligence network.

Since Bao Dai had encouraged the sects against Diem, a confrontation was inevitable. To win support, Diem called a Popular Revolu-

---

[16] For a balanced, scholarly review of Diem's administration, see Robert Scigliano, *South Vietnam: Nation Under Stress* (Boston, 1964).

[17] Shaplen, *op. cit.*, pp. 121-25, treats the significance of this victory on continued U. S. support to Diem.

tionary Committee of pro-government delegates in April 1955. Guided by Nhu, this group urged Diem's elevation to Chief of State. Bao Dai dismissed Diem, but was ignored. In a nation-wide referendum in October, 98.2 per cent of the voters chose Diem over Bao Dai. While unnecessary rigging bloated the count, the referendum clearly evidenced Diem's popularity. Diem then proclaimed Vietnam a republic with himself as president, and received recognition from the United States and other friendly nations. The following March, a constituent assembly was elected.[18]

While Diem consolidated his power, his government resettled over 900,000 refugees from the North. At the same time, some 60,000 to 100,000 Viet Minh moved to the North. Diem's government permitted free movement northward, but the Communists prevented possibly several hundred thousand from migrating to the South. Conversely, 32,000 petitions protested the Viet Minh's abduction of youths to the North, but the ICC could take no effective action, partly because the DRV permitted only Communist interpreters. The DRV also sabotaged an agreement in 1955 for exchanging postal cards. Messages to the North, when delivered, caused addressees to suffer threats or punishments. Thousands of cards sent south carried propaganda slogans and calls for rebellion, and Hanoi complained when these were not delivered.[19]

[18] Some critics of the U. S. Vietnam involvement have questioned the legitimacy of the Diem administration which succeeded the Bao Dai government. They contend that Bao Dai's abdication forfeited all claims to head the Vietnamese government. However, while the DRV proclaimed independence in 1945, it received no diplomatic recognition until 1950, at about the time the major Western non-Communist countries recognized Bao Dai's government. France treated the Bao Dai government as a sovereign state in the 1954 negotiations for independence and subsequent agreements. (See Allen B. Cole, ed., *Conflict in Indochina and International Repercussions: A Documentary History, 1945-55* [Cornell, N. Y., 1956], p. 199) Diem's victory in the 1955 plebiscite gave him a clear mandate to form a government. Three subsequent national elections strengthened this mandate. Conversely, the North had a shaky claim to legitimacy. The legality of Bao Dai's abdication could be questioned, because under the protectorate agreements, Vietnamese emperors could make no important political decisions without French approval. The DRV mandate to rule was based on coercion, not legality or popular approval as expressed at the polls. After the controlled elections of 1946, no elections were held by the DRV for sixteen years.

[19] Diem's ending of this exchange has been unfairly cited as an example of his refusal to cooperate. For Diem's viewpoint, see Government of Viet Nam, *Violations of the Geneva Agreements by the Viet Minh Communists* (Saigon, 1959), pp. 89-91.

Though not openly refusing ICC requests, the North Vietnamese by subterfuge and delaying tactics hampered ICC activities. Diem's government rejected the legality of the Geneva agreements and of the ICC, but generally, though reluctantly, facilitated its work. The DRV had an intelligence network feeding information on which to base charges. The South had no comparable system in the North. While the ICC could readily observe the main Southern ports and airports for military shipments, there was no such freedom in the North. Consequently, reported violations in the South were investigated and sometimes condemned, while gross transgressions in the North often went unchecked. The ICC's composition compounded the problem. The Communist Polish representative generally sided with the North, and until invaded by China, the Indians were highly critical of Diem. Only the Canadians gave South Vietnam a sympathetic hearing, while endeavoring to be impartial in their judgment.[20]

South Vietnamese defenses were greatly reduced by France's withdrawal and the national army's reduction. But between 1954 and 1956, North Vietnam's army increased from 7 to 20 divisions and Chinese technicians and laborers helped rebuild military facilities. To French and South Vietnamese complaints, the ICC admitted they needed an army of investigators. Diem charged that even where they could freely investigate as in the discovery in the South of Viet Minh arms caches containing formidable arsenals, the ICC refused to recognize violations, simply labelling the dumps abandoned arms. Diem also protested the presence of Viet Minh forces in the South. Government troops eliminated some of these, but many remained to propagandize and attack refugee relocation camps, strengthened by infiltrators from the North.

Despite this harassment, refugee resettlement proceeded rapidly. Major aid came from private Catholic groups as two-thirds of the refugees were Catholic, and from the U. S. government, which assisted all aspects of the operation. About 133,000 refugees were urban craftsmen, businessmen or professionals, and 90,000 were fishermen. But

[20] An Indian ICC staff member, B. S. N. Murti, author of *Vietnam Divided: The Unfinished Struggle* (New York and Bombay, 1964), tends to be critical of the South. Robert Scigliano, *op. cit.*, pp. 152-156, discusses the Polish refusal to cooperate and resultant ICC problems. Consequently, the first eleven ICC reports charged the South with some 150 violations while charging North Vietnam with one. The Canadians and Indians stated "the number of formal citations in itself is no fair measure of the degree of cooperation received from either party." (ICC, *Eleventh Interim Report*, February 1, 1960 to February 28, 1961, p. 25.)

over 700,000 were farmers, needing land, seeds, and plows. In the largest operation at Cai San in the far south where 47,000 were resettled, Vietnamese taxi drivers operated 100 tractors 18 hours a day, preparing fields for cultivation. Some 20,000 refugees dug 100 miles of irrigation canals in only 90 days. Resettlement was not without errors and problems, however. Ten thousand imported buffaloes and oxen had to learn Vietnamese commands. Wet rice farmers were resettled in dry-rice highlands, and small landholdings did not always provide a livelihood. Land taken from Montagnard tribes without compensation created frictions, and northerners settled in southern villages were resented as "foreigners."

Resettlement merged with agrarian reform. Because of French land concessions, about half the cultivated Mekong delta land was held by 2.5 per cent of the landowners, while some 600,000 were tenant farmers. Land rents reached 50 per cent of the crop, and usurious loans cost 5 to 10 per cent monthly interest. Viet Minh agitators had exploited peasant discontent and had expelled many larger landlords, lowered or eliminated rents, and "given" land to peasants. Diem began reforms in 1955 by setting rents at 15 to 25 per cent according to productivity, and extending rent contracts to five years. But many tenants had been paying no rent and were warned by the Viet Minh against signing contracts. Conversely, landlords demanded retroactive rent. Future discontent was fostered when Diem settled refugees on uncultivated lands but required rent contracts instead of selling or giving the land. In 1956, a land redistribution measure limited rice landholdings to 247 acres with the excess to be sold to landless peasants with 6-year payment periods. In 1957, the National Agricultural Credit Office (NACO) was created to provide low interest loans to farmers, fishermen and craftsmen. NACO also helped farmers organize cooperatives for processing and marketing produce and for jointly purchasing equipment.

The Viet Cong opposed the land reform with violence and propaganda, and, unfortunately, Diem's program proved inadequate. Prices for land redistributed were often too high and payment periods too short. Redistribution moved slowly, partly because many government officials were landholders. Only one-tenth of the tenant farmers received land, and some were sold tracts the Viet Minh had given them. Although the 247 acre base was large, loopholes permitted even larger holdings. Some opposition leaders accused government officials, including Diem's family, of acquiring land intended for redistribution.

Meanwhile, Diem was building a centralized administration. The constitution promulgated October 29, 1956 permitted the president to suspend laws in an emergency, rule by decree when the legislature was not in session, and make quarterly appropriations when the assembly failed to pass the budget.[21] The constituent assembly became the first National Assembly with a three-year term. With no constitutional provisions for local government, Diem organized a centralized system of appointive officials down to the hamlet level. This completed the destruction of the traditional village councils, which, though hardly democratic, had represented local interests. Outsiders could rarely secure comparable local cooperation. Adapting Viet Minh tactics, Diem also organized the population into five-family groups with several linked into larger units. These provided village-level information, propaganda, and organization channels. Diem's destruction of village autonomy has been criticized for weakening local resistance to Communist penetration.

The Geneva agreements anticipated reunification elections in July 1956 under ICC supervision, but details were vague. The United States and South Vietnam had refused to sign the agreements. When France, who had signed, withdrew her forces and disavowed responsibility, North Vietnam protested and widely propagandized its willingness to conduct the elections. For Diem, the 1955 referendum was more than a choice between himself and Bao Dai. Three months earlier, Diem had clearly stated that reunification elections must be free and that he viewed this impossible with a totalitarian Communist regime ruling the North.[22] In effect, the vote for Diem was also a vote for an anti-Communist government in the South. Diem believed discussions with the DRV in mid-1955, as projected in the Geneva agreements, might have caused his overthrow. Pro-election demonstrations in Saigon at that time received little popular support, but the anti-Communist refugees were easily aroused for demonstrations against the Geneva agreements and the ICC. The United States backed Diem's decision. On June 1, 1956, Assistant Secretary of State Robertson asserted, ". . . we support President Diem fully in his position that if elections are to be held, there must first be conditions which preclude intimidation or coercion of the electorate. Unless such conditions exist there can be

[21] For the texts of the constitutions of both North (1960) and South (1956) Vietnam, see Bernard B. Fall, *The Two Vietnams* (New York, 1963), pp. 399-431.
[22] Dennis Warner, *The Last Confucian* (New York, 1964), p. 106.

no free choice." [23] Had free elections been possible, Diem might well have won. [24] In 1956, South Vietnam was more prosperous than it had been in a decade and Diem's popularity was at its peak, while North Vietnam was at that time verging on a state of rebellion.

The Diem government itself permitted something less than real freedom. Working broadly within the constitutional framework, Diem and his advisers closely controlled the country, justifying restrictions by the growing Communist subversion directed and aided from the North. Whether a more democratic approach might have more effectively combatted communism may be freely but inconclusively debated, since it was not tried. Diem and his family imposed their will especially through the Can Lao, the NRM and, after 1960, the Republican Youth, which trained "youths" from 18 to 50 for hamlet self defense. The Can Lao provided secret elite direction of the government, ferreting out dissenters, while the NRM and Republican Youth permitted mass control. These and government-directed mass organizations such as the Farmers' Associations and Madame Ngo Dinh Nhu's Women's Solidarity Movement, which added a paramilitary corps in 1962, were used for indoctrinating the rural populace. The press was curbed by various harassments, including imprisonment of editors.

Such devices manifested Diem's preference for controlling rather than leading. His government was personal and often arbitrary. Intruding into the smallest details, Diem paralyzed official initiative. He retained the inefficient colonial-type bureaucratic system and civil service, filling the former French-held positions with inexperienced Vietnamese. Diem's distrust of those who had served the French or Bao Dai restricted his choice of top officials. Corruption was a serious problem, inasmuch as official morality had declined seriously during French rule. Moreover, there were few civil servants properly trained to operate a modern state. Less than 2 per cent had college degrees and only 4 per cent, including teachers, had completed secondary

---

[23] Committee on Foreign Relations, U. S. Senate, *Background Information Relating to Southeast Asia and Vietnam,* June 16, 1965, p. 72.

[24] It has been claimed that Ho Chi Minh, as the hero of the independence movement, would have won an election in 1954. This is possible had the election involved only Ho's name. However, had the issue been presented in 1954 or 1956 as a choice between a non-Communist and a Communist government, the vote quite probably would have gone against the Communists who had already aroused considerable fear and mistrust. Even before partition, the Viet Minh had failed in their efforts to sabotage the 1953 local and municipal elections held by the Bao Dai government.

school. In addition to attracting several hundred degree holders back to Vietnam from France and elsewhere, Diem greatly expanded education to fill the gap. By 1962, the South had 12,000 students in three universities as compared with one university and fewer than 700 students for all Indochina in 1939. Secondary school enrollment increased from 20,000 in 1954 to 228,000 in 1962, and elementary attendance from 400,000 to 1.4 million. A National Institute of Administration was also created to train government officials.

From the beginning, Diem faced problems created by the Communists, called Viet Cong (Viet Communist) in the South. Diem's government took over areas controlled for years by the Viet Minh. While the main Viet Minh forces were withdrawn to the North in 1954-55, the Communists left behind arms caches, thousands of secret agents, armed propaganda units and guerrilla bands. These were used to maintain the Viet Minh underground network and to sabotage the government's reconstruction efforts. These agents and guerrillas had to be eliminated and the populace won over in order to create effective government.[25] Vietnamese army units re-establishing control were accompanied by civic action and propaganda teams to explain the new government, distribute needed supplies, and encourage villagers to rebuild public facilities and undertake self-help projects. Though the program met success in some areas, it foundered in red tape. To maintain security in the countryside, Diem organized a rural civil guard. But this decentralized force was ill-trained, poorly equipped, and generally ineffective. Even less effective were the village self-defense units.

While Diem inherited a large army, its conventional French training and equipment were ill-suited to combat guerrilla warfare. Many Vietnamese military leaders, including General Duong Van Minh, favored antiguerrilla training, but American advisers, reasoning from Korea's experience, followed conventional patterns in reorganizing and equipping Vietnam's 150,000 man army. After the Viet Cong insurgency began to mount, however, a few Ranger-type units were organized.

[25] The situation in the South was further complicated by the presence of armed bands of non-Communist remnants of the defeated Binh Xuyen and sect forces whose activities were sometimes confused with the Communists'. However, Bernard B. Fall, in "South Viet-Nam's Internal Problems," *Pacific Affairs,* September 1958 (reprinted in Fall's *Viet-Nam Witness* [New York, 1966], pp. 169-96), points out with maps the coincidence of DRV complaints of government retaliation against former Viet Minh with areas of Communist terrorism. Only through an extensive espionage network could Hanoi have received the information on which to base its complaints.

The Communists first concentrated attacks on isolated civil guard and self-defense units, but by 1958-9, they were ready to attack regular army units. Schooled in conventional warfare techniques, the Vietnamese army seemed unable to adjust to fighting under guerrilla conditions.

Infiltration of retrained southerners from the North had accelerated after Hanoi became alarmed by Diem's early successes and the defection of many Viet Minh agents. By the end of 1955, 6000 Communist agents were reported to have infiltrated back into the South, including a North Vietnamese army general to organize guerrilla warfare.[26] Radio Hanoi beamed a barrage of propaganda, attacking every action of Diem's government. Hanoi's decision to overthrow Diem was apparently made at about the time the constituent assembly elections indicated strong support for him. The Lao Dong party established a Central Reunification Department in 1956 to supervise the Southern insurrection, and a Reunification Commission was subsequently created as a DRV government organ. In 1960, Hanoi organized the National Front for the Liberation of South Vietnam. A year later, the People's Revolutionary party was formed as the southern branch of the North Vietnamese Communist party.[27]

By that time, the Viet Cong had mounted a rural insurgency patterned on the pre-Geneva Viet Minh tactics. These closely resembled those of Communist liberation movements in China, Greece, Malaya, the Philippines, Laos, and, more recently, Thailand. The process is simplified in a society with a tradition of submission to authority. A few armed propagandists fan the grievances of village malcontents into hatred and open violence against local authority. Police stations are attacked to gain arms. As the malcontents become an armed gang, other villagers are forced to attend indoctrination sessions. Communism is not mentioned, but everyone is promised what he most wants—lower rents or taxes, free land, education. Acts of terror increase. Unpopular officials and opponents within the village are killed or terrorized, and all witnesses are made participants to involve them, willingly or unwillingly, in acts of open opposition to the government. Government

[26] United Press dispatch from Saigon, November 24, 1955. This figure is undoubtedly too high and probably included agents infiltrated along with northern refugees. French officials complained to the ICC of the infiltration, but the ICC did not consider the complaint since it did not come under any article of the Geneva agreements, according to B. S. N. Murti, *op. cit.*, p. 91.

[27] These steps are documented and discussed in greater detail in Chapter Six.

efforts to bring order are exploited as repression of the popular will. Terrorism spreads to include teachers and health workers, and all who serve the government. Once a village is under control, it becomes a base for more rapid subversion of neighboring villages by armed agitation and propaganda platoons.[28] Into such bases poured men and arms infiltrated from the North to build a guerrilla army. Diem fought back with propaganda, organization, and force. The mass political organizations waged counter-propaganda and offered Personalism as a counterdoctrine. Those difficult to persuade were confined for indoctrination at Reeducation Centers, and a presidential ordinance permitted arbitrary imprisonment of dangerous persons. A national emergency was proclaimed in October 1961, and the National Assembly gave Diem extraordinary powers. In 1959, Diem adapted Malaya's experiences by regrouping peasants from insecure areas into fortified rural cities or *agrovilles* which were to offer security and such amenities as clinics, schools, and electricity. Without enough competent and honest officials to execute a program of this magnitude, it was doomed. To show impressive progress, some officials forced the peasants into agrovilles before the amenities were available, creating discontent, which the Communists exploited. Other officials reported completion of nonexistent agrovilles. Only 22 of the projected 80 agrovilles were even partly completed when planning shifted in 1961 to fortifying "strategic hamlets" nearer the peasants' fields. They were to elect civic committees and to have local self-defense units. Again the peasants had to build fortifications and move their houses with little or no recompense. The hamlet program also moved too rapidly. Some officials reported hamlets fortified and safe that they had not dared visit. To encourage movement into the hamlets, the government proclaimed "free kill" zones outside the "secure" areas, open to random artillery or bombing. As the Viet Cong focussed their attacks on the fortified hamlets, the peasant received no respite.

In Saigon, Diem's strong rule forced any opposition into conspiracy and intrigue. Parties not following the government line did not receive certification, and opposition often brought imprisonment or "re-educa-

---

[28] Arthur J. Dommen's *Conflict in Laos, The Politics of Neutralization* (New York, 1964), pp. 129-32, describes this pattern as used by the Pathet Lao to subvert Lao villagers. The resemblance to Viet Cong tactics is no coincidence since the Pathet Lao are also directed by the DRV. Dommen quotes one observer's description of the technique as "a propaganda sentence punctuated by a terrorist period" (p. 132).

tion." Many opponents left for France. Of those remaining, Dr. Phan Quang Dan proved most persistent. An active nationalist associated with the VNQDD, Dan had refused to serve in Ho Chi Minh's cabinet and had been an adviser to Bao Dai. After studying at Harvard, Dr. Dan returned in 1955 to lead opposition elements, until his imprisonment in 1960. The factionalized opposition briefly achieved some unity in April 1960, when 18 political leaders signed a manifesto calling for political and economic reforms and the elimination of Diem's family influence from government. Except for the Cao Daist Phan Khac Suu, the Caravelle group, as they were called, remained aloof from an unsuccessful coup in November 1960, but all were arrested and some were imprisoned without trial until Diem's death.

The 1960 coup had a mixed civilian and military leadership, including Colonel Nguyen Chanh Thi. The coup group quickly seized their Saigon objectives, but lacking clear plans, negotiated with Diem for reforms. The president stalled until loyal forces arrived, and the coup collapsed. The evidence of dissatisfaction frightened Diem and Nhu into creating a legal opposition, the National Union Front, chaired by the respected Dai Viet party leader Phan Huy Quat. But when the Front called for political reforms and release of political prisoners, Diem withdrew his support and the movement disappeared.

Meanwhile, assembly elections in 1959 produced another pro-Diem legislature. Diem was relected president in April 1961. In both elections, the NRM and Civil Servants League backed the government candidates. Reports indicated opposition candidates were harassed, arrested, or disqualified on petty pretexts. Despite this, government candidates polled only 57 per cent of the vote in the cities and less than half in Saigon, although they received 84 per cent in the countryside. Diem won only 64 per cent of the Saigon vote, but 95 per cent from the rest of the country. Though elected by a substantial majority, Dr. Dan was disqualified on unsubstantiated charges of election law violations. The elections have been widely debunked as rigged, and certainly they fell short of Western democratic standards. There were undoubted government pressures to bring voters to the polls, yet each vote registered a protest against the Communists who had worked frantically to sabotage the elections.[29] While 82 per cent of the registered voters voted in 1959, over 90 per cent cast ballots in 1961 when the Communists tried hardest to enforce a boycott of the elections.

[29] Scigliano, *op. cit.,* pp. 75-100, has a good treatment of elections and politics under Diem.

End of the Diem Regime

Despite his faults, Diem had brought relative order and prosperity to a devastated land and had prevented a Communist takeover. Though his government was dictatorial, he preserved a constitutional framework and held four national elections. A traditional scholar-ruler, he accepted full responsibility, believing his actions necessary to save Vietnam. However, Diem and his family were pathologically self-righteous, assuming all criticism of them to be inspired by colonialism or communism. They judged foreign advice contrary to their thinking to be based on ignorance of Vietnamese values and needs. Diem found irritating the succession of Americans with their sometimes conflicting advice. For its part, the U. S. valued Diem's militant anticommunism, considering Vietnam important to Southeast Asian defenses. In urging reforms, Americans moved cautiously to avoid undermining Vietnamese sovereignty, though considerable pressure was sometimes exerted. Diem's suspiciousness isolated the American mission and cut them off from reliable information, even as Diem was himself prevented from learning the truth by sycophantic subordinates and by his inability to listen.

Although he tried hard, Diem failed to stem the Viet Cong insurgency. Government propaganda relied heavily on anti-Communist themes, though the Viet Cong rarely mentioned communism. His unwillingness to trust subordinates prevented the development of more positive and imaginative approaches. He ran the war personally, treating generals like junior officers and stifling aggressive plans. After two disgruntled pilots bombed Diem's palace in February 1962, Diem impounded the air force's larger bombs. The coup attempts fortified Diem's distrust of everyone except his family. Decision making became a family affair. His brother Nhu was chief political counselor; another brother Canh, though he held no official position, ruled central Vietnam virtually as a governor, and a third brother Thuc headed the Vietnamese Catholic church. Nhu and his wife increasingly dominated Diem. As his power grew, Nhu developed signs of megalomania, withdrawing more frequently to his opium pipe, and rejecting all guidance except that from his power-mad wife or his brother Archbishop Ngo Dinh Thuc.

As the Ngo Dinh clan progressively antagonized the foreign press, criticism grew. The American mission, committed to support Diem, was under pressure to control American correspondents who in turn sharply criticized the Mission. Contributing to the growing cleavage was the ambivalence of the American role.[30] While the U. S. had not concurred in the Geneva agreements and while the DRV had violated nearly every clause, the U. S. was reluctant for diplomatic reasons to admit it was providing military assistance beyond the Geneva limitations. When newsmen pointed out these discrepancies or revealed government failures that Diem was not aware of, American officials sometimes felt impelled to more staunchly defend him.

Few observers anticipated the role Buddhists would play in Diem's overthrow. By 1963, however, the General Buddhist Association (GBA), which in 1954 united most Buddhist groups in the South, counted a million lay members, 2000 monks, including many who had fled the North, 600 nuns, and a youth organization exceeding 70,000. Buddhist leaders claimed a following of 80 per cent of the population, though active Buddhists are much less than half that percentage. Under Diem, the Buddhist reform movement extended into social welfare. A feeling of government discrimination created a growing self-awareness. Diem's government, whether intentionally or not, favored Catholics, who held a disproportionately high number of official positions, partly because the French had given them educational advantages, but also because Diem preferred Catholics. Can Lao membership was mainly Catholic. By a 1950 decree, Catholics enjoyed special legal advantages. The official doctrine of Personalism was taught to government officials in a Catholic university. Madame Nhu, a Catholic convert, especially antagonized the Buddhists by pushing through the Assembly her Family Bill and Law for the Protection of Morality, which imposed Catholic standards on family relations and her own puritanical morality upon the entire nation.

Buddhist-Catholic antagonisms grew, stimulated by politically ambitious Buddhist monks. The flashpoint came in May 1963 over the display of religious flags. Though Catholics had just flown their flags to commemorate the anniversary of Archbishop Ngo Dinh Thuc's consecration as bishop, a law forbidding the use of any except the national flag was invoked to stop the Buddhists from doing the same for Buddha's birthday. The government yielded when the Buddhists defied the ban, but Thich (Venerable) Tri Quang, Buddhist leader of Hue, raised

[30] The dilemma of the American mission is ably treated in John Mecklin, *Mission in Torment* (Garden City, New York, 1965). Mr. Mecklin was Director of the United States Information Service in Saigon during this critical period.

the cry of repression and organized protest demonstrations, which ended with a number of Buddhists wounded and killed. Responsibility was not clearly placed, but the monks blamed the government. After painstaking negotiations, Diem and the Buddhists reached a *modus vivendi*, which outraged Nhu, who organized protest demonstrations against the government. This action welded the Buddhists into a unified resistance, supported on political grounds by many with little concern for religion. An Inter-sect Committee was formed to handle negotiations and coordinate antigovernment activities under Thich Tri Quang and Thich Duc Ngiep. The monks displayed a talent for publicity, country-wide coordination, and planning of theatrical protests, including the self-immolation of seven monks. Tri Quang began to evidence political ambitions that many observers felt violated Buddhist doctrine.[31]

The U. S. and other foreign missions urged the government to make concessions, but the Nhus demanded that the Buddhists be crushed, insisting they were Communist-led. As Diem vacillated, on August 21, just before the arrival of the new U. S. Ambassador Henry Cabot Lodge, Nhu masterminded attacks on unarmed pagodas by the elite Vietnamese Special Forces, who had been diverted from antiguerrilla activities to palace guard duty. The brutal roundup of monks ended support for the Diem regime at home and abroad. When students and teachers demonstrated for the monks, several thousand youths were arrested and high schools and colleges were closed. This heavy-handed repression alienated many officials, military officers, and professionals whose children were manhandled and jailed. Though most were soon released, stories spread of the torture of those still held as leaders. The U. S. suspended subsidies for Vietnamese imports and for the Special Forces until they returned to combat. Nhu acrimoniously charged Americans and various other foreign representatives in Saigon with plotting a coup. Following a comment by General de Gaulle that a neutral Vietnam would receive French assistance, Nhu began secret negotiations with the Communists.[32]

[31] Among the early journalist critics of the militant Buddhists was Marguerite Higgins, whose observations have been largely substantiated. See her *Our Vietnam Nightmare* (New York, 1965). Higgins also presented a favorable view of Diem, contrary to most correspondents who sympathized with the Buddhists, such as David Halberstam, *The Making of a Quagmire* (New York, 1965).

[32] Jean Lacouture, *Vietnam: Between Two Truces* (New York, 1966), pp. 82-5, believes these contacts were to be used "to blackmail the Americans."

Emboldened by the withdrawal of U. S. support, several army officers plotted Diem's overthrow.[33] One group seems to have been led by Colonel Do Mau and General Tran Thien Khiem, while another included Generals Tran Van Don, Duong Van Minh, and Le Van Kim. Do Mau and Khiem joined with other officers who were plotting with some students and workers, and the Don group secured the cooperation of First and Second Corps commanders, General Do Cao Tri and Nguyen Khanh. Meanwhile, in collusion with Diem's most trusted general, Ton That Dinh, Nhu plotted to seize leadership from Diem. Nhu's cleverness was used against him when Dinh was won over by the opposition generals who had joined forces.

On November 1, this military coalition moved smoothly into Saigon. They quickly occupied the main government offices and surrounded Diem's palace. Unable to rally support, Diem and Nhu fled, but shortly thereafter surrendered in a Catholic church in Cholon. The two brothers were killed by police officers while being taken to coup headquarters and were buried in secret graves. The end of the Diem regime was celebrated with jubilance in Saigon's streets. The withdrawal of U. S. aid had implied American willingness for a change, and many journalists claimed the U. S. had approved the coup plans. However, Ambassador Lodge tried earnestly to save the lives of Diem and Nhu. He stated flatly that the U. S. was not involved, but had been trying to bring changes in Diem's policies by legitimate means.

Military Government

The military junta began its administration with strong popular support and high hopes. Promising elections and civilian rule within twelve months, the junta replaced the National Assembly with a Military Revolutionary Council (MRC), chaired by the popular General Duong Van Minh, who became Chief of State. Diem's vice-president, Nguyen Ngoc Tho, a Southern Buddhist, became premier. Though generals took over key ministries, top bureaucratic levels remained largely unchanged. However, Diem's secret police, the NRM, Can Lao, and Women's Solidarity Movement were disbanded. Colonel Pham Ngoc Thao, one of the coup members, was assigned to recreate Vietnam's political life. Under his guidance, a Council of Notables composed of respected academic and professional figures was organized to draft a new constitution, but it disintegrated into futile debates. Efforts

[33] Shaplen, *op. cit.*, pp. 188-211, gives a good account of the plotting. See Mecklin, *op. cit.*, pp. 189-279, for a different viewpoint.

to strengthen political organizations by regrouping the sixty-odd splinter parties into four "fronts" floundered in harping criticism and factional strife.

While the generals maneuvered for power, the insurgency sharply accelerated. During 1963, the Viet Cong had overrun 8 per cent of the hamlets in two provinces near Saigon. Viet Cong-initiated actions soared from 500 in September 1963, itself a record, to 3500 in November and 5000 a week five months later. Of the 8600 strategic hamlets purportedly completed, about one in five was viable militarily. The U. S. urged completion of the hamlet project after proper consolidation, but Vietnamese leaders, wanting to reassure villagers, favored hamlets only in safe areas.

Before General Minh could implement a reform program, he was pushed aside on January 30, 1964, by Generals Nguyen Khanh, Do Mau, and Tran Thien Khiem. The pretext was a rumored neutralist coup by others of the junta following an unpopular French proposal for neutralization of Vietnam. After exiling the suspected generals to Dalat, Khanh persuaded Minh to remain chief of state, while Khanh became premier and chairman of the MRC. He named three vice-premiers, General Khiem became minister of defense, Dr. Phan Huy Quat, minister of foreign affairs, and Harvard-trained Nguyen Xuan Oanh, minister of national economy. Other posts were filled by representatives of the VNQDD, Hoa Hao, Cao Dai, and Dai Viet.

Proclaiming an anticommunist, antineutralist and anti-French policy, Khanh advanced a program of urban and rural development. He promised a civilian government with a constitution, but dismissed the Council of Notables previously assigned this task. All able-bodied citizens were ordered mobilized for military service or village improvement. Strategic hamlets, renamed New Rural Life Hamlets, were to become centers from which security and government authority would spread on the old French "oil slick" theory. Local autonomy was to be restored and land squatters were assured tenure with long-term purchase rights. Urban industrialization and improved social services were projected.

Americans were more impressed than were Vietnamese. Many of the latter resented Khanh's ousting of the popular General Minh. While students feared Khanh's mobilization, intellectuals distrusted his promises and disdained his common origins (his mother had run a bar). When politicians encouraged by Khanh's efforts to organize effective parties proposed a parallel all-civilian cabinet, Khanh declared the army was the only "disciplined force capable of leading the country." The bureaucracy countrywide was demoralized by Khanh's purge of Can Lao and "Diemists" and by his Revolutionary Court, which sentenced Diem's brother Ngo Dinh Canh to death. Growing urban discontent progressively paralyzed government initiative. The mass turn-overs of province and district chiefs following the November and January coups disrupted both civil and military activities.

Meanwhile, in January most of Vietnam's Buddhist sects and organizations joined in the United Buddhist Association (UBA). Its most active bureau, the Institute for Secular Affairs, was headed by Thich Tam Chao, leader of the northern refugee monks. Thich Thien Minh, a militant activist, directed the Youth Bureau, while Tri Quang rejected any responsible public position. To appease the Buddhists, Khanh, himself a Buddhist, recognized the UBA and donated land for a national pagoda, which helped the activists when their political involvement caused their expulsion from Saigon's main pagoda. Khanh also annulled the Catholics' favored legal status and authorized a Buddhist chaplain corps for the armed forces. Despite these gestures, Buddhists soon charged Khanh with repression. Military commanders complained the chaplains were subverting discipline by advising soldiers not to obey "unjust" officers.

Taking advantage of these disruptive forces, Viet Cong activities mounted. Infiltration from North Vietnam of about 2000 per month was matched by local recruitment. Increasing quantities of Communist-bloc weapons arrived by land and sea. In response, U. S. forces increased to over 22,000 by the end of 1964.[34] General Maxwell Taylor's appointment as Ambassador in June 1964 indicated a stronger U. S. military stance, while the naming of career diplomat U. Alexis Johnson as Deputy Ambassador implied an equal concern for political and social reform. Following the attack by DRV PT boats on two U. S. destroyers in the Gulf of Tonkin in August, U. S. aircraft bombed North Vietnamese naval bases. President Johnson took this occasion to assure the world that the U. S. would stay in Southeast Asia as long as the struggle required and would "meet aggression with firmness and unprovoked attack with measured reply."

General Khanh, apparently considering the moment opportune for

[34] The Viet Cong and its Front long claimed to be fighting only with weapons captured from government forces. However, by mid-1965, they had captured only 40,000 weapons while losing 25,000 in battle. The V. C. forces then totalled 70,000 main forces and 90,000 irregulars. In February 1965, a DRV cargo ship sunk off Phu Yen Province had a cargo of rifles and machine guns and many tons of other equipment of Communist-bloc origin. Subsequently, even larger quantities of Communist-bloc military equipment have been captured from the VC.

establishing a dictatorship, declared a national emergency and assumed total authority. Next came a constitution, the Vung Tau Charter, which gave nearly absolute powers to the president. To this position, the MRC elected Khanh, displacing General Minh. Outraged students demonstrated, joined and encouraged by Buddhist monks who charged repression by former Can Lao and Diemists. Communists infiltrated demonstrations to induce religious strife, and mobs blocked Saigon's thoroughfares. Violence spread to Hue and Danang. Religious tensions mounted as politically ambitious monks assiduously sought to undermine Khanh's government.

Faced with continuing strife and Buddhist intransigence, Khanh withdrew the Vung Tau Charter and resigned. For an interim government, the MRC selected a triumvirate—Generals Minh, Khanh, and Khiem. After a "rest" in Dalat during which Saigon remained in chaos and Buddhists in Hue and Danang organized "revolutionary committees," Khanh returned to bring temporary order. He promised a civilian government and a national congress, but when he organized an interim cabinet with heavy civilian representation, the generals eliminated from power seized Saigon on September 13, 1964. Khanh was in Dalat, but some younger officers, including Air Commodore Nguyen Cao Ky, opposed the dissidents. Ky's support proved decisive, for the armed planes circling over the coup headquarters brought capitulation without bloodshed.

Failure of Civilian Government

While the young officers exerted a growing political influence, a High National Council (HNC) appointed by Minh completed provisional organization of a civilian government. The transfer took place October 26, with the HNC's chairman, Cao Dai leader Phan Khac Suu, replacing General Minh as chief of state. Former Saigon mayor Tran Van Huong became prime minister with a civilian cabinet of "technicians." Khanh remained commander-in-chief and head of a new Armed Forces Council, while Minh and Khiem were assigned abroad.

A combination of factors doomed civilian government. Catholic and Buddhist groups, their differences intensified and political ambitions whetted by the summer's riots, demonstrated against Huong, charging they had not been adequately consulted on political matters. U. S. efforts to support Huong stimulated Buddhist vituperation. When the young generals dissolved the HNC for obstructing their military purges, the U. S. expressed strong interest in the continuation of civilian rule. Khanh and Huong reached a limping compromise, which the Buddhist militants unbalanced by persistent opposition. Charging the government with "criminal persecution," they organized student demonstrations in Danang, Hue, and Saigon, sacked the USIS library and cultural center in Hue and marched before the U. S. Embassy in Saigon. Promising to restore order, Khanh induced the Armed Forces Council to dismiss the Huong government in late January.

In mid-February, a joint military-civilian Legislative Council was set up under Dr. Phan Huy Quat, the former foreign minister. Quat's largely civilian cabinet attempted a balanced representation of minority religious groups with a Buddhist majority. Many had belonged to the 1960 Caravelle group. Almost immediately a pro-Catholic faction led by Colonel Pham Ngoc Thao attempted yet another coup. While it failed to take over the government, the coup did oust General Khanh, who in fifteen months had antagonized every faction. Though "honorably exiled" as an ambassador-at-large, Khanh was later charged with misuse of government funds and took refuge in Europe.

This political maneuvering was overshadowed by military events. In early February, the Viet Cong attacked American installations at Pleiku in the highlands and Qui Nhon on the coast, possibly to impress USSR Premier Kosygin, then visiting Hanoi. In line with President Johnson's repeated warnings that DRV aggression could bring attacks on the North, American and South Vietnamese planes answered by twice bombing North Vietnamese military targets. To "clear the decks," American dependents were evacuated from South Vietnam, and American bombers and fighters began flying combat missions.

Barely had Quat's ministry taken office than it was embarrassed by a Buddhist peace campaign led by Yale-educated Thich Quang Lien of the Buddhist Secular Affairs Institute. The peace group advocated a "Reconciliation Committee" to reunify and neutralize Vietnam following withdrawal of all foreign troops and advisers and the disbanding of the Liberation Front. Premier Quat refused to consider negotiations until North Vietnamese aggression against the South ended. Thich Quang Lien was permitted to go abroad, but his lay followers were arrested and three hard core unrepentants were exiled to North Vietnam as a lesson to all. The more moderate Buddhist activists of Saigon asserted their anticommunism by passing, over Tri Quang's protests, a motion denouncing Communist terrorism and efforts to subvert Buddhism. However, many observers distrusted the militant Buddhists, and the Catholics' wariness of all Buddhists, including Dr. Quat, mounted.

Despite this, Quat's prestige grew until in early May 1965, the

Armed Forces Council entrusted "full control" to him. His finest achievement was the holding of provincial and municipal advisory council elections that month. In apparently the fairest elections Vietnam had seen, 3.5 million of 4.5 million registered voters cast ballots despite Viet Cong terrorist harassment. However, continued bickering among the religious, political and military factions left Quat little time for governing. Supported by First Corps Commander Nguyen Chanh Thi, the Buddhists pressured the replacement of officers who had incurred their displeasure. These included some of the most anti-Communist leaders, many of whom were Catholic. In response, the Catholics, led by the militant refugee Father Hoang Quynh and supported by Cao Dai and Hoa Hao elements, organized a "struggle" movement to defend their rights. On May 20, a group of junior officers and civilians, many supporters of Colonel Thao, were charged with plotting to assassinate the premier. Their arrests increased Catholic agitation and forced a cabinet crisis that broke when Chief of State Phan Khac Suu refused to recognize Premier Quat's right to dismiss cabinet officers. When asked by Quat to mediate, the "young Turk" generals ousted both Suu and Quat and installed a war cabinet on June 11.

Escalation and Demonstration

Ten of the young generals formed a National Leadership Committee. The Catholic former vice-premier General Nguyen Van Thieu became chief of state, while the nominally Buddhist Nguyen Cao Ky (meanwhile promoted to Air Marshal), became prime minister. Shortly after Ky's government was formed, Henry Cabot Lodge returned to Saigon as U. S. Ambassador. Most observers gave the flamboyant and aggressive Ky small chance for success, but the 35-year-old flyer showed remarkable staying power. Though Ky had avoided politics aside from his coup breaking, his colleagues chose him over stronger figures, notably First Corps Commander General Nguyen Chanh Thi. Ky entered enthusiastically into his duties. He declared war on North Vietnam to put the country on a war footing and broke relations with France because of de Gaulle's pressure for neutralization. He doubled the soldiers' pay, halved that of high officials, and offered a program of austerity and reform. Proud of his personal honesty, Ky attacked war profiteering and official graft.

When Ky became premier, the Communists appeared to have raised the insurgency to Giap's phase three, the general offensive. Government control of the delta had declined until the major cities were virtually besieged. North Vietnam's growing infiltration of military and political personnel and supplies combined with the political chaos in the South had brought staggering Viet Cong victories during the first half of 1965. As early as 1962, the DRV's systematic invasion had become so open that it was condemned in a majority report of the ICC, Poland abstaining.[35] With the exhaustion of the reservoir of South Vietnamese who had gone north in 1954, the infiltration had become almost totally North Vietnamese army personnel by 1964. Infiltration mounted to over 5000 a month in mid-1966 but apparently declined somewhat by late 1966.

To help counter this escalation, U. S. forces in Vietnam entered combat in June 1965. By early 1967, U. S. strength in Vietnam had risen to nearly 400,000 men, not including the Seventh Fleet operating offshore. In addition, 44,000 Koreans, 4000 Australians, and small New Zealand, Philippine, and Thai contingents had joined the allied forces. The South Vietnamese Army (ARVN) had grown to 325,000 regular and 420,000 paramilitary troops, with most of both being volunteers. The enemy main force numbered 50,000 North Vietnamese and 70,000 Viet Cong army regulars, backed by 150,000 Viet Cong irregulars, 40,000 political cadre, and 20,000 logistical support troops. In their "rear base" in North Vietnam, the "People's Army of Vietnam" (PAVN) had about 225,000 regulars, 200,000 paramilitary, and large trained reserves, which Ho Chi Minh officially called to arms in August 1966. Some 80,000 Chinese supplemented DRV manpower.

While the allies were far short of the ten-to-one ratio considered necessary to defeat guerrillas, this ratio no longer applied. Enemy main forces concentrated in the highlands had switched to regular army tactics, although smaller units continued guerrilla actions in the deltas. Moreover, B-52 and other bombers, artillery and helicopters could direct overwhelming force against Communist troops anywhere in the South. These factors changed the nature of the war. In 1966, the relative ease with which allied forces penetrated main Viet Cong strong-

[35] International Commission for Supervision and Control in Vietnam, *Special Report to the Co-Chairmen of the Geneva Conference on Indo-China* (Saigon, June 2, 1962), pp. 7-9, reported evidence the DRV had sent arms and armed personnel to the South, had conducted armed attacks against the forces of South Vietnam, and was "inciting, encouraging and supporting hostilities in the zone of the South, aimed at the overthrow of the government in the South." While noting South Vietnam's pleas of acting "in the face of aggression," the ICC also charged the South with violations by receiving arms from the U. S. beyond Geneva limitations.

holds containing tunnel networks, supply dumps, and underground centers, indicated a declining Viet Cong morale. At the same time, the amount of men and material from the North was limited and made increasingly costly by accelerated bombing. ARVN forces progressively cleared the guerrilla-infested delta, while the allies concentrated on enemy forces north of Saigon. Early in 1967 U. S. forces also entered the delta fighting.

During 1966, the Communists lost a weekly average of over 1000 killed and 150 prisoners, plus 385 defectors through the increasingly effective South Vietnamese "Open Arms" (Chieu Hoi) program. Uncounted others were killed in B-52 raids, and about two were wounded for each man killed in battle. Defectors, prisoners, and diaries of infiltrators tell of the terrible toll from malaria and hardship. Enemy losses, therefore, may outstrip gains from infiltration and conscription.[36] Communist losses, moreover, included highly trained cadre replaceable only by lengthy indoctrination, made impossible by allied attacks. Only by recruiting boys as young as 13 years and women in local forces did the Viet Cong maintain their manpower. With greatly expanded U. S. participation, American casualties inevitably rose. The total allied combat casualties, however, were but a fraction of those of the Communists. ARVN had a high desertion rate, but few defected to the Viet Cong, and many returned to their units after a period of "French leave." New regulations reduced this rate in late 1966. Prisoner interrogation revealed the Viet Cong also have high desertion rates.

Some journalists claimed large Viet Cong and DRV units had taken refuge in the Cambodian and Lao jungles. Prince Norodom Sihanouk of Cambodia has vehemently denied the Viet Cong presence but in a series of radio broadcasts in November, 1966, the Prince accused the Cambodian Communist Pracheachon party of being "lackeys of the Viet Minh" and of conspiring to overthrow the Cambodian government. The Lao government has repeatedly complained of DRV invasions.[37] In June 1966, the U. S. offered to assist the ICC in patroling the Cambodian border areas, including suspected Viet Cong supply bases at the terminus of the Ho Chi Minh "trail," the network of paths and semi-improved roads running from North to South Vietnam through Laos.

[36] Joseph Alsop, *Washington Post,* September 28 and September 30, 1966, believed enemy losses greatly exceeded gains from infiltration and conscription and that many enemy units were hollow shells. Other observers believed the enemy was overcoming losses.

[37] For a discussion, see Joseph Alsop, "The Sanctuaries," and "The Sanctuary Problem Again," *Washington Post,* September 19 and October 17, 1966.

Some observers believed Communist efforts to mass forces in the highlands in 1966 were aimed at seizing control of one or more provinces in which the Liberation Front might declare a government that could invite diplomatic recognition. However, allied operations, aided by intelligence from Viet Cong defectors and prisoners, frustrated such plans. Yet, there was no sign of a quick end to the war at the end of 1966. PAVN forces remained relatively untapped and Red China could send even more men, although Mao Tse-tung's Cultural Revolution made Chinese aid less certain. While unable to launch a major offensive, the Viet Cong could still maintain a high level of terrorist and small-scale actions. If, as some observers expected, the enemy main forces abandoned conventional warfare in the highlands for guerrilla tactics in the densely-populated lowland, they could be more difficult to handle.

During 1965 and 1966, however, Viet Cong relations with the peasants deteriorated. When they launched their victory drive in 1965, the Viet Cong increased their taxation and conscription. Dropping their pose as persuasive peasant leaders, they took what they needed by force, and peasant hostility grew. Some villages attacked Communist tax collectors; others expelled Viet Cong soldiers because they brought government attacks; still others fled en masse. The flood of over one million refugees to government-held areas cost the Viet Cong heavily, for abandoned villages produced no rice. They vented resentment by terrorist attacks on refugee centers and resorted to mass kidnapping to repopulate deserted areas. The flow of intelligence from peasants, an important clue to attitudes, markedly increased. With the escalation, the Viet Cong and DRV virtually dropped the pretense of the Liberation Front being a peasant-based South Vietnamese revolution, though the DRV still officially denied the presence of North Vietnamese forces in the South. Defectors and prisoners indicated the North Vietnamese had progressively taken command of the weakened Viet Cong main force, with resultant North-South frictions.[38]

The influx of Americans and construction of bases, combined with the Viet Cong's economic war, brought new shock waves to the battered South Vietnamese economy. Viet Cong strategy aimed to isolate and economically strangle the cities they could not safely attack. Until the major U. S. escalation, it appeared the strategy might work. By blocking canals and roads, rural areas were cut off from urban manufactures and the city from food, and prices soared. As thousands of Americans

[38] Joseph Kraft, "The Road to Peace," *Washington Post*, October 5, 1966, suggested Hanoi was reversing this trend by building up Nguyen Huu Tho, the Liberation Front chairman.

entered the country with dollars to spend, urgent measures were required to restrain inflation. The piastre was devalued, new import taxes were imposed, and the flow of required imports was increased. Prices in general nearly doubled in 18 months up to mid-1966, but hurried imports of food and consumer goods kept the effects from being as severe on the most basic consumer items. Government efforts to control profiteering and official peculation intensified, but lack of adequately trained personnel made it practically impossible to fully police even Saigon's economy.

The growing American presence became painfully evident to middle-class Vietnamese who found it difficult to get taxis or were ousted from rented houses by landlords desiring to rent to Americans at higher prices. Also, many Vietnamese were offended by the numerous bars and other pleasure facilities catering to American servicemen. In late 1966, steps were taken to greatly reduce the number of servicemen in Saigon to alleviate friction and congestion. Yet, thousands of Vietnamese finding high paying jobs with the Americans enjoyed an economic boon. New cities springing up along the coast at Cam Ranh Bay, Chu Lai and other bases drained a labor supply reduced by government and Viet Cong recruitment. The American bases also provided jobs for a refugee flood exceeding the proportions of the 1954 exodus from the North. Other refugees were resettled on vacant lands, but many of the very old and the very young had to be supported in temporary shelters. This presented a heavy burden for the Vietnamese government which lacked trained administrative personnel. Increasingly, the U. S. and refugee relief agencies working closely with provincial officials moved in to fill the gap.

After his first 100 days in office, Ky pledged a war on poverty, illiteracy, corruption, and inefficiency. Renewed emphasis was placed on training rural reconstruction cadre. Earlier programs had fallen short of success because of lack of security, bureaucratic snarls, shifts of personnel during government upheavals, and an inadequate supply of rural-oriented and properly motivated administrative personnel. Rural leadership had been decimated by the Communist assassination and kidnapping of tens of thousands of village officials, teachers, and other potential leaders. During 1964, experiments had begun with U. S. guidance in training rural workers for village action work. Ky's government with considerable U. S. assistance revised and amplified the plans. During 1965 and 1966, 30,000 rural reconstruction personnel were trained to bring social, economic and political reforms to the villages. Armed platoons of about 60 persons, divided into specialized teams, organized village defenses and government, stimulated self-help projects to build housing and improve agriculture, surveyed villagers' needs and desires, and ferreted out Viet Cong infrastructure. Such platoons moved into newly freed areas to help meet villagers' needs and to create the mechanism and will to resist a Viet Cong return. Liberation of the delta by ARVN forces progressed more rapidly, however, than these platoons were available, and despite their training, the rural workers inevitably met with frustrations and failures that brought the program under considerable criticism.

The problems of pacification are enormous, for a few organized guerrillas can terrorize large areas. In the Philippines and Burma, guerrillas exerted control with only 5 to 10 per cent active supporters. Estimates of the population controlled by the Viet Cong in Vietnam at the end of 1966 varied, with about 20 per cent accepted by many, while the government controlled about 55 per cent, with the remainder contested. Government "control" is a relative term, meaning basically the existence of a functioning administration and reasonable security. However, a small group of determined people indistinguishable from the general populace can make any place unsafe any time. Even in the United States a lone "mad sniper" can demoralize a city, and organized gangsters can baffle police for years. Terrorist techniques, combined with a highly developed propaganda and indoctrination system, are very difficult to combat, especially when directed against isolated peasant communities. Critics of the pacification program sometimes expected the Vietnamese government to maintain greater security during an insurrection than is available at night in some American cities. To accelerate the pace of pacification, a shift of military emphasis was ordered. The burden of fighting Communist main forces was to be undertaken by the allied troops during 1967, while the Vietnamese regular army would support pacification in the lowlands by fighting Viet Cong guerrillas and working with rural development activities, thus simultaneously increasing local security and improving the people's welfare. While foreigners could provide technical and economic assistance, only Vietnamese could inspire, direct, and achieve an effective social revolution at the rice-roots level.

Ky early sought to make peace with the minority groups. Building on overtures of the Quat government, Ky improved relations with the Hoa Hao, whose villages had resisted Communist infiltration. He gave them legal recognition and organized Hoa Hao military units under regular Vietnamese army officers. These units had limited utility, however, due to the Hoa Hao's loyalty to their own group and insistence on autonomy. A more serious minority problem was that of the Montagnards, who after long misrule and exploitation, feared and disliked the Vietnamese who treated them with contempt. Diem had stirred unrest by appropriating their lands for refugees and pressing their assimilation into Vietnamese culture. The Communists infiltrated the Montagnards to exploit their grievances and cultivate their desires for autonomy, but without great progress. American Special Forces teams had marked success in organizing the Montagnards into irregular units to oppose Viet Cong penetration, but their efforts were frequently undermined by the Vietnamese army officers who worked with them. In 1964, five Montagnard camps rebelled, killing 31 Vietnamese superiors. Led by Y Bham Enoul, a Rhadé tribal leader who had been jailed by Diem and had briefly served as Director of Montagnard Affairs under Khanh, dissident tribesmen organized the United Front for the Liberation of the Oppressed Race (FULRO). This rebellion caused the Vietnamese to suspect the U. S. of encouraging Montagnard autonomy as had the French, but the Americans, who liked and were liked by the tribal peoples, only wanted a fair deal for them. While FULRO extremists demanded an autonomous state, most asked only recognition of their land rights and tribal customs, representation in local government, and equal services with the Vietnamese. Khanh's government promised greater recognition and equal status, but these promises were so badly kept that a new rebellion occurred in September 1965. Ky mixed firmness with compromise and the rebellious Montagnards reaffirmed their loyalty to the government. How long this peace would last remained in question.

At the Honolulu Conference in February 1966, Generals Ky and Thieu and other top Vietnamese leaders met with their American counterparts, including President Johnson and four cabinet secretaries. The conference dramatically placed U. S. support behind the Ky government, but emphasized not merely military victory but also rural reconstruction and South Vietnam's social and political revolution. The Honolulu Declaration committed the Ky government to encourage national unity and broaden popular participation in nation-building by a democratic constitution and an elective government. The U. S. pledged its support for free elections and maintenance of the "principles of self determination" and "government by the consent of the governed . . ."

After returning from Honolulu, Ky reshuffled his cabinet to emphasize social revolution and began plans for constituent assembly elections. But the Honolulu pledges opened the flood gates of political agitation as various groups sought to seize the political initiative. In a country without viable political parties or a tradition of free debate, demonstrations and "struggle" movements had become methods of political expression and religious groupings had organized as political forces. A political-religious confrontation was touched off in March 1966 by the dismissal of General Nguyen Chanh Thi, who treated the First Corps region as a fief and ignored Premier Ky's orders. Militant student and Buddhist leaders of Hue and Danang led by Thich Tri Quang, whom Thi had cultivated, organized massive protest demonstrations supporting Thi and demanding the removal of the Catholic Chief of State Thieu. The agitation grew more strident as it was infiltrated by Viet Cong. The highly organized militants aided by elements of the civil service, police, and army, virtually cut the northern provinces from Saigon's control, imposed strikes and closed schools at will. The activists, however, met little success in Saigon and other cities, where most students and Buddhists were disgusted with the misuse of religion by political monks. Thi was forgotten, as Tri Quang and his "strugglers" focused on demands for immediate constituent assembly elections and civilian control, ignoring the Honolulu pledge and rejecting Ky's timetable for preparing a constitution.

Proceeding with his program despite a militant Buddhist boycott, in April Ky convened a representative congress which recommended plans for elections and the time and manner for transfer to civilian rule. An Election Law Drafting Committee assembled in May. Tri Quang attempted a tactical retreat, but the Viet Cong-infiltrated agitators in Hue and Danang were not easily quieted. Government control was forcibly reasserted in Danang in June, but resistance continued in Hue. This agitation brought on ten self-immolations before the demonstrations subsided. To placate the militants, Ky added ten civilians to the military directorate, but he rejected demands that the directorate be empowered to select a new premier and chief of state. When moderate Buddhist leader Thich Tam Chau returned from abroad, he denounced both Tri Quang and the demonstrators. Quang then embarked on a hunger strike, calling for a boycott of the September elections.

The Election Law promulgated June 19 created 117 electoral districts with nine reserved for Montagnards. Local election boards representing government and nongovernment elements were to screen candidates with a central board to review appeals. Following the practice established in insurgency situations in Greece, Malaya, and the Philippines, Communists were prohibited from candidacy. Neutralists, interpreted as persons working for a foreign power against national interests, were also excluded, but all adults over 18 were eligible to vote. The government made strenuous efforts to screen candidates fairly, to permit free discussion in electioneering, and to make citizens aware of the elections and the issues involved. Both the Viet Cong and militant Buddhists urged their followers to boycott the elections or to spoil their ballots if "forced" to vote. The government deployed all its military and police forces to counteract Viet Cong terrorism and to safeguard the polls.

The election results proved a phenomenal victory for the government. The foreign diplomats and some 500 foreign newsmen who observed the voting throughout the country on September 11, found no significant evidence of government manipulation or coercion of voters or of malpractice in ballot counting. Eighty per cent of all registered voters cast ballots with local results ranging from 65 per cent in Saigon and 83.9 in Buddhist Hue to over 92 per cent in provinces where the Viet Cong were strongest. Only 5 per cent of the ballots countrywide and 11 per cent in Hue were spoiled. The results were humiliating to both the Viet Cong and the militant Buddhists, supporting some pre-election estimates that each had a following of no more than 10 per cent of the population. The voters clearly defied Communist terrorism, which killed 19 and injured 120 on election day.

The new constituent assembly represented all walks of life. Notably, 33 Catholics won seats as compared to 44 Buddhists. With over half the representatives under 44 years old, much young blood enlivened Saigon's war-weary political life. While elder statesman Phan Khac Suu was elected chairman, the young men took control. Although considerable jockeying for leadership ensued as new political forces and blocs developed, the assembly proceeded with writing its constitution with less bickering and greater independence than any Vietnamese assembly had previously displayed. As the assembly organized, Ky found it necessary to reshuffle his cabinet to placate dissatisfaction over excessive use of police powers by the Saigon police and Southerners' complaints of inadequate representation in the government. While it appeared likely that the military would continue to have a significant role, the Ky government promised to return to military duties after elections under the new constitution.

6: The Communist North

In view of the Viet Minh's military victory over the French, the question has been raised frequently as to why the Communists accepted the division of the country at Geneva. Certainly there was international pressure on them to do so and also the expectation that the South would fall in two years without fighting. But the Viet Minh were themselves in desperate circumstances. They had been fighting from the jungles and mountains for eight years at an increasingly terrible cost. Also casualties were high among the laborers who swarmed over jungle trails carrying supplies from China. Nearly everyone in the resistance suffered malnutrition, exhaustion, and disease. Having lost only 4 per cent of their Indochinese forces at Dien Bien Phu, the French could have continued the war, possibly with direct American involvement in the fighting. While a pro-Chinese faction led by Truong Chinh might have welcomed Chinese intervention, Ho Chi Minh and General Vo Nguyen Giap feared that the Chinese, if invited in, might never leave.

When the Viet Minh returned to Hanoi, they found it more difficult to build than to destroy a government and economy, though the North had nearly all the industry and mineral resources of Vietnam. While it had over half the population, its smaller area included less food-growing terrain than the South. Communication, transportation, and irrigation facilities were badly damaged. The French had removed much of the factory and office equipment and machinery, because the Viet Minh refused to guarantee French investments against confiscation. Communist belligerence also frightened out all but a few French technicians who remained one year to run essential public services. Only by agreeing to pay for it with coal deliveries for 15 years, did the DRV save part of the coal-mining equipment.

[145]

Rehabilitation and Political Consolidation

As in other Communist-controlled countries, all aspects of life in the DRV—politics, economics, social engineering, and the strategy of war or peace—serve the interests of the Party's goal of achieving a Communist society. Intermediate objectives are set by a series of development plans. The DRV's First Three Year Plan (1955-57) aimed at rehabilitating agriculture, industry, transportation and communications and preparing for collectivization and industrialization. It was also a period of political consolidation during which the united-front stage of the revolution ended. Following the surfacing of the ICP as the Lao Dong or Workers' Party in 1951, the Party hierarchy paralleled that of the DRV government, with Party organisms directly or indirectly controlling equivalent government bureaus at each level. Some non-Party men were given important-sounding offices but were flanked by Party men.

Even before the Geneva Conference, measures for close physical and thought control had been imposed in Viet Minh areas.[1] Everyone was enrolled in cells, whose members reported on each other and conducted criticism and self-criticism sessions. Children were encouraged to inform on their parents. All above the age of six were organized into a network of overlapping front associations based on age, sex, occupation, and special interests. Trusted Party cadre held the important offices and directed the meetings to serve Party ends, while simulating democratic procedures. To coordinate Party direction of these associations, the Lien Viet (United Front) was merged with the Viet Minh in 1951. It was further broadened into the Fatherland Front in 1955 to add "non-communist" political machinery for the absorption of South Vietnam by the expected 1956 elections. The Front's platform called for a two-stage reunification—a loose confederation with separate legislatures for the North and the South, followed by full integration. Although no reunification elections occurred, the Fatherland Front was maintained as a device for internal population control and indoctrination and for international propaganda.

Long range plans for purging traditional rural leaders through land reforms and for collectivizing agriculture had been announced in 1950 by Party Secretary General Truong Chinh, who was strongly motivated

---

[1] Hoang Van Chi, a former Viet Minh, vividly describes these techniques in *From Colonialism to Communism* (New York, 1964).

by Red Chinese experiences in these areas. In March 1953, remnants of the 1946 National Assembly met to rubber-stamp a Population Classification decree. All people, rural and urban alike, were divided into classes and subclasses, ranging from landlords to landless laborers. Elaborate formulas equated money, fish, or other forms of income with fixed quantities of rice. A two-stage "agrarian reform" began with a rent reduction campaign in 1953, which lowered rents and absolved debts, followed by a land reform campaign (1954-56), which confiscated money, property, and land from the more prosperous.[2]

Accompanying both stages was the punishment of "feudalists" for "crimes" against society. To direct the reform, Truong Chinh used Chinese Communist advisers and Vietnamese cadre trained in China. By terror and propaganda, Communist agitators incited the villagers to lodge accusations against their more prosperous neighbors. Although the few truly rich landlords had fled to the South, each village had to fill a quota of "feudalists." Estimates of the number killed range up to 100,000.[3] About half a million were driven from their homes and lands, some to prison or hard labor; others, including women and children, starved because people feared to aid them.

As purge excesses brought local Party factional strife, 12,000 Party members were jailed. Top Party leaders, sharply critical of Truong Chinh's dogmatic and inflexible attitude, tried to stem the purge with a "Mistakes Rectification" campaign that filled Hanoi's newspapers and journals for months with details of the reign of terror. In October 1956, Vo Nguyen Giap discussed the Party's errors in a remarkably frank speech before the Lao Dong Party Central Committee:

We . . . executed too many honest people . . . and, seeing enemies everywhere, resorted to terror which became far too widespread. . . . While carrying out our land reform program, we failed to respect the principles of freedom of faith and worship . . . in regions inhabited by minority tribes we have attacked tribal chiefs too strongly, thus injuring instead of respecting local customs and manners. . . . When reorganizing the Party we paid too much importance to the notion of social class instead of adhering . . . to political qualifications alone. Instead of recognizing education to be the first essential, we resorted exclusively to organizational

[2] See Hoang Van Chi, op. cit., for details and Allen B. Cole, ed., Conflict in Indo-China and International Repercussions: A Documentary History, 1945-1955 (Ithaca, N. Y., 1956) for the texts of the decrees, pp. 139-147, 150-56.

[3] Gérard Tongas, a leftist professor teaching in Hanoi, estimated 100,000 in his J'ai vécu dans l'enfer communiste du Nord Viêt-Nam et j'ai choisi la liberté (Paris, 1960), p. 222.

measures such as disciplinary punishments, expulsion from the Party, executions, dissolutions of Party branches and cells. Worse still, torture came to be regarded as a normal practice during party reorganization.[4]

Though the purge gradually spent itself, the peasants remained alienated. In November, villagers openly revolted in heavily Catholic Nghe An, Ho's home province. This uprising and other lesser disturbances were brutally suppressed by regular army units. According to DRV reports, the land reform transferred some 2.25 million acres of land, 115,000 farm animals, 1,846,000 farm implements, and 71,000 tons of foodstuffs to 2.1 million peasant families with about 8.3 million members. This amounted to about 1/70 of an animal, 1/5 of a farm implement, 19 pounds of food and ⅓ acre of land per person. Half of the land distributed had been commonly owned and helped pay for village government, communal rites, and charities. Land redistribution brought a sharp drop in food production, partly because the people were demoralized and partly because land was taken from the most experienced cultivators and given to the poorest peasants, who were not always skilled farmers. The rebellions and purge excesses caused Truong Chinh's removal as Party chief, although Chinese support kept him in the Party Central Committee. Assuming Truong Chinh's position (renamed First Secretary), Ho Chi Minh managed to hold the Party together. One basic goal of the reform was achieved, however—the destruction of the traditional rural elite.

The elimination of troublesome intellectuals followed. At partition, the Communists, who needed all available skills, convinced many intellectuals not to migrate by bestowing liberal rewards and decorations and government employment. In this permissive climate, intellectuals contributed to the criticisms of the Mistakes Rectification campaign. Their criticism first focused on the Party's virtual military dictatorship that left little room for intellectual leadership. Later attacks were broadened, stimulated by the Hungarian uprising and by China's Hundred Flowers campaign. Several intellectual journals flourished briefly, all critical of the Lao Dong party and the government.[5]

With both countryside and city aligned against them, the Lao Dong party leaders moved cautiously to regain command. Critical journals were closed by indirect means, such as strikes of their workers and

[4] *Nhan Dan* (Lao Dong party newspaper), October 31, 1956.
[5] Hoang Van Chi quotes articles from these journals in his *The New Class in North Vietnam* (Saigon, 1958).

stoppages of paper supplies. In December 1956, a presidential decree strengthened government controls over the press. Intellectuals were organized into a union with permission to publish its own journal under Party guidance. Through the mass associations, Party agitators incited a wave of anti-intellectualism. Critical intellectuals were forced to make humiliating public apologies. Millions of signatures were collected demanding their punishment as "enemy agents," and leading intellectuals were arrested as agents of Diem. Some died in prison; others were "re-educated" by labor in mines or factories after indoctrination courses designed to teach a "proletarian viewpoint." The purge of the intellectuals and the indoctrination movement spread to teachers and students and finally to the Party itself, extending over several years.

The dislocations caused by the reform and purges prevented realization of the first plan's economic goals.[6] However, the first steps toward socialization of agriculture were taken. Concurrently, city merchants were impoverished by confiscatory capital taxes ranging up to 50 per cent on merchandise stocks. Even street vendors were victimized. Without the usual commercial imports and with local production disrupted, stores emptied of nearly everything. Famine was averted only by rice rationing and by emergency food imports. Burma supplied rice under a three-way agreement with the USSR, and China provided food and clothing. Technical aid and capital equipment for rehabilitation were provided by all Communist-bloc countries, either as cash grants or loans, with China contributing over half of the total. Such aid helped restore rail links with China and put back into limited production the Hon Gay coal mines, Haiphong cement works, Nam Dinh textile mills, and a few other plants. Otherwise progress toward reconstruction was slow.

"Socialist Transformation"

The second development plan (1958-60), calling for a "socialist transformation" by the transfer of the instruments of production to the state, was drawn up with Russian and Chinese help, but it aimed too high and its goals were cut back annually. No dependable statistics are available, but food production apparently declined while the

[6] See William Kaye, "A Bowl of Rice Divided: The Economy of North Vietnam," in P. J. Honey, ed., *North Vietnam Today, Profile of a Communist Satellite* (New York, 1962), pp. 104-16.

population grew by about 500,000 yearly. Industrial output increased modestly, but from a low base point. Although a foundation for industrialization was to be prepared, the principal plan objective was political —to increase Party control and to move the economy toward collectivization. By 1960, practically all private industry, commerce, and transportation were under state control and 75 per cent of the craftsmen and small traders were organized into cooperatives.

With less success, Party cadre undertook extensive campaigns to effect Truong Chinh's 1950 plan for agricultural collectivization. Individual farmers were first induced to form mutual aid teams that shared tools, draft animals, and labor. Then they were organized into low level cooperatives in which they pooled land, labor, and equipment, while retaining ownership and receiving shares in produce based upon their acreage and labor. As rapidly as the cooperatives were functional, Party organizers urged reluctant farmers to convert them into state-owned collective farms. For peasants who had received land in the redistribution, this completed the full cycle inasmuch as they became agricultural workers on state-owned collectives, bossed in work gangs by Party cadre. Pressured by high taxes and the need for tools and farm animals, 85 per cent of the landowners had joined mutual aid teams or producers' cooperatives by 1960, though only 12 per cent had moved into collectives. Continual meetings, Party pressures, and changes demoralized the peasantry and unquestionably contributed to the Party's failure to achieve its 1958-60 production goals, despite progress in rebuilding dikes and reclaiming abandoned land. To offset these failures and placate the farmers, the state permitted them small private garden plots, which soon provided 55 per cent of the farmers' income. Despite this lesson, the Party dogmatically pushed for rapid collectivization, apparently with strong urging from Communist China.

The period of the second plan brought a new constitution, promulgated on January 1, 1960, after extensive popular discussion and consideration.[7] This constitution, like Diem's, declared Vietnam a single nation from north to south. A long preamble attacked the French and American "imperialists and their henchmen." The role of the Communist party was not defined in the main text of the constitution. However, the preamble defined the country as a "people's democratic state" based on an alliance between the workers and peasants under the leadership of the working class, and made clear that the Lao Dong or

[7] Bernard B. Fall, The Two Viet-Nams (New York, 1963), pp. 399-416, presents the full text.

Workers' party would lead the government and the people in building socialism in the North and struggling for national reunification. The economic and social section emphasized state ownership of the means of production and subjected ownership of private property to state "guidance." Equal rights for all regardless of sex, race, religion or property status were guaranteed but qualifications stressing the duties of the individual and the priority of the state's interests effectively negated them. The constitution provided for a strong president, a vice-president, and a premier. National Assembly electoral districts consigned heavier representation to the cities than to rural areas, reflecting the same distrust of peasants shown in the Soviet constitution. Minority peoples were reserved one-seventh of the total seats. The National Assembly was proclaimed the highest state organ, but its functions were largely delegated to a Standing Committee resembling the Soviet Presidium. A Special Political Council of top officials seemed designed to prevent the president or premier from becoming overly powerful.

In May 1960, the first national elections in the North since 1946 were held. Over 99 per cent of the electorate voted, but there was no secret ballot and little choice, with only 458 Party-selected candidates for 362 contested seats. Members of the 1946 assembly representing the South were carried into the new body. Truong Chinh was chosen president of the Assembly, Ho was reconfirmed as DRV president, Pham Van Dong continued to serve as premier and foreign minister as he had since 1955, while army commander-in-chief Vo Nguyen Giap remained minister of defense.[8] National elections in 1964 made no change in leadership. Local government was dominated as before by popularly elected People's Councils. Like the mass associations, these councils provide for Party-directed popular discussion on a principle called "democratic centralization." Power is held by Party stalwarts at each level, but Party-controlled debate of all decisions and actions is encouraged. Great effort is exerted to persuade the people that Party decisions are not only correct, but also represent the popular will. Before an action is undertaken, it is introduced through Party channels at local meetings. There it is discussed and conclusions are presented to higher levels as a request from the people. Thus objections to a policy are talked out or necessary modifications made. This was essentially the process followed in preparing the new constitution.

[8] P. J. Honey, ed., *North Vietnam Today*, pp. 47-59, gives an authoritative view of the top DRV leaders. Also see Honey, *Communism in North Vietnam: Its Role in the Sino-Soviet Dispute* (Cambridge, Mass., 1963).

DRV Expansionism

Having consolidated Party control, the DRV was ready for a major escalation of the war in the South. Reunification was increasingly vital to the Northern economy, for the failures to enlarge food production jeopardized the whole development program. Before partition the North had exchanged its manufactures for rice from the South, but Diem refused to continue this trade which might support Communist aggression. By winning the South, the DRV hoped to feed its own people and to secure rice and rubber for export to support industrialization. Without the South, the DRV was reduced to perennial mendicancy.

Important to winning the South was the supply route through Laos. Even before the Communists had won North Vietnam by pursuing the "line of the united front," they had adopted the same line for Laos. When the Party re-emerged in 1951, it declared that it had the "duty to help the Laotian and Cambodian revolutionaries" and "revolutionary movements in other countries." The name Workers' (Lao Dong) Party was selected because it facilitated "actions to help these revolutionary movements." [9] Because many Lao Dong members feared losing control of the Lao and Cambodian parties, a top secret party directive explained, "The Vietnamese party reserves the right to supervise the actions of its brother parties in Cambodia and Laos." [10] Prince Souphanouvong, leader of the Communist Pathet Lao, had been in contact with Ho Chi Minh since World War II. His Vietnamese wife was a high Lao Dong party member. The Viet Minh invasions of Laos in 1953-54 brought large Lao areas under Viet Minh control and established "secure bases" for the Pathet Lao. Viet Minh forces have remained in Laos ever since, supporting the Lao insurgents in violation of the Geneva agreements of 1954 and 1962. They also built and guarded the Ho Chi Minh trail. This network has been connected with South China by roads across northern Laos constructed under the direction of a large Chinese "economic and cultural" mission from Peking, headed by a general specializing in guerrilla warfare and in the tribal peoples of the area.

More recently, a Hanoi-Peking supported insurgency has been mounting in Northeastern Thailand. This area has a Lao-speaking

---

[9] P. J. Honey, "North Vietnam's Worker's Party," *Pacific Affairs*, XXXV, No. 4 (Winter, 1962-3), 375-383.

[10] Arthur J. Dommen, *Conflict in Laos: Politics of Neutralization* (New York, 1964), p. 73.

population with a Communist-infiltrated Vietnamese minority. A clandestine radio, Voice of the People of Thailand (VOPT), initiated appeals for revolution in 1962. On October 1, 1964, the New China News Agency reported the Thai Communist Party's call for the formation of a united front. Two months later, VOPT formally announced a Thailand Independence Movement (TIM) to overthrow the Thai government. On January 1, 1965, the Lao Dong journal *Nhan Dan* announced the proclamation of a Thailand Patriotic Front. News organs in Peking and Hanoi and the Liberation Radio in South Vietnam supported the calls for revolution. Radio Peking on April 19, 1966 said the Chinese have an "inescapable duty" to support the Thai movement and warned that "a single spark could start a prairie fire." In late 1965, TIM merged with the Patriotic Front and, on December 15, Radio Peking said of the Front, ". . . the only way . . . to destroy the enemy and to score a final victory is to enlarge the struggle into a people's war." Hanoi and Peking continued to support the rising violence in Thailand during 1966 by propaganda and by training guerrillas and propaganda cadre.

In 1956, Communist cadre in South Vietnam were ordered to step up their agitation and political efforts. In that year, a DRV general and 100 infiltrated propaganda agents were reported to be holding training courses for sabotaging Diem's constituent assembly elections.[11] In Hanoi, the Lao Dong party created a Central Reunification Department to supervise operations in the South and direct the training and infiltration of the cadre who had gone north in 1954-55. The Viet Cong, however, won little real political following. Control over villages could be secured by persuasion backed by terrorism and government operations could be disrupted in the countryside, but this failed to win the intellectual and professional groups. After an inspection tour into the South in 1958, Le Duan, a top Party official and a former southern guerrilla leader, recommended a South Vietnamese National Liberation Front under a southern branch of the Lao Dong party, backed by a South Vietnamese "liberation army."[12] These recommendations were approved by the Party Central Committee in May 1959. On May 14, 1959, the Party newspaper *Nhan Dan* called for "all necessary forms and measures . . . [to] achieve the goal of the revolution." As early as August 1958, however, a radio program calling itself

[11] *Newsweek*, February 13, 1956, pp. 47-8.
[12] See George Carver, "The Faceless Viet Cong," *Foreign Affairs*, April, 1966, pp. 347-472.

the voice of the Liberation Front had begun broadcasting instructions to the Viet Cong forces.

On July 10, 1959, Ho Chi Minh wrote in an article in *Red Flag*, a Belgian Communist journal, that the North Vietnamese were building socialism in "only one part of the country while in the other part we still have to direct and bring to a close the middle class democratic and anti-imperialist revolution." The following January, the chief military strategist General Vo Nguyen Giap said, "The North has become a large rear echelon of our army. . . . The North is the revolutionary base of the whole country. . . ." [13] Following the promulgation of the constitution, the government created a Reunification Commission which was chaired by the same DRV army general (a specialist in guerrilla war), who headed the Party's Reunification Department. In September 1960, Le Duan, named first secretary of the Lao Dong party after his trip to the South, told the Third Congress of the Party in Hanoi, "Parallel with the building and consolidation of North Viet-Nam, bringing it to socialism, our people should endeavor to maintain and develop the revolutionary forces in South Vietnam. . . ." He warned that the struggle "will be long, drawn out and arduous," and will combine "many varied forms of struggle—from elementary to advanced, legal and illegal. . . ." To assure victory for the "revolutionary struggle," Le Duan recommended that "the South Viet-Nam people, under the leadership of the Marxist-Leninist Party and the working class, should endeavor to build a worker-peasant-army coalition bloc, and set up a broad national united front. . . ." [14] On September 10, the Congress issued a resolution directing the establishment of a "broad national united front" in South Vietnam. [15] Three months later, the National Front for the Liberation of South Vietnam (NFL) was proclaimed in terms almost identical with those of the Lao Dong party Resolution. On May 18, 1961, the Liberation Front radio announced that the ". . . decision of the Third Congress of the Lao Dong party concerning the revolution . . . in South Vietnam has been correctly executed by the delegates of the party for South Vietnam and the different echelons of the Party. . . ." [16]

[13] *Hoc Tap*, January, 1950.

[14] From a Lao Dong Party Central Committee Political Report, quoted in Department of State, *A Threat to the Peace: North Viet-Nam's Efforts to Conquer South Viet-Nam* (Washington, 1961), Part II, Appendix A, pp. 4-5.

[15] Resolution of the Third National Congress of the Lao Dong Party adopted at Hanoi, September 10, 1960, quoted in Department of State, *op. cit.*, pp. 1-3.

[16] Communist sources maintain the Front was created by "non-Communists" to protect themselves from Diem's oppression. Wilfred Burchett, a writer for

The Liberation Front's 10-point Manifesto was an ambiguous document. While promising a representative government of national union, it added that "patriotic eminent citizens must take over for the people the control of the economic, political, social and cultural interests. . . ."[17] Promised freedoms were qualified by such words as "essential" and "normal," and the door was left open for confiscation of business, industry, and private property, and the introduction of a socialist state. Initial announcements of the Manifesto promising agrarian reform apparently aroused concern in the South, for the excesses of the North were well known. Later broadcasts dropped these references.

It seems that some South Vietnamese Communists were disturbed by the instructions to include in the front intellectuals, bourgeoisie, and wealthy peasants whom the Communists ordinarily consider unreliable. A Party directive explained:

In the present situation of South Viet-Nam, the Central Committee supports integration of these elements into the Front, not because the Party is going to entrust these classes with heavy responsibilities in the revolutionary liberation of South Viet-Nam, but only to utilize their abilities and their prestige in order to push forward the revolution and to give more prestige to the People's Front for the Liberation of South Viet-Nam.

This line of conduct is only a temporary policy of the Party. When the revolution is crowned with success, this policy will be revised. Then the Party will act overtly to lead the revolution in South Viet-Nam.[18]

But the NFL did not attract many "national bourgeois," intellectuals, or other middle class figures, who knew of the Northern purges. The best recruit for NFL chairman was Nguyen Huu Tho, a little-known

Moscow papers, gives this view in *The Furtive War: The United States in Vietnam and Laos* (New York, 1963). Some non-Communists advance variations of this approach. French scholar Philippe Devillers in "The Struggle for Unification," in *North Vietnam Today,* ed. J. P. Honey, pp. 25-46, accepts the Party's role, but says the southern Communists only reacted to Diem's attacks. Hanoi, then following the Soviet "peaceful coexistence" line in the Sino-Soviet dispute, gave support because it feared losing control of the southern movement. This view does not stand up under the weight of evidence that Communist terrorism not only did not stop but steadily accelerated after 1954 and that Diem's "repression" of former Viet Minh was initiated by that terrorism and not the reverse.

[17] See Fall, *op. cit.,* pp. 439-443, for the text of the program as broadcast over the Liberation Radio.

[18] Captured document reproduced in facsimile and translation in Department of State, *A Threat to the Peace,* Part II, Appendix P, pp. 96-7.

provincial lawyer, who had a long record of Communist associations as did the other top Front leaders. Subsequently, not a single nationally known non-Communist personality has supported the NFL, though some served jail sentences for opposing Diem or succeeding governments. Many of the associations that supposedly created the Front seem to have remained on paper. Captured documents and statements of prisoners and defectors make clear the Party maintained a close control over those that did exist and over all military forces of the Front. A "Research Document on the Organization of Peasants' Associations," captured in Bien Hoa February 8, 1961, states, "The Front's policy should be in deep harmony with the laboring class and should be placed under the leadership of the Lao Dong Party of Viet-Nam. . . ." [19]

In January 1962, the People's Revolutionary Party (PRP) was announced as an independent Marxist-Leninist party, but a captured secret Party instruction dated December 7, 1961, explained to Lao Dong party members in the South:

In regard to the foundation of the People's Revolutionary Party of South Viet-Nam, the creation of this party is only a matter of strategy; it needs to be explained within the party; and, to deceive the enemy, it is necessary that the new party be given the outward appearance corresponding to a division of the party (Lao Dong) into two and the foundation of a new party, so that the enemy cannot use it in his propaganda.

Within the party, it is necessary to explain that the founding of the People's Revolutionary Party has the purpose of isolating the Americans and the Ngo Dinh Diem regime, and to counter their accusations of an invasion of the South by the North. It is a means of supporting our sabotage of the Geneva agreement, of advancing the plan of invasion of the South, and at the same time permitting the Front for Liberation of the South to recruit new adherents, and to gain the sympathy of non-aligned countries in Southeast Asia.

The People's Revolutionary Party has only the appearance of an independent existence; actually, our party is nothing but the Lao Dong Party of Viet-Nam (Viet-Minh Communist Party), unified from North to South, under the direction of the central executive committee of the party, the chief of which is President Ho. . . . [20]

The PRP leadership remains secret, but evidence indicates it is headed by top Lao Dong party men, many of whom are southern born as is Pham Van Dong, the DRV premier, who represents a southern con-

[19] Facsimile and translation in Department of State, op. cit., pp. 85-6.
[20] Translated in Department of State, Aggression From the North: The Record of North Viet-Nam's Campaign to Conquer South Viet-Nam (Washington, 1965), Appendix G., p. 57. Also see P. J. Honey, "North Vietnam's Workers' Party," Pacific Affairs, XXXV, No. 4 (Winter, 1962-63).

stituency in the DRV National Assembly, having been carried over from the 1946 assembly.[21]

Socialist Construction

Despite the heavy war drain, the Party pressed socialism in the North. Hanoi's literature and broadcasts revealed that the second economic plan failed badly, especially in agriculture. Yet, the first Five Year Plan (1961-65) moved the emphasis from "socialist transformation" to "socialist construction." The Lao Dong Party Congress of September 1961 called for building a "balanced and modern socialist economy," with priority for heavy industry. Agriculture was to be completely collectivized to serve industrialization. After serious crop failures in 1962, a three-year plan was launched to improve agricultural management, but urgent radio appeals from Hanoi during 1966 indicated the farming community did not respond well to the pressures. In addition, there were shortages of fertilizer, equipment, and labor because of the war, and in 1963 large areas suffered from drought and flood. To relieve food shortages and population pressures and to develop new export crops such as rubber, several hundred thousand people were resettled in the highlands. Though they met serious problems, including malaria and hostile tribesmen, the forced migration continued under special impetus to decentralize both the population and industry for war purposes. Despite the various strenuous efforts for improvement, food production remained static. While increases in industry outpaced agriculture, this progress did not compensate for the growing agricultural deficits.

Mining operations, particularly of coal, provided most of the exports, which dropped sharply after the bombing began. Light industries, a large part remaining handicrafts, supplied 90 per cent of the limited consumer goods. Textiles, coal, and cement production went far above prewar levels, but paper and other industries progressed far more slowly. New hydroelectric and thermal electric plants increased power output several hundred per cent before being damaged in the bombing. Production at the Thai Nguyen iron-steel complex, however, remained low.

[21] At the Geneva Conference on Laos in July 1962, a DRV delegate inadvertently disclosed that four Lao Dong Party Central Committee members were not listed publicly since they were "directing military operations in South Vietnam." P. J. Honey, *loc. cit.* For extensive documentation of Communist control of the Liberation Front and the PRP, see Douglas Pike, *Viet Cong: The Organization and Techniques of the National Liberation Front of South Vietnam* (Cambridge, Mass., 1966).

Through their successive plans, the North Vietnamese claimed great strides in the field of education and social welfare. After 1954, a concerted campaign to eliminate illiteracy sent students to the hamlets to teach adults. Villagers were required to pass spelling tests before crossing bridges or entering markets. School construction and teacher training were pressed in all development plans. By 1964, the school enrollment stood at nearly 2.8 million or about 55 per cent of the school-aged children, with 26,000 in universities and 80,000 in vocational training, according to government reports.[22] There were also adult schools run by cooperatives and factories. Special efforts were made to bring education in their own languages to the major tribal groups. While the quantitative educational achievements were impressive, qualitatively there was much to be desired. All teaching was required to further Communist indoctrination. Teachers were watched for possible political deviation, and at times, as in 1958, were sent into forced labor to assure a proper proletarian viewpoint. Complaints in Hanoi literature of the low technical and cultural level of workers and Party leaders indicated that this political emphasis had seriously affected education. However, other complaints indicated the political education was not completely successful. In a speech on Hanoi radio October 22, 1966, Ho attacked such evils as "individualism and commandism" and "bureaucratic and overbearing manners," which would indicate that many Party members still tend to act selfishly and arbitrarily, ignoring the principle that the good Communist must always place the Party above himself and must lead rather than command the people.

In public health, the DRV claimed progress equal with that in education. In 1964, the government reported that the number of hospitals had increased from 47 in 1939 to 480 in 1964. All lowland villages and 80 per cent of the highland ones reportedly had medical and maternity stations. According to DRV reports, the health and medical services stressed prevention and combined Eastern and Western medicines. Village education emphasized personal and public hygiene. While the level of medical and health training was low, considerable improvement in public health had been achieved.

Problems of Escalation

Original expectations of large Communist-bloc aid were not fully met. Foreign technical advisers often proved inefficient from the Viet-

---

[22] Gérard Tongas, op. cit., states that North Vietnamese statistics are published only to support propaganda. While teaching in North Vietnam, Tongas became highly critical of the DRV educational system.

namese viewpoint, while the advisers complained the Vietnamese would not take advice. These complaints resembled some heard in South Vietnam. Some reports indicated the USSR temporarily stopped or reduced assistance in 1963, when Hanoi failed to back Moscow against Peking. However, after the U. S. began to bomb North Vietnam, new aid was promised from both Moscow and Peking. War needs made a shambles of economic planning, and a second five-year program to have begun in 1966 was abandoned in favor of an emergency two-year plan. Destruction from the bombing mounted steadily as hundreds of planes daily attacked communications, transportation, military bases, and other facilities supporting the war in the South. A quarter million Vietnamese and some 80,000 Chinese were reported to be kept busy repairing the damage. Power plants and fuel depots went up in flames even in the outskirts of Hanoi and Haiphong, but these centers with the major concentrations of industry were spared for humanitarian, psychological, and diplomatic reasons. The raids also grew increasingly costly to the Americans as thousands of anti-aircraft guns and missiles arrived from China and the Soviet Union. Inevitably, there were mounting North Vietnamese civilian casualties from misplaced and jettisoned bombs and from falling anti-aircraft shells and rockets.

Within North Vietnam as within the United States a debate has occurred over the course to be pursued in the war. The North Vietnamese have tried to effect a balance between the doctrines of the USSR and Communist China.[28] An article in Hoc Tap in March 1964 recognized two forms of liberation movements, political (i.e., the Soviet's) and armed (the Chinese). Each is suitable under certain circumstances, but both should receive support from the socialist camp. In South Vietnam, explained Hoc Tap, both forms of struggle were being used. DRV leaders, however, had long been divided into factions ranging from extreme pro-Peking liberation war proponents to extreme pro-Moscow peaceful coexistence orientations. The pro-Chinese group was headed by Truong Chinh, who had not completely recovered from the disgrace of the agrarian reform excesses. General Vo Nguyen Giap, considered the head of the pro-Soviet group, evidenced anti-Chinese sentiments but, as defense minister and commander-in-chief, most certainly was directing the strategy of the war in the South, which has appeared to follow the Peking hard line rather than the Soviet soft line.

[28] See P. J. Honey, *Communism in North Vietnam: Its Role in the Sino-Soviet Dispute* (Cambridge, Mass., 1963), and King Chen, "North Vietnam in the Sino-Soviet Dispute 1962-64," *Asian Survey*, IV, No. 9 (September, 1964), 1023-36.

Somewhere between the extremes was Party First Secretary Le Duan, who was thought to have supported a hard line in pursuing the war and opposing negotiations, and for this reason was believed to have Chinese backing. Ho Chi Minh usually played a conciliatory role. He was thought to have feared the possible consequences of accepting larger Chinese aid and resisted China's past pressures to break with Moscow. Such a break was made less likely in October 1966, when the Soviet bloc of nations pledged $1 billion in additional aid and seemed to be made more remote by the chaos caused in China by the Cultural Revolution. Ho had good reason to be aware, however, that Vietnam was a pawn in the Sino-Soviet dispute.

But some observers believed the pawn may have boxed in the major powers. China's belligerence helped push North Vietnam into aggression against the South, but both China and the less enthusiastic Soviets appeared to feel bound to keep Hanoi supplied with the sinews of war at whatever cost, because Communist-bloc prestige and its liberation war theory were at stake. As the war continued, the leaders of North Vietnam and the Liberation Front searched for a safe position in the Sino-Soviet quarrel. In an editorial in the September 1966 *Hoc Tap*, the Hanoi leaders indicated irritation at being pushed by both sides. The editorial asserted that with 36 years of successful revolutionary experience, the Vietnamese Communists, while still ready to learn "from select experiences of fraternal parties," could guide their own revolution and knew what was best for Vietnam.[24] However, Hanoi's radio and periodicals increasingly alluded to internal Party strife, popular unrest, and even small-scale open resistance. Party journals contained numerous exhortations that implied growing difficulties in maintaining production in industry and agriculture. But DRV leaders, while differing among themselves over strategy, still refused to end their military aggression and rejected opportunities to negotiate an end to hostilities. Meanwhile both North and South Vietnam continued to suffer the horrors of war.

[24] "Let Us Step Up the Theory-Formulating Task of the Party," *Hoc Tap*, September, 1966; also broadcast over Radio Hanoi, October 2, 1966.

7: Efforts for Peace

Rarely has peace been so widely sought as it was in Vietnam. International organizations, coalitions, national leaders, and private individuals all endeavored to end the conflict. The United States energetically and thoughtfully pursued peace, encouraged the efforts of others, and solicited assistance from the world's leaders of all political orientations. Yet every effort was rebuffed by the Viet Cong, Hanoi, and Peking.

Why was this intransigent position maintained? There was first Hanoi's objective of reunifying Vietnam under Lao Dong party control, which has been discussed and documented in earlier chapters, as has been DRV interest in Laos. There was also the view of Hanoi, Peking, and, to a lesser degree, Moscow that Indochina was a testing ground for Communist-led wars of liberation. This position was made evident at the Tricontinental Solidarity Congress in Havana in January 1966, when delegates of Communist and extreme left-wing parties of 82 countries set up machinery for coordinating liberation movements world-wide. A twelve-nation directorate, including Communist China and the USSR, created a Committee for Assistance and Aid to National Liberation and Fighting Movements, a Secretariat, and a Tricontinental Committee to Aid Vietnam. Havana became the center for these organs and for training guerrillas and political agents.

One might well have asked whether Hanoi and her allies would accept anything less than complete victory in South Vietnam. The idea of a neutralist settlement was advanced on occasions. The United States expressed no opposition to a neutralist solution but insisted that true neutrality must include genuine independence, free from any form of outside threats or subversion. A neutralist government on a "troika" formula was tried in Laos in 1962, but when the Communists could not gain control they refused to cooperate. In July 1963, while the Buddhist crisis was developing in South Vietnam, Liberation Front and Hanoi propaganda suggested a neutralist solution might be possible if Diem sent away his American advisers and established a coalition government. This move was supported by President de Gaulle. Subsequently, as the Communists scented total victory, neutralist themes were largely abandoned. On January 7, 1966, Chinese Premier Chou En-lai, in discussing Moscow's reported advocacy of a troika formula for Vietnam, said, "In actual practice this formula failed in Laos. How can we let South Vietnam follow this pattern and repeat the failure of Laos?" [1]

Another frequently suggested solution was U. N. mediation. After DRV torpedo boats attacked U. S. Seventh Fleet vessels in August 1965, the late U. N. Ambassador Adlai Stevenson explained American retaliatory attacks before the United Nations. The U. S. accepted a Soviet proposal to invite a North Vietnamese representative to provide information for the Security Council. Hanoi replied, with Peking's support, that the U. N. had no right to examine the problem and that any "wrongful decision" by the Security Council would be "null and void." All subsequent suggestions of a U. N. solution have been equally rejected by Hanoi and Peking.

The Vietnamese Communists have issued two separate but similar proposals stating their terms for ending the war. On March 22, 1965, the Liberation Front radio broadcast a set of conditions known as the "five points." They asserted:

1. The United States violated the Geneva agreements by assisting South Vietnam.

2. The Front will continue fighting "to kick out the U. S." in order to "liberate South Vietnam" and build an "independent, democratic and peaceful" country and advance toward reunification with the North. ". . . all negotiations are useless unless the U. S. withdraws its troops and its support of the Saigon government" and "as long as the NFLSV— the only genuine representative of 14 million South Vietnamese people —does not have the decisive voice."

3. Vietnam is one nation and the Front pledges ". . . to stand side by side with the Laotian and Cambodian people in their struggle against their common enemy . . ."—the United States and its allies.

4. The Front has the right to receive aid from abroad while the U. S. introduces troops into South Vietnam.

5. The Front will continue to fight until complete victory.

[1] Chou En-lai interview with visiting Japanese left-wing politicians, in Peking, January 7, 1966, published in the Japanese monthly, Sekei, March 1966.

Refining this proposal, the following month DRV Premier Pham Van Dong offered a more subtly worded four-point proposal calling for:

1. Complete withdrawal of the U. S. forces from the South, dismantling of U. S. bases and abolition of U. S. military alliance with the South, and cessation of U. S. attacks on the North "in accordance with the Geneva agreements."

2. The temporary continuation of the division of Vietnam but with strict adherence to the military provisions of the Geneva truce.

3. The settlement of the internal affairs of South Vietnam "by the South Vietnamese people themselves in accordance with the program of the National Liberation Front without any foreign interference."

4. "The peaceful reunification" of Vietnam to be settled "by the Vietnamese of both sides without any foreign interference. . . ." [2]

Neither the Front's five points nor the DRV's four points left much room for discussion, compromise, neutral solution, or coalition. Both essentially demanded a total victory for the Communists. Both emphasized a return to the Geneva agreements of 1954 at which time the Liberation Front did not exist. The Communists' repeated demands that the Front receive recognition as the "sole genuine representative of the South Vietnamese people" completely ignored the South Vietnamese government which participated in the Geneva conferences co-equally with the DRV. Communist China supported Hanoi's emphasis upon the Geneva accords while taking a hard line against negotiations until June 1966, when Peking declared the Geneva agreements were "already non-existent," and consequently were no vehicle for negotiations.[3] This reversal undoubtedly embarrassed Hanoi's leaders who maintained their previously stated position.

Meanwhile, on June 22, 1965, South Vietnam's Foreign Minister released Saigon's own four-point peace proposal, which stated:

1. North Vietnam must stop its aggression, dissolve its instrumentalities in the South such as the Liberation Front, and withdraw its troops and political agents.

2. South Vietnam can decide its own future through established democratic procedures without outside interference.

3. When the aggression from the North ceases, foreign forces which have assisted in the defense of the South would be withdrawn; however,

[2] *Vietnam News Agency* release, Hanoi, April 12, 1965.
[3] *People's Daily*, Peking, June 24, 1966.

the government reserved the right to call upon assistance again if aggression was renewed.

4. There must be an effective guarantee of South Vietnamese independence. The government's basis for settlement focused upon the crucial fact that the war was created through the deliberate and calculated plans of the Communist leaders of Hanoi.

The U. S. government repeatedly stressed American desires for a peaceful settlement that would leave South Vietnam free of outside coercion. At Johns Hopkins University on April 7, 1965, President Johnson called for "unconditional discussions." The President's offer was made in response to a proposal of 17 nonaligned nations for negotiations without preconditions. Hanoi suggested that some of the 17 nations had cooperated reluctantly or were ill informed, while Peking called their appeal a trick "by the Tito clique." [4] That same month, Peking and Hanoi refused to receive a special British envoy. In May 1965, the U. S. temporarily stopped air attacks against the North to encourage possible negotiations, but Hanoi called this a "trick." She also rejected a peace bid by the Canadian Commissioner on the ICC.

In June, Hanoi, Peking and Moscow refused a peace mission sent by five British Commonwealth nations. Peking criticized the British government's ". . . consistent efforts to serve as an errand boy to the U. S. and peddle Johnson's peace talks hoax." [5] Harold Davies, a British Labor member of Parliament with past DRV contacts, reportedly found the DRV leaders "wholly unyielding" on a visit to Hanoi in July. A joint appeal by India's Premier Shastri and Yugoslavia's President Tito for a halt of air raids and the convening of a conference was rejected by Hanoi radio August 5, ". . . because it carefully avoids referring to U. S. aggression. . . ." To U. N. Secretary General U Thant's efforts to reassemble the participants in previous Indochina conferences, Pham Van Dong replied that Hanoi had no desire to discuss peace, that the U. S. must accept the DRV and Front terms, and that efforts by third countries to mediate would be unsuccessful. Soviet approaches also received short shrift. In November, Peking charged the USSR with trying to help the U. S. ". . . find a way out of Vietnam." [6]

With the approach of Christmas 1965, President Johnson ordered

[4] *Vietnam News Agency,* Hanoi, April 19, 1965: *People's Daily,* Peking, April 22, 1965.
[5] *People's Daily,* Peking, June 21, 1965.
[6] *Ibid.,* November 11, 1965.

a longer pause in the bombing and initiated a world-wide "peace offensive." Vice-President Hubert Humphrey and other top government figures journeyed to numerous capitals, letters went to many heads of state, and U. S. Ambassadors explained the U. S. Vietnam policy and desire for a peaceful solution. Peking belittled the attempt by saying, ". . . monsters and freaks of all description are scurrying hither and thither and raising a lot of dust with their sinister activities."[7] Again the DRV termed the bombing pause a "trick."

About this time, Britain's Prime Minister Wilson proposed to the USSR a joint appeal to Hanoi for discussions. When Soviet Party Secretary Shelepin went to Hanoi shortly thereafter, some observers speculated he might persuade Ho Chi Minh to talk peace. Others noted his mission included a missile expert. If the mission sought peace, it failed. On January 28, 1966, Ho sent letters to several countries reiterating that only the Front could represent South Vietnam in negotiations.

In connection with Vice-President Humphrey's visit to the Far East during the peace offensive, the U. S. issued a 14-point summary of its previous statements concerning peace in Southeast Asia. The 14 points represent the most complete official statement of the U. S. position:

1. The Geneva Agreements of 1954 and 1962 are an adequate basis for peace in Southeast Asia;
2. We would welcome a conference on Southeast Asia or on any part thereof;
3. We would welcome "negotiations without preconditions" as the 17 nations put it;
4. We would welcome unconditional discussions as President Johnson put it;
5. A cessation of hostilities could be the first order of business at a conference or could be the subject of preliminary discussions;
6. Hanoi's four points could be discussed along with other points which others might wish to propose;
7. We want no U. S. bases in Southeast Asia;
8. We do not desire to retain U. S. troops in South Viet-Nam after peace is assured;
9. We support free elections in South Viet-Nam to give the South Vietnamese a government of their own choice;
10. The question of reunification of Viet-Nam should be determined by the Vietnamese through their own free decision;

[7] *Ibid.*, December 31, 1965.

11. The countries of Southeast Asia can be non-aligned or neutral if that be their option;

12. We would much prefer to use our resources for the economic reconstruction of Southeast Asia than in war. If there is peace, North Viet-Nam could participate in a regional effort to which we would be prepared to contribute at least one billion dollars;

13. The President has said, "The Viet Cong would not have difficulty being represented and having their views represented if for a moment Hanoi decided she wanted to cease aggression. I don't think that would be an insurmountable problem."

14. We have said publicly and privately that we could stop the bombing of North Viet-Nam as a step toward peace although there has not been the slightest hint or suggestions from the other side as to what they would do if the bombing stopped.[8]

China and Hanoi flatly rejected this statement, saying, "To hell with the 14 points."[9]

Many people found it difficult to understand why the Vietnamese Communists rejected all peace efforts and continued a war that threatened to destroy their past gains. Perhaps the answer lay in the religious fervor of the controlling clique, who may have become victims of their own intensive indoctrination and propaganda, which isolated them from the non-Communist world. Because they believed statistics must serve the needs of "politics" and propaganda, they could have lost contact with reality as did the Red Chinese in their "Great Leap Forward" and their "cultural revolution." Each Communist field commander had to maximize his gains and minimize his losses for propaganda purposes. Constantly playing back their exaggerated claims, they sometimes seemed unable to separate fact from fiction.

Marxist-Leninist dogma assures the Communists they are riding the wave of the future and by inexorable historical logic, victory is certain. Time is on their side, for imperialist nations with their bourgeois leadership lack the staying power to fight a protracted war. The Communists are sure they can deceive and divide the "deaf-mute" bourgeoisie with their propaganda and front technique and that internal and international public opinion will force the United States to withdraw from Vietnam. Toward this end, Peking and Hanoi direct their propaganda resources with world-wide aid from Communists and their sympathizers. They especially work to create feelings of guilt

[8] Department of State Press Release, January 7, 1966, no. 4.
[9] New China News Agency, Peking, January 11, 1966.

in the American public by presenting the image of a giant nation attacking a struggling underdeveloped country. They know the United States has vast technical superiority, but they are convinced that propaganda-fed anti-war sentiments will sap American will to fight, as they did in France in 1954. Hanoi's leaders are said to have believed the 37-day bombing pause was forced upon President Johnson by anti-war agitation in the United States. Consequently, they rejected negotiations, expecting America would soon abandon South Vietnam. Subsequently, they were buoyed by hopes the Buddhist struggle movement would cause the southern government to collapse and by the expectation President Johnson would be repudiated in the November 1966 elections. As old hopes vanished, they seized at new straws.

Vietnamese Communists firmly believe Lenin's doctrine that wars to expand communism are "holy" and "just," while any efforts to oppose Communist aggression are "unjust." They are also deeply committed to Mao Tse-tung's dogma that the "people," led by the Party, will triumph if they keep fighting regardless of human cost as at Dien Bien Phu. It is the people not weapons that win wars. For years, the North Vietnamese boasted of the ragged Viet Minh guerrillas who defeated 500,000 French Union forces, a victory that seemed to prove the theories of Giap and Truong Chinh of the inevitability of a "people's" victory in a liberation war. In July 1964, the Party journal *Hoc Tap* asserted, "This revolution can and should be settled only by the use of revolutionary acts and the forces of the masses to defeat enemy forces. It absolutely cannot be settled by treaties and accords. . . ." In another significant *Hoc Tap* article of December 1966, Party military theorist Hoang Minh Thao emphasized that the "leadership of the Party in the war must be strict, direct and total from the Party central committee to the Party *chi bo* [low level cadre]." Thao said, "The united national front is one of the decisive factors which dictate the success of the revolution and the people's war in our country." But he pointed out, "The front must be placed under the leadership of the Party. . . ." Thao stressed the Communist conviction that their "people possess sufficient material and spiritual forces to prosecute a long war" and "to endure it for 10 years, 15 years, 20 years or longer . . . ," adding that no foreigners "can match this determination."

The Communists have clearly laid down the challenge for free nations to prove that their people can and will when requested defend small countries from Communist attempts at conquest by the front technique and liberation wars. On July 12, 1966, President Johnson reaffirmed the American intention of meeting this challenge in Vietnam. In an address at Hot Springs, West Virginia, the President restated America's views on the needs for peace in four points:

1. First is the determination of the U. S. to meet our obligations.
2. The second essential for peace in Asia is to prove to aggressive nations that the use of force to conquer others is a losing game.
3. The third essential is the building of economic strength among the nations of Free Asia.
4. There is a fourth essential for peace in Asia which may seem the most difficult of all: reconciliation between nations that now call themselves enemies.

A variety of individuals and organizations seeking peace have had informal contacts with DRV and Front representatives around the world. Sometimes, these have brought indications of a relaxation of Communist demands, but every time these feelers were surfaced in the press, Hanoi heatedly denied them. When Signor La Pira, former mayor of Florence, returned from a visit to Hanoi, he reportedly passed a message to President Johnson through Italian Foreign Minister Fanfani, then President of the U. N. General Assembly. The message was said to have indicated the DRV might negotiate without prior U. S. withdrawal and that Ho would go anywhere and meet anyone. The DRV denied the report, saying the U. S. had "cooked up a legend about 'Hanoi's desire to negotiate' in an attempt to sow confusion." [10]

Throughout 1966, all peace efforts were rejected by Hanoi and Peking, with Moscow taking an increasingly hard public stand. In July 1966, the USSR rejected mediation efforts by Indian premier Indira Ghandi, U. N. Secretary General U Thant, and Prime Minister Wilson, saying the Soviets would not initiate negotiations or a new Geneva conference without Hanoi's assent. Moscow no longer appeared to be urging caution on Hanoi. In August Premier Shelepin declared the USSR would use restraint to avoid a third world war, but would also do everything they could to expel U. S. forces from Vietnam. By early 1967, it was not yet clear what effect the internal dislocations in China caused by her "cultural revolution" would have on Peking's hard line in supporting revolutions worldwide. Some Chinese statements were interpreted to imply North Vietnam might have to fight alone and not depend too heavily on outside support; yet the number of Chinese technicians aiding North Vietnam was increasing and some

[10] Hanoi Radio, December 30, 1965.

press dispatches from Vietnam reported that Lu tribal troops from South China had entered Northern Laos.

Still another approach was offered in July 1966, by U Thant, who advanced a three-stage mutual de-escalation plan calling for: (1) cessation of bombing of the North, (2) scaling down of military operations by all parties, and (3) negotiations among all parties actually fighting. Western observers pointed out that cessation of bombing was not "mutual" unless matched by an end of Hanoi's infiltration. The U. S. was said to have explored the proposal with Soviet intermediaries, but Hanoi reportedly rejected point 2 since to agree to it would be to admit that she had troops in the South. Hanoi was also believed to fear losing control of the southern Communists if they thought Hanoi was abandoning them. Subsequently in his annual report to the General Assembly on September 18, U Thant stated his position regarding the failure of peace efforts: "I remain convinced that the basic problem in Vietnam is not one of ideology, but one of national identity and survival. I see nothing but danger in the idea so assiduously fostered outside Vietnam that the conflict is a kind of holy war between powerful ideologies . . . it cannot be resolved by force, but by patience, and understanding, in the framework of a willingness to live and let live."

Cambodia and France, who oppose United States policy in Vietnam, have both made peace feelers and recommendations. In August 1966, Cambodian Chief of State Prince Norodom Sihanouk suggested in a speech that a settlement might be achieved if the United States would hold talks with the Liberation Front. About the same time, Jean Sainteny, de Gaulle's special envoy, returned from Hanoi with the message that the DRV might negotiate if the United States made appropriate gestures such as a bombing moratorium. These feelers caused some critics of the U. S. to point to Algiers where the French gained stature by reaching agreement with the Algerian liberation movement. However, this comparison was rejected by some western commentators who pointed out that Algiers was a colony seeking independence, while South Vietnam was a sovereign country trying to maintain independence with American aid. As for a unilateral bombing pause, journalists and scholars who are opponents of Communist expansion recalled that in Korea, the Communists had accepted negotiations when a major American offensive threatened to break through enemy lines. Though the U. S. ended its offensive, continued fighting during two years of truce talks cost 90,000 American casualties.

Prior to a visit of General de Gaulle to Cambodia, Washington reportedly informed the French anew that the U. S. was prepared to abide by the Geneva agreements and would negotiate, either secretly or publically, with Hanoi to arrange a mutual phased withdrawal of forces by both sides.[11] If General de Gaulle received the message, he gave no public response. In Cambodia, he proposed a unilateral American withdrawal from Vietnam without reference to North Vietnam's forces. During the same month, Pope Paul VI appealed to all parties to end the war. While appreciating the Pope's concern, the U. S. felt constrained to send Ambassador Averell Harriman to Rome to explain how Hanoi had used the 37-day bombing pause to increase military shipments to the South. On the same trip, Harriman discussed with other European leaders the fact that pressure upon the U. S. for unilateral concessions only encouraged Hanoi to continue the war.

A further U. S. peace move was made in September by the U. S. Ambassador to the United Nations, Arthur Goldberg. He told the General Assembly that the U. S. was prepared to pull back its forces as others withdrew theirs under U. N. or other international supervision. He said the U. S. would stop the bombing if given assurance Hanoi would reduce its military activities, and he suggested that the obstacles to Viet Cong participation in negotiations were more imaginary than real. Goldberg again stressed that U. S. aims were limited to aiding South Vietnam and that the U. S. was not engaged in a "holy war," wanted no colonies, bases or alliances, and did not seek unconditional surrender or the overthrow of Hanoi's government or the exclusion of any segment of the South's population from "peaceful participation in their country's future."[12] U Thant called the speech an important statement, but the Soviet delegate termed it "familiar old sounds and tunes." DRV Premier Pham Van Dong said it was another effort to mask war intensification.

The fear that peace might be concluded on terms inadequate to stop Communist aggression in Southeast Asia has caused some alarm. Australian Minister of External Affairs Paul Hasluck warned: "It would be dangerous to world peace" if hostilities ceased on terms giving "encouragement to further subversion and terrorism in Southeast Asia and other parts of the world in accordance with doctrines and practices originated in or inspired or supported by Peking."[13] Thailand's Foreign Minister Thanat Khoman also warned of accepting

[11] *Washington Post* and *Washington Star*, September 10, 1966.

[12] *Washington Post*, September 23, 1966. Interestingly, in late 1966 and early 1967, after Ambassador Goldberg's denial that the U. S. was engaged in a "holy war," Hanoi and Liberation front broadcasts repeatedly referred to their own struggle as "holy" or "sacred."

[13] *Ibid.*, September 28, 1966.

terms too favorable to the Communists and attacked "uninformed" persons "whose proposals to end the war benefit only Communist aggressors." [14]

An all-Asian peace conference was proposed at a meeting of the foreign ministers of Thailand, Malayasia, and the Philippines in August 1966. Though Hanoi called the idea "shopworn merchandise," it was encouraged by Washington. It remained in the planning stage by late 1966, but the proposal and the need for establishing a consensus on peace terms among the allied nations resulted in a conference of the chiefs of state of the seven allies fighting in South Vietnam, at Manila in late October. The principle result of the conference was a communique presenting terms for peace in Vietnam. This communique pledged the removal of allied forces from South Vietnam following "close consultation" as Hanoi withdrew its "military and subversive forces" and stopped infiltration, and "the level of violence thus subsides." The allied withdrawal was to be completed no later than six months "after the above conditions have been fulfilled." Meanwhile, the allies would continue "military and all other efforts as firmly and as long as may be necessary." [15]

The communique further assured the completion of South Vietnam's constitution-making processes on schedule, with village and hamlet elections following national assembly elections in 1967. The Ky government also agreed to devote more resources to rural reconstruction and to prepare a National Reconciliation Program to grant amnesty to all who had been "coerced or misled into casting their lot with the Viet Cong." In a Declaration on Peace and Progress in Asia and the Pacific, the communique stressed the need to be free from aggression, to conquer hunger, illiteracy and disease, to build security, order, and progress, and to seek reconciliation and peace throughout Asia and the Pacific. All nations in the region were invited to join in fulfilling these needs in peace and harmony. Communist nations were assured, "We do not threaten the sovereignty and integrity of our neighbors, whatever their ideological alignment." The Manila Declaration and its goals were intended as statements of general principles to which other Asian nations, including Indonesia, India, and Japan, might subscribe.

During the conference, it was reported that through Hungary's Foreign Minister Janos Peters the Communists had advanced new peace proposals, softening demands for prior withdrawal of allied forces and complete acceptance of the Front's program before nego-

[14] *Ibid.*, September 28, 1966.
[15] *Washington Post*, October 26, 1966.

tiations. But, whatever Hanoi told the Hungarians, there was no public retreat from the hard line. Hanoi, Peking, and the Viet Cong called the Manila meeting "a war conference" aimed at escalating the war. China repeated demands for unconditional allied withdrawal and said the communique "smacks of gunpowder." [16] Ho Chi Minh told a French journalist, ". . . some people of good will, deceived by U. S. propaganda have advised us to negotiate with the aggressors at all costs. They have forgotten that to end this war there needs only that the United States undertake to withdraw." Ho added that the DRV stood firm on its own four points and the five points of the Liberation Front, embodying the provisions of the Geneva agreements as "the only correct basis to settle the Vietnam problem." [17]

Despite Hanoi's public rigidity, some observers still believed the Lao Dong leaders might make peace if they could negotiate out of hearing of Peking and without having to publicly admit they had invaded the South. On the other hand, it seemed clear the DRV intended to keep control of the Communist apparatus in the South and were suspicious of being "sold out," as they had convinced themselves they were in 1954. Certainly, the southern Communists who had fought long and hard would feel betrayed and would be thoroughly demoralized if peace came without victory. There also remained the fear China might exert overwhelming pressure or invade Vietnam if Peking considered that the area might fall into hostile hands. Caught between the horns of several dilemmas and torn internally by pro-Soviet, pro-Peking, and neutralist factions, the Lao Dong party was in an awkward position. Meanwhile, Hanoi presented a bold front to the world, hailing "big victories" and proclaiming, "The political and moral strength of our army and people is invincible." [18] At the same time, Hanoi hoped for a break in American will to fight, believing the key factor in the war was not U. S. military power, but the American "rear . . . the political situation at home and abroad, the morale of its army and people and its own ability to conduct the war." [19]

Whether Americans had the stamina to continue to fight a protracted war in Vietnam remained to be seen. Many Americans found it difficult

[16] *New China News Agency,* Peking, October 28, 1966.

[17] Interview reported on Hanoi Radio, October 30, 1966.

[18] *Nhan Dan,* Hanoi, November 17, 1966.

[19] DRV Chief of Staff, quoted in *Wall Street Journal,* August 10, 1966. In late 1966 and early 1967, there were various rumors of possible negotiations that might include some softening of Hanoi's terms. However, it remained uncertain whether these would bear fruit or were examples of Communist psychological war-

to understand an undeclared war being fought in a distant land. Also, as a people dedicated to human liberty and proud of their own revolutionary heritage, some too uncritically accepted the Communist propaganda that the Viet Cong represented a truly popular uprising. They were unaware of the degree to which united front and liberation war techniques have been designed to distract the world's attention from actual Communist objectives and actions. Many could not distinguish between the anti-Vietnam war propaganda, organized and orchestrated by international organizations and Communist fronts, such as those set up by the Tricontinental Congress in Havana, and legitimate debates on American, as well as Vietnamese, goals and needs. To understand such a war as that in Vietnam required historical perspective with some knowledge of Communist goals and techniques and of the West's past successes in frustrating Communist subversion in Greece, Malaysia, and elsewhere.[20]

In an editorial reviewing the results of the Manila Conference, the *Economist* of London concluded, "Mr. Johnson's policy is starting to pay off—though the Communists will make one more try to break the American will to fight." The editorial compared events in Southeast Asia with those in Southeast Europe in 1947. When President Harry Truman committed the U. S. to defend Greece and Turkey, he gave non-Communists a power center around which to rally and started a conflict within the Communist camp between those favoring aggressive pursuit of the Greek insurrection and those favoring tactical retreat. Yet, not until two and a half years after the Truman declaration did the Communists abandon their efforts to conquer Greece by arms. The *Economist* saw the same process underway in Southeast Asia: "Five years ago, a stable Southeast Asia looked like a pipe dream. Now there may be a chance of bringing peace to that shattered region."[21]

fare designed to create the impression that the U. S. was rejecting negotiations. In previous similar instances, Hanoi's terms had proved to be the same—a capitulation of the Allies based on the Front's five points and Hanoi's four points. Some observers were hopeful that the disarray in Communist China might have given Hanoi greater freedom of action to mitigate her position.

[20] For a more detailed discussion on the different viewpoints and the debate regarding the Vietnam war, see Frank N. Trager, *Why Vietnam?* (New York, 1966) and Ralph K. White, "Misperception and the Vietnam War," *Journal of Social Issues*, XXII, No. 3 (July 1966), 1-164.

[21] Editorial, "The Pacific Concensus," *Economist*, October 29, 1966, pp. 445-46.

Suggested Readings

The literature on Vietnam until recently was mainly in French. The best bibliography of the older works is Cecil C. Hobbs (Library of Congress), *Indochina: A Bibliography of the Land and People* (Washington: 1950). More recent surveys of the literature in English and French are Joseph Coates, *Bibliography of Vietnam* (Washington: 1964); and Stephen N. Hay and Margaret H. Case, *Southeast Asian History: A Bibliographic Guide* (New York: 1962). Later studies and periodical articles on Vietnam can be located through volumes of the *Journal of Asian Studies*, especially the annual bibliography issues. For North Vietnam, consult U. S. Department of State External Research Division, Research Paper No. 142, *The Democratic Republic of Viet-Nam: A Bibliography* (Washington: 1964).

General Studies

Two useful geographies of Southeast Asia are Ernest H. G. Dobby, *Southeast Asia* (7th ed., London: 1960); and Charles A. Fisher, *Southeast Asia: A Social, Economic and Political Geography* (London: 1964). The best general histories of Southeast Asia are John F. Cady, *Southeast Asia: Its Historical Development* (New York: 1964); and D. G. E. Hall, *A History of Southeast Asia* (rev. ed., London and New York: 1964). Most useful for the early Indian colonization of Southeast Asia is George Coedès, *The Making of Southeast Asia* (Berkeley: 1964), a translation by H. M. Wright of *Les états hindouisès d'Indochine et d'Indonésie* (Paris: 1964).

In more specialized fields, Kenneth P. Landon, *Southeast Asia: Crossroads of Religion* (Chicago, 1949) is one of the few studies of its kind. George McTurnan Kahin, ed., *Government and Politics of Southeast Asia* (rev. ed., Ithaca, N. Y.: 1964) has excellent general material. Older political studies still of interest are: Rupert Emerson, Lennox A. Mills, and Virginia Thompson, *Government and Nationalism in Southeast Asia* (New York: 1942); Rupert Emerson, *Representative Government in Southeast Asia* (Cambridge, Mass.: 1955); and William L. Holland, ed., *Asian Nationalism and the West* (New York: 1953).

Studies dealing with the tactics and spread of communism are: Cyril

[174]

E. Black and Thomas P. Thornton, eds., *Communism and Revolution: The Strategic Uses of Political Violence* (Princeton: 1964), which has an informative chapter, "The Viet Minh Complex," by George Modelski, dealing with Vietnam and Laos; J. H. Brimmell, *Communism in Southeast Asia* (London and New York: 1959); A. Doak Barnett, *Communist Strategies in Asia, A Comparative Analysis of Governments and Parties* (New York: 1963); Robert A. Scalapino, ed., *The Communist Revolution in Asia: Tactics, Goals and Achievements* (Englewood Cliffs, N. J.: 1965); and Frank N. Trager, ed., *Marxism in Southeast Asia* (Stanford: 1959), which has an excellent chapter on Vietnam by I. Milton Sacks.

For international relations, Russell H. Fifield, *The Diplomacy of Southeast Asia: 1945-1958* (New York: 1958) is the best study in its field. Kenneth T. Young, Jr., *The Southeast Asia Crisis* (New York: 1965) examines U. S. interests and the role of international law; while economic and foreign aid problems are covered in Amos A. Jordan, Jr., *Foreign Aid and the Defense of Southeast Asia* (New York: 1962); and John D. Montgomery, *The Politics of Foreign Aid* (New York: 1962).

Among the general anthropological and sociological studies in English are: John F. Embree and William L. Thomas, Jr., *Ethnic Groups of Northern Southeast Asia* (New Haven: 1950); Gerald C. Hickey, Frank M. LeBar, and John K. Musgrave, *Ethnic Groups of the Mainland Southeast Asia* (New Haven: 1964); Robbins Burling, *Hill Farms and Padi Fields: Life in Mainland Southeast Asia* (Englewood Cliffs, N. J.: 1965); and Victor Purcell, *The Chinese in Southeast Asia* (London: 1965).

VIETNAM—GENERAL AND PRE-1945

Among the very few general popular surveys on Vietnam are: Ann Caddell Crawford, *Customs and Culture of Vietnam* (Rutland, Vt. and Tokyo: 1966); and Ellen Hammer, *Vietnam, Yesterday and Today* (New York: 1966). The most informative general study is Special Operations Research Office (American University), *U. S. Army Area Handbook for Vietnam* (Washington: 1962).

The only history generally available, Joseph Buttinger, *The Smaller Dragon, A Political History of Vietnam* (New York: 1958), covers only to 1900 and relegates much important detail to footnotes. Nguyen Van Thai and Nguyen Van Mung, *A Short History of Vietnam* (Saigon: 1958) is useful for its Vietnamese viewpoint. Nguyen Phut Tan, *A Modern History of Viet-Nam (1802-1954)* (Saigon: 1964) provides valuable details on the Tayson Rebellion and Vietnamese nationalist movements. Le Thanh Khôi, *Le Viet-Nam, histoire et civilisation* (Paris: 1955), the best general history, is influenced by the author's Marxist outlook.

For the French conquest and administration, see John Cady, *The Roots of French Imperialism in Eastern Asia* (Ithaca, N. Y.: 1955), covering the period 1840-1861; Roger Levy, *French Interests and Policies in the Far*

East (New York: 1941); Stephen H. Roberts, *History of French Colonial Policy* (*1870-1925*) (London: 1929); and Thomas E. Ennis, *French Policy and Developments in Indochina* (Chicago: 1936).

Two valuable sociological reports on the same village are Gerald C. Hickey, *Village in Vietnam* (New Haven and London: 1964); and James B. Hendry, *The Small World of Khanh Hau* (Chicago: 1964). A pioneer work on the Vietnamese peasant is Pierre Gourou, *The Peasants of the Tonkin Delta* (2 vols., New Haven: 1955), translated from his 1936 French study. Recent works on the mountain tribes are John D. Donoghue and others, *People in the Middle: The Rhadé of South Viet Nam* (East Lansing, Mich.: 1962); Gerald Hickey, *The Major Ethnic Groups of the South Vietnamese Highlands* (Santa Monica, Cal.: 1964); and G. Bertrand, *The Jungle People: Men, Beast and Legends of the Moi Country* (London: 1959).

VIETNAM SINCE 1945

The best scholarly studies in English on the early post World War II period are Ellen J. Hammer, *The Struggle for Indochina* (Stanford: 1954); and Donald Lancaster, *The Emancipation of French Indochina* (London: 1961). *The Two Viet-Nams: A Political and Military Analysis* (rev. ed., New York: 1964) by Bernard B. Fall, a French author long resident in the United States, is generally critical of U. S. policy. Two outstanding French works on the period are Philippe Devillers, *Histoire du Viet-Nam de 1940 à 1952* (Paris: 1952); and Paul Mus, *Viet-Nam: Sociologie d'une guerre* (Paris: 1952). For the military history of the Viet Minh war against France, see Bernard B. Fall, *Street Without Joy* (Harrisburg, Pa.: 1961); Edgar O'Ballance, *The Indo-China War, 1945-1954: A Study in Guerrilla Warfare* (London: 1964); George K. Tanham, *Communist Revolutionary Warfare: the Vietminh in Indochina* (New York: 1961); and Truong Chinh, *Primer for Revolt: The Communist Takeover in Viet-Nam* (New York: 1963), a facsimile of two studies of Viet Minh military and political tactics, *The August Revolution* (Hanoi: 1958) and *The Resistance Will Win* (Hanoi: 1960).

For the Diem period, Robert Scigliano, *South Vietnam: Nation Under Stress* (Boston: 1963) provides a scholarly, balanced view. B. S. N. Murti, *Vietnam Divided: The Unfinished Struggle* (New York: 1964) presents the problems of the International Control Commission. Stephen Pan and Daniel Lyons, *Vietnam Crisis* (New York: 1966), is favorable to Diem and the U. S. commitment in Vietnam. The most useful of the journalists' accounts is *The Lost Revolution: U. S. in Vietnam, 1945-66* (rev. ed., New York: 1966), by Robert Shaplen, who believes Ho Chi Minh might have become a Tito with different handling. Other journalists' views are: Malcolm W. Brown, *The New Face of War* (Indianapolis: 1965), and David Halberstam, *The Making of a Quagmire* (New York: 1965), which are critical of the Diem government; and Marguerite Higgins, *Our Vietnam Nightmare* (New York: 1965), which supports Diem and attacks the militant Buddhists. Denis Warner, *The Last Confucian* (New York: 1963) is a knowledgeable assessment by an Australian journalist; and Bernard Newman, *Background to Viet-Nam* (New York: 1965) is by an English journalist. For a portrait of Diem, see Anthony T. Bouscaren, *The Last of the Mandarins: Diem of Vietnam* (Pittsburgh, Pa.: 1965). Jean La-couture, *Vietnam: Between Two Truces* (New York: 1966) is a sensational and often inaccurate account with an anti-American bias. John Mecklin, *Mission in Torment* (Garden City, N. Y.: 1965) gives an account of Diem's last year by a U. S. official in Saigon at the time.

Among the useful collections of articles and lectures are the "Vietnam" issue of *Asia* (New York, fall, 1965); Wesley R. Fischel, ed., *Problems of Freedom: Vietnam Since Independence* (East Lansing, Mich.: 1961); Richard W. Lindholm, ed., *Viet-Nam, the First Five Years* (East Lansing, Mich.: 1959); and Bernard B. Fall, *Viet-Nam Witness, 1953-66* (New York: 1966).

Nghiem Dang, *Vietnam: Politics and Public Administration* (Honolulu: 1966) is a scholarly work by a former Vietnamese official. The best economic studies are R. W. Lindholm, *Economic Development Policy With Emphasis on Vietnam* (Eugene, Ore.: 1964); Frank C. Child, *Essays on Economic Growth, Capital Formation and Public Policy in Vietnam* (Saigon, 1961); and United Nations, Economic Survey Mission to the Republic of Viet-Nam, *Toward the Economic Development of the Republic of Viet-Nam* (New York: 1959). Specialized works on development problems are Milton E. Osborne, *Strategic Hamlets in South Vietnam: A Survey and a Comparison* (Ithaca, N. Y.: 1965—Cornell University Southeast Asia Program, Data Paper No. 55); and George K. Tanham, ed., *War Without Guns: American Civilians in Rural Vietnam* (New York: 1966).

The critics of the American commitment to Vietnam have produced more books than the defenders. Among the more balanced studies is Victor Bator, *Vietnam, A Diplomatic Tragedy: Origins of the United States Involvement* (Dobbs Ferry: 1965). Hans J. Morgenthau, *Vietnam and the United States* (Washington: 1965) gives the view of a leading critic. For a scholarly defense of the U. S. commitment with the historical developments leading to it, see Frank N. Trager, *Why Vietnam?* (New York, 1966). Ralph K. White, "Misperception and the Vietnam War," *Journal of Social Issues*, XXII, No. 3 (July, 1966), pp. 1-164, presents a critical psychological analysis of the various viewpoints toward the war.

Documents on the Vietnam conflict may be found in Allen B. Cole, ed., *Conflict in Indo-China and International Repercussions: A Documentary History, 1945-1955* (Ithaca, N. Y.: 1956) and in two collections of readings, selected to present a critical view of the U. S.: Marcus G. Raskin and Bernard B. Fall, eds., *The Vietnam Reader* (New York: 1965) and Marvin Gettleman, ed., *Vietnam* (New York: 1965). The official U. S. statements with documentation are found in two Department of State publications: *A Threat to the Peace: North Vietnam's Effort to Conquer South Vietnam* (Washington: 1961), and *Aggression From the North: the Record of North Viet-Nam's Campaign to Conquer South Vietnam* (Washington: 1965). Also consult the reports and hearings of the U. S. Senate Foreign Relations Committee, especially its *Background Information Relating to Southeast Asia and Vietnam* (Washington: 1965).

NORTH VIETNAM AND THE VIET CONG

The earliest study of the Viet Minh in English is Bernard B. Fall, *The Viet Minh Regime, Government Administration in the Democratic Republic of Vietnam* (Ithaca, N. Y.: 1954). Hoang Van Chi, *From Colonialism to Communism, A Case History of North Vietnam* (New York: 1964) gives an inside view by a defector. P. J. Honey, *Communism in North Vietnam: Its Role in the Sino-Soviet Dispute* (Cambridge, Mass.: 1963) emphasizes problems within the Communist bloc; and P. J. Honey, ed., *North Vietnam Today* (New York: 1962) reprints articles from the *China Quarterly*, vols. IX and X. Jay Mallin, *Terror in Vietnam* (Princeton, N. J.: 1966) portrays Viet Cong terrorism. Douglas Pike, *Viet Cong: The Organization and Technique of the National Liberation Front of South Vietnam* (Cambridge, Mass.: 1966) is a thorough, scholarly analysis of the Communist front operation.

The Communist viewpoint may be found in *The Furtive War, the United States in Vietnam and Laos* (New York: 1963) and *Vietnam: Inside Story of the Guerrilla War* (New York: 1965) by Wilfred B. Burchett, an Australian correspondent for *Pravda* and other Communist journals. For a significant work by a North Vietnamese leader, see Vo Nguyen Giap, *People's War, People's Army: The Viet Cong Instruction Manual for Underdeveloped Countries* (New York: 1961).

Index